ARCHAEOLOGICAL SURVEY OF INDIA.

ANNUAL REPORT

1915-16

ARCHAEOLOGICAL SURVEY OF INDIA.

ANNUAL REPORT

1915-16

EDITED BY

SIR. JOHN MARSHALL,

Kt., C.I.E., M.A., Litt. D., F.S.A.

Hon. A.R.I.B.A., Director General of Archaeology in India.

GYAN

Published by

Gyan Publishing House
5, Ansari Road
Daryaganj, New Delhi-110002
Phone: 011-47034999, 9811692060
E-mail: books@gyanbooks.com

Distribution Network
gyanbooks.com
India, USA, Canada, UK, Australia, France

ISBN : 978-81-212-2544-1 (HB)
First Published, 1918

2nd Impression 2021

Printed at: Gyan Press, Delhi.

Archaeological Survey of India.
Annual Report
1915-16
Author: Sir. John Marshall

ARCHÆOLOGICAL SURVEY OF INDIA.

ANNUAL REPORT

1915-16

EDITED BY

SIR JOHN MARSHALL, Kt., C.I.E., M.A., Litt.D., F.S.A.,

Hon. A.R.I.B.A., Director General of Archæology in India.

CALCUTTA

SUPERINTENDENT GOVERNMENT PRINTING, INDIA

1918

Agents for the Sale of Books Published by the Superintendent of Government Printing, India, Calcutta.

IN EUROPE.

Constable & Co., 10, Orange Street, Leicester Square, London, W.C.

Kegan Paul, Trench, Trübner & Co., 68-74, Carter Lane, E.C., and 25, Museum Street, London, W.C.

Bernard Quaritch, 11, Grafton Street, New Bond Street, London, W.

P. S. King & Sons, 2 & 4, Great Smith Street, Westminster, London, S.W.

H. S. King & Co., 65, Cornhill, E.C., and 9, Pall Mall, London, W.

Grindlay & Co., 54, Parliament Street, London, S.W.

Luzac & Co., 46, Great Russell Street, London, W.C.

W. Thacker & Co., 2, Creed Lane, London, E.C.

T. Fisher Unwin, Ltd., 1, Adelphi Terrace, London, W.C.

Wm. Wesley & Son, 28, Essex St., Strand, London.

B. H. Blackwell, 50 & 51, Broad Street, Oxford.

Deighton, Bell & Co., Ltd., Cambridge.

Oliver and Boyd, Tweeddale Court, Edinburgh.

E. Ponsonby, Ltd., 116, Grafton Street, Dublin.

Ernest Leroux, 28, Rue Bonaparte, Paris.

Martinus Nijhoff, The Hague, Holland.

IN INDIA AND CEYLON.

Thacker, Spink & Co., Calcutta and Simla.

Newman & Co., Calcutta.

R. Cambray & Co., Calcutta.

S. K. Lahiri & Co., Calcutta.

B. Banerjee & Co., Calcutta.

The Indian School Supply Depôt, 309, Bow Bazar Street, Calcutta, and 226, Nawabpur, Dacca.

Butterworth & Co. (India), Ltd., Calcutta.

Rai M. C. Sarcar Bahadur and Sons, 90/2A, Harrison Road, Calcutta.

The Weldon Library, 18-5, Chowringhee Road, Calcutta.

Standard Literature Co., Limited, Calcutta.

Lal Chand & Sons, Calcutta.

Higginbotham & Co., Madras.

V. Kalyanarama Iyer & Co., Madras.

G. A. Natesan & Co., Madras.

S. Murthy & Co., Madras.

Thompson & Co., Madras.

Temple & Co., Madras.

P. R. Rama Iyer & Co., Madras.

Vas & Co., Madras.

E. M. Gopalakrishna Kone, Madura.

Thacker & Co., Ltd., Bombay.

A. J. Combridge & Co., Bombay.

D. B. Taraporevala, Sons & Co., Bombay.

Mrs. Radhabai Atmaram Sagoon, Bombay.

Sunder Pandurang, Bombay.

Gopal Narayan & Co., Bombay.

Ram Chandra Govind & Son, Kalbadevi, Bombay.

A. H. Wheeler & Co., Allahabad, Calcutta and Bombay.

N. B. Mathur, Supt., Nazir Kanun Hind Press, Allahabad.

Rai Sahib M. Gulab Singh & Sons, Mufid-i-Am Press, Lahore.

Rama Krishna & Sons, Lahore.

Supt., American Baptist Mission Press, Rangoon.

Manager, the "Hitavada," Nagpur.

S. C. Talukdar, Proprietor, Students & Co., Cooch Behar.

A. M. & J. Ferguson, Ceylon.

Manager, Educational Book Depôts, Nagpur and Jubbulpore.*

Manager of the Imperial Book Depôt, 63, Chandney Chauk Street, Delhi.*

Manager, "The Agra Medical Hall and Co-operative Association, Ltd." (Successors to A. John & Co., Agra).*

Supt., Basel Mission Book and Tract Depository, Mangalore.*

P. Varadachary & Co., Madras.*

H. Liddell, Printer, etc., 7, South Road, Allahabad.*

Ram Dayal Agarwala, 184, Katra, Allahabad.*

D. C. Anand & Sons, Peshawar.*

Manager, Newal Kishore Press, Lucknow.*

* Agents for the sale of Legislative Department publications only.

CONTENTS

LIST OF PLATES

PLATE

EXCAVATIONS AT TAXILA, 1915-16.[1]

DHARMARĀJIKĀ STŪPA.

AT the Dharmarājikā Stūpa my operations were mainly directed to clearing away the great heaps of débris towards the northern side of the plateau and so opening up the southern face of the monastery which I assume to have occupied this part of the site. Whether it will be necessary to dig much further in order to reach the wall of this monastery, is not yet apparent. A series of walls of the semi-ashlar and later types of masonry have already been found extending from building H as far as the eastern limits of the plateau, but it has yet to be determined if these are the remains of the monastery itself or of a row of chapels in front of it. Probably, it will be found that the latter is the case, and that they are chapels similar to those which I shall presently describe in the north-east corner of the excavated area. The accumulation of débris along the line of these structures is some 15 to 20 feet in height, and, as it consists largely of colossal stones fallen from the ruined buildings, the task of excavating it is necessarily a slow and laborious one.

In front—that is, on the south side—of the stretch of walls referred to above and towards their western end, are three small circular stūpas designated U^1, U^2, and U^3 on the plan (Pl. I), which closely resemble one another in point of size and construction, and which were clearly built at one and the same period. They are now standing to a height of between 3′ 6″ and 4′ 6″ above their foundations, and vary in diameter from 10′ 9″ to 11′ 0″. They are built of semi- Stupas U^{1-3}.

[1] The following is a list of the abbreviations and references used in this article.

Abbreviations and references.

A. S. R.	Archæological Survey Reports.	M.	Monogram.
B. M.	British Museum.	M. M.	Mora Moradu.
b. s.	below the surface.	Mon.	Monastery.
C. S. R.	Cunningham's Survey Reports.	P. M.	Punjab Museum.
Dh.	Dharmarājikā Stūpa.	Sk.	Sirkap.
I. M.	Indian Museum.	Ss.	Sirsukh.
Lc.	Lālchak.		

Numbers printed thus: 125 × 68′ indicate the particular square in Sirkap in which an object has been found.

ashlar masonry with a torus and scotia base moulding of kañjūr. Like most of the other structures of the same age on this site, the torus moulding is bevelled off in three edges, but this bevelling may have been for the convenience of the masons when cutting the stones, and it may well be that the stucco with which the kañjūr was subsequently covered was round instead of angular in section. Two of these stūpas (U^2 and U^3) yielded no relics, but in the third (U^1) I found, near the top of the structure and at a height of 4′ 3″ from the ground level, an earthenware pot much like a modern flower pot (Pl. IV, *4*), with a casket of Gandhāra stone (Pl. IV, *3*) inside, and the damaged bottom of another casket of the same material (Pl. IV, *5*) placed over the lid for protection. The diameter of the earthenware pot is $7\frac{5}{8}$″, that of the relic casket $4\frac{1}{2}$″, and that of the protecting casket $5\frac{9}{16}$″. Inside the relic casket were the following articles (Pl. IV, *6-16*) :—

(1) Bone relic, $1\frac{5}{16}$″ long.
(2) 32 thin discs of beaten gold, whole or fragmentary, varying from $\frac{7}{16}$″ to $\frac{3}{4}$″ in diameter.
(3) Oval gold leaf, $\frac{9}{16}$″ long.
(4) Minute cylindrical ring of gold.
(5) Minute cylindrical ring of silver, $\frac{3}{8}$″ diameter.
(6) Fragments of silver leaf apparently belonging to discs.
(7) 6 pearl beads and fragments of mother-of-pearl.
(8) Piece of rock crystal, uncut, $1\frac{1}{8}$″ × $\frac{7}{8}$″.
(9) Cornelian gem of scaraboid shape, polished but not engraved; $\frac{15}{16}$″ long.
(10) 114 pierced beads of various shapes—round, 24-sided, amygdaloid, lenticular, octagonal and irregular; one in form of monkey and two of tortoise. The materials used are cornelian, green jasper, topaz, limestone, aquamarine, garnet, amethyst, mother-of-pearl, crystal, ruby, bone and glass. One of the cornelian beads is of the shape and make common in Maurya times.
(11) Broken fragments of banded agate, highly polished and finely bored, probably of Maurya date. $1\frac{1}{2}$″ × $1\frac{3}{8}$″.
(12) Unpierced amygdaloid bead of yellowish brown stone, $\frac{15}{16}$″ long.
(13) 33 pieces of coral, pierced.
(14) Miscellaneous pieces of rock crystal, topaz, and aquamarine.
(15) 4 coins of Maues, Apollodotus and Spalahores, and one defaced and uncertain.

In the near vicinity of this stūpa there also came to light a few objects of copper including a crescent-shaped piece, a ring and an antimony rod, as well as a broken Gandhāra relief (No. 1507) representing Śiva (?) standing in front of his bull Nandi. Assuming that the identification of the standing figure with Śiva is correct, this will make another interesting addition to the very few examples of Gandhāra sculptures portraying Brahmanical subjects.

Stūpas P^{12} and N^{20}

Two other stūpas which were cleared in this part of the site are those numbered P^{12} and N^{20} in the plan, both situated in the near vicinity of the large stūpa N^4. All that now remains of the former is the plinth, which is

9′ square and 2′ 9″ high. It is composed wholly of kañjūr stone coated with stucco and is relieved around the base with the usual torus and scotia moulding. In the centre of the structure was a square relic chamber long since rifled of its contents, the walls of which were finished internally with a coating of lime plaster. In view of the fact that this chamber is not set square with the walls of the stūpa, and in view also of the fact that it descends to a somewhat lower level than the foundations of the walls, it is legitimate to assume that it may have belonged to an earlier edifice on the same site. Abutting against the north and east sides of the plinth, as well as at the north-east corner, are three later additions in the shape of rectangular plinths which once no doubt supported shrines for images. The earliest of these additions was the one on the north, then came the one on the east, and last of all the one at the north-east corner. All three are constructed of semi-ashlar masonry of limestone, and the two on the north and east sides are provided with cornices of kañjūr; the other has been destroyed to a point below the line of the cornice. The only small antiquities found in the excavation of this building were a small lidless casket of slate (No. 608) decorated with cross hatchings and an iron arrow-head (No. 558).

The plinth of the other stūpa (N^{26}) is square, built of kañjūr stone covered with stucco, and subsequently enlarged to 11′ 6″ by the construction of a semi-ashlar wall on its four sides. It is in too ruinous a condition to call for any particular notice.

Chapel N^{18}.

Still further to the east—that is, in the extreme north-east corner of the excavated area—I brought to light a singularly interesting group of edifices. At this point there is a broad passage going due north past the side of the stūpa N^{4}, flanked on either side by stūpas and image chapels, and apparently leading to another chapel at its northern end. Of these chapels there are two on the west of the passage and, so far as can be seen at present, four on the east—all of semi-ashlar stone construction and very solidly built. Most striking among them is N^{18} (Pl. II *b*) at the extreme northern end on the east side. It stands on a plinth raised 3′ 6″ above the ground level, access to which is provided by a broad flight of four steps. Its walls, which are singularly massive and obviously intended to carry a great weight, are nearly 5′ in thickness, and its interior measurements 17′ 9″ by 14′ 9″. When excavated from the débris, it was standing to a height of approximately twelve feet, but, to judge by what is left of the chief image, it must once have had an elevation of at least 40 feet. The image in question, doubtless of the Buddha, is of colossal proportions and stands opposite the entrance on a low plinth measuring 10′ 1″ by 5′ 11″. Unfortunately, only the feet and lower part of the raiment have survived, but the length of the foot (5′ 3″ from heel to toe) indicates that the figure had an approximate height of 35 feet. To the left of this colossal statue and on a smaller plinth against the northern wall of the shrine is a seated but headless figure of the Buddha, 5′ 8″ in height including the pedestal (Pl. III *a*); the halo is circular and large enough to surround the whole figure from head to foot. On the south side of the shrine, again, there is a third standing image, of which the whole upper part above the thighs is now destroyed; and placed against the east wall, between this and the main image, is a fourth standing figure of smaller dimensions (Pl. III *c*). Its head and right hand are missing; but otherwise it is in a tolerably good state of preservation and the plastic treatment of the feet and left hand are singularly good. A large head found in the débris near this chapel probably belongs to the third of these images. In all of these statues, as well as in others of the same period, the core is composed either of kañjūr stone roughly fashioned to the shape of the figure, or of mud and small kañjūr stones combined together, or of mud alone; and the stucco which covers this core and in which all the features and other details are made out, is composed of almost pure lime plaster. Red paint is found in several instances still adhering to the robes, and no doubt other pigments as well as gilding were employed, as they were also employed in the case of the Gandhāra sculptures, for their further embellishment.

Chapel N^{17}. The next chapel towards the south, N^{17}, which was built subsequently to the preceding one, is of smaller dimensions, measuring internally 9′ 2″ wide by 9′ 8″ deep, with a plinth 2′ 10″ in height. The northern wall of this chapel is less substantially built than the southern, being a foot less in thickness. The reason for this difference is that, the chapel being built against the already existing structure N^{18}, its northern wall received lateral support from it and did not therefore require to be so strong, whereas its southern wall had no such support until the chapel N^{16} was subsequently erected against it. In the interior of the chapel are the remains of three standing images, also presumably of the Buddha, though nothing is now left of them save the lower parts of the drapery and feet. The latter are singularly well preserved and remarkable for the excellence of their modelling. A head (No. 893) belonging to one of the three, was found on the floor of the shrine. It is of the usual conventional type but without the customary *ūrṇā*; the curve of the mouth is beautifully modulated; (Pl. III *g*).

The combined width of the two adjoining walls of the chapels described above, that is, the southern wall of N^{18} and the northern wall of N^{17}, amounts to 7′ 5″. Against the western face of these two walls and between the flights of steps giving access to the shrines there was erected at a later date a small shrine built in the semi-ashlar style, of which only the plinth has escaped destruction. The western façade of this plinth is adorned with four Corinthian pilasters resting on a torus moulding and surmounted by a frieze and dentil cornice. In the central bay between the pilasters is a trefoil niche containing a seated figure of the Buddha, apparently in the attitude of meditation.

Chapel N^{16}. Adjoining N^{17} on its south side, is another smaller chapel (N^{16}), approached by a flight of 3 steps and containing a square stūpa. The latter is 5′ 1″ square, constructed of kañjūr, stuccoed over and coarsely replastered later on. It is standing to a height of 1′ 9″, is decorated with a row of lion heads surmounted by a frieze of stunted Corinthian pilasters alternating with niches of the same shape as those on the Main Stūpa, with which it is no doubt approximately contemporary.

Chapel N^{20}. The two chapels on the opposite (west) side of the passage stand on a common plinth with a partition wall between them, and must therefore have been erected at one and the same time. In the one to the north (N^{28}) are two pedestals for statues, but the statues themselves have disappeared. In the one to the south are the remains of what appears to have been a long pedestal on the north side, but there are no longer any traces of images.

Stūpas S^8 and S^9.

The only other buildings at the Dharmarājikā that remain to be mentioned are three small stūpas on the western side of the main edifice. Two of these (S^8 and S^9) are comprised in the ring of small stūpas which were erected in the Śaka-Pahlava period and must have fallen to decay before any of the chapels could be reared upon their ruins. The former consists of a square plinth and circular drum, and is constructed of rough rubble with a torus moulding of kañjūr near the base of the latter. The same material may be assumed also to have been employed for facing the upper part of the structure, just as it was employed in the case of D^1 and D^2 in the south-west quadrant of the circle. In penetrating into the interior of this stūpa some difficulty was experienced owing to the walls of the later chapels being carried almost directly across its centre, and, as these walls could not be removed, it was necessary to sink a shaft alongside of them and then cut laterally beneath their foundations. In this way the relic chamber was reached at a depth of 6′ and was found to be of small dimensions ($9\frac{1}{2}'' \times 8\frac{3}{4}'' \times 11''$ deep) and constructed of kañjūr blocks. Inside it were four copper coins (Nos. 797-800) of Azes I and Maues, and a steatite casket well turned on the lathe (Pl. IV, *27*) which contained the following articles (Pl. IV, *17-26*) :—

1. Miniature casket of gold, diam. $\frac{5}{8}''$ (Pl. IV, *26*).
2. Safety pin of gold with diamond-shaped bezel surrounded by a double line of granulations and inlaid with opaque blue stone. Length $1\frac{5}{8}''$ (Pl. IV, *25*).
3. Safety pin of gold with plain diamond-shaped bezel. Length $1\frac{7}{16}''$ (Pl. IV, *24*).
4. Safety pin of gold with plain leaf-shaped bezel. Length $1\frac{1}{4}''$ (Pl. IV, *23*).
5. Six small beads of ruby, garnet, amethyst and rock crystal. Five are pierced and one unpierced (Pl. IV, *17-22*).

In the gold casket were five minute beads of bone, a round bead of ruby, three small pieces of silver leaf, a piece of coral, a fragment of stone and a bone relic. Lying beside this stūpa were two small stucco heads (Nos. 945 and 829), one to the south and the other to the west.

The second stūpa (S^9) is for the most part concealed by the later chapels erected over it. All that is now visible is the eastern side of the square plinth, which is constructed of rubble faced with kañjūr and covered with stucco. In the centre of this plinth was a circular relic chamber, 1′ 1″ in diam. and 1′ 4″ deep, with a heavy slab of coarse conglomerate stone ($2'\ 7'' \times 2'\ 6'' \times 6\frac{1}{2}''$) over the top. The casket enshrined in this chamber is exceptional in that it is of ivory (Pl. IV, *1*). It measures 4″ in diameter, and, like the caskets of stone, is turned on the lathe, but it differs from them to this extent, that the concentric circles with which the lid and base are decorated are raised in relief instead of being incised. Inside it was another smaller reliquary of ivory of cylindrical shape, decorated externally by dividing the surface into eleven horizontal sections each with a convex surface (Pl. IV, 2). Besides this smaller casket there were also in the larger receptacle the following articles:—

(1) 7 more or less broken discs of silver, varying in diameter from ½" to ⅞", convex in shape and very thin. There appear to have been discs of wood fitted into the concave side.

(2) 2 gold discs, of smaller size, damaged.

(3) Fragment of twisted gold wire.

(4) 2 pieces of coral.

(5) 11 small beads of gold, amethyst, pearl, bone, and (?) iron pyrites.

(6) Fragments of glass paste and limestone.

Stūpa S^7.

The third and last stūpa deserving notice (S^7) is situated immediately at the back of the circle of chapels. The original structure, which probably dates from the latter half of the first century A.D., is 13' 10" square and of rough rubble masonry, approximating to the small diaper style. Its present height is 4' 3". The relic chamber, which was 8¼" square and 2' deep, contained no relics. Along the east and part of the north side of the stūpa is a later addition of 3rd-4th century A.D., which for some obscure reason seems never to have been continued round the other sides. It is faced with squared and well-dressed kañjūr blocks formerly covered with stucco, and was originally adorned, on the east side, with a row of six slender pilasters set at intervals of 3' 7" on a well moulded and elaborate base.

The following is a list of some of the minor or detached antiquities found at the Dharmarājikā Stūpa.

A.—Stone Objects.

1. Fragment of frieze, 1' 10½" long, with Amorini bearing a garland and flying Gandharvas in bold relief. The winged figures are particularly successful. Gandhāra stone. B^{22}, floor. No. 963. (Pl. V, 7).

2. Rider on horseback, 6¾" high. Badly damaged. Gandhāra stone. Débris. No. 1082.

3. Makara head in relief, 1' ¼" × 9¼". Of early school. Stone hollowed out behind. Greyish-white sandstone. Débris. No. 1071.

4. Small flying figure in relief, 3" high, with halo and hands outstretched in attitude of worship. Main Stūpa, East gate. 2' b.s. No. 1547.

5. Figure in relief, 5⅛" high, seated on conventional lotus; halo behind head. Gandhāra stone. Main stūpa, East gate. 2' b.s. No. 1470.

6. Head in relief, 6⅛" high, much mutilated. Gandhāra stone. Mon. S[1], 12' b.s. No. 1344.

7. Lid of a casket, diameter 2⅞", with handle, decorated with incised linear designs. Slate. Mon. S, 8' b.s. No. 1539.

8. Two tablets of reddish porous stone and yellowish sandstone, respectively, 4¼ × 3¼ × 1⅜" and 4⅜ × 3¼ × ¾"; used as flesh rubbers. Mon. S, 7' b.s. No. 1424

[1] Mon. S here refers to a trench running east and west on the south side of the monastery; Mon. N to a trench on its north side.

9. Large stone lamp, 1′ 1″ long, much broken, with projecting handle at back and linear decoration in relief around rim. Gandhāra slate stone. Mon. **S**, 10′ b.s. No. 1269.

10. Head of Bodhisattva in alto relievo, 1′ 2″ high, with halo at back and canopy above. Surface damaged. Mon. **S**, 10′ b.s. No. 1162.

11. Head of Buddha, 5¾″ high. Hair arranged in short curls over head and *ushṇīsha*. Left ear, nose and *ūrṇā* damaged; slight moustache. Best period. Modelling good. Gandhāra stone. Mon. **S**, 8′ b.s. No. 1185. (Pl. V, *f*).

12. Small head of an ascetic (?) in relief; 2⅝″ high. Gandhāra stone. Mon. **S**, 10′ b.s. No. 1215.

13. Head in the round, 3¾″ high. Hair arranged in corkscrew curls starting from the crown. Tip of nose, chin, eyebrows and ears damaged. The crown of the head is much flattened. Gandhāra stone. Mon. **S**, 10′ b.s. No. 1167.

14. Standing figure of Bodhisattva (?) in low relief, 4¼″ high. His right elbow resting on smaller figure at side. Delicate workmanship. Fine-grained, grey stone. Mon. **S**, inside chamber. No. 1027.

15. Bodhisattva head, 6″ high, with decorated turban, tiara and ear ornaments. Front of face damaged. Mon. **S**, inside chapel. No. 881.

16. Head, 4¾″ high. Hair arranged in fine strands and bound with beaded fillet. The back of the head is missing and the face damaged. Mathurā sand-stone. Mon. **S**, 11′ b.s. No. 371.

17. Finger ring, diam. 1⅛″, of banded agate. Mon. **S**, 10′ b.s. No. 1375.

18. Bottom of steatite casket, diam. 2″, of grey slate. Turned on lathe and decorated with lines. Mon. **N**, 6′ b.s. No. 1127.

19. Bodhisattva, 7½″ high, seated on lotus in *dhyāna-mudrā*, with a devotee seated on stool on either side. Gandhāra stone. **N**[5], south. 2′ b.s. No. 1093.

20. Gandhāra bust and head in relief, 5″ high. Much damaged. **N**[17], 2′ b. top of stūpa. No. 674.

21. Winged figure of cupid in the round, ht. 4⅜″. Face damaged and legs below hips missing. Greenish Gandhāra slate. **N**[17], 2′ b. top of stūpa. No. 673.

22. Head in low relief, 3½″ high. Hair arranged in a knot over forehead and flowing back over the ears. Gandhāra stone. **P**[2], north (débris). No. 1381.

23. Frieze of cupids bearing garland, 1′ 7¼″ long. Gandhāra stone. **P**[4] south (débris). No. 1196.

24. Standing figure in relief, 11¼″ high, with flying figure at side appearing over proper left shoulder. Wears *dhotī*, scarf and ornaments. Feet and arms damaged. Style and modelling good. Gandhāra stone. **P**[5], north. 6′ b.s. No. 1137.

25. Bottom of casket of grey amethyst steatite, diameter 2″, decorated with cross hatchings. **P**[12], S. corner of structure, 2′ b.s. No. 608.

26. Bottom of miniature casket, diameter 1″, rim partially broken. Slate stone. **R**[3], 2′ 6″ b.s. No. 364.

27. Lion's head, 5″ high, kañjūr stone. **S**[3], west of débris. 2′ b.s. No. 30.

28. Draped figure of (?) Buddha, 7¼" high. Head, hands and feet missing, Gandhāra stone. T^2, 3′ b.s. No. 718.

29. Carved slate votive dish of grey schist, diameter 4½", divided into 4 quadrants with circular depression in centre. Two quadrants contain lotus leaves, the third a winged *makara*, and the fourth a figure with fish-tailed legs. T^2, 2′ b.s. No. 613. (Pl. V, *b*).

30. Bottom of steatite casket, diameter 1¾", decorated with lines and cross hatchings. T^2, 3′ b.s. No. 867.

31. Lamp of grey schist, 3" long, coarse workmanship. T^2, 1′ b.s., inside an earthen jar. No. 205.

32. Śiva (?) standing in front of bull. 6¼" high. Upper part above waist missing. Gandhāra stone. U^1, east. 8′ b.s. No. 1507.

B.—Stucco Objects.

1. Architectural fragment in form of flower, diameter 9¼", with acanthus-like leaves. In middle of flower but not at right angles to its face, a square hole is drilled. B^{22}, east. 3′ b.s. No. 1227.

2. Left foot, 5½" high, with traces of red paint, toes damaged. Main stūpa, East gate (débris). No. 1148.

3. Standing figure (male), 7¼" high. Left leg, both arms and head missing. Well modelled. Nude except for scarf and necklace. Main stūpa, East gate (débris). No. 1490.

4. Head, 3⅜" high, with corkscrew curls springing from crown of head and confined by heavy fillet; traces of red colour. Main stūpa, East gate (débris). No. 1474.

5. Head, 3¼" high. Flowing hair confined by cap with tasselled top. Main stūpa, East gate (débris). No. 1475.

6. Small head, 2⅝" high, with conical Persian cap and hood or veil behind. Nose and chin damaged; eyes, eyebrows and hair painted grey black; peak of cap, veil and fillet red; and red lines also on forehead and cheeks. Mon. S, 8′ b.s. No. 1563.

7. Head, 3⅞" high, with moustache and elaborate head dress. Nose damaged and right side of face missing. N^4, north. 3′ b.s. No. 504.

8. Right hand, 11½" long. Coarse workmanship; fingers damaged; first and second fingers wear rings with bezels. N^9, inside stūpa. 6′ b.s. No. 226.

9. Head from relief, 5¼" high. Face twisted towards left proper; ears and nose damaged; fillet bound round head. N^{11}, east; débris. No. 1376.

10. Mask of lion's head. Ht. 3". N^{13}, east. 2′ b.s. No. 1405.

11. Large head of Buddha, 13¼" high. Conventional type (belonging to one of the standing figures). Well modulated mouth. No *ūrṇā*. N^{17}, inside chapel. No. 893. (Pl. III, *g*).

12. Left hand, 9½" long. Tip of ring finger broken; also middle of little finger holding end of garment. Belongs to standing figure on south wall of shrine. N^{18}. No. 815.

13. Head of ascetic with drawn features, ht. 4¾". Deep-set eyes. Right side of skull missing. Striking forceful expression. Earlobes protracted. **P**^{8}, north. 6′ b.s. No. 1141. (Pl. III *f*).

14. Bracket figure 6¾" long. Gaping mouth; face damaged: traces of red pigment. **R**^{3}, 4′ b.s. No. 93.

15. Head, 4¾" high, with nose, chin and lower lip damaged. Features and hair treated in strikingly bold manner. Well modelled brow and cheeks. **R**^{3}, 2′ b.s. No. 178.

16. Head of an animal. (?) Bull. 2¾" high. **R**$_{3}$, 9′ b. top of wall. No. 334.

17. Head, 4½" high. With deep set eyes and gaping mouth, like a gargoyle. **R**^{3}, 2′ 6" b.s. No. 360.

18. Head. 2⅝" high. **S**^{6}. 2′ 6" b.s. No. 68.

19. Head, 2⅜" high; wears ear-rings and fillet. **S**^{6}. 2′ 6" b.s. No. 69.

20. Head, 3⅜" high, similar to preceding but crowned with conical cap **S**^{6}, 1′ b.s. No. 53.

21. Head, 3¾" high. Hair confined by turban tied in knot over r. ear. In fair preservation. Traces of red-brown pigment. **S**^{6}. 2′ 6" b.s. No. 179.

22. Torso and head of female, 6" high. Right arm and r. ear missing: left shoulder and one hand damaged. Wears armlets, bangles and headdress. The ring around neck appears to be the upper edge of a garment. **S**^{6}. 1′ 6" b.s. No. 54.

23. Head, 4½" high, with ornamental headdress. Left ear missing; otherwise well preserved. Hair falling in curls over r. ear; ring in r. earlobe. Charmingly delicate features. **S**^{6}. 2′ 6" b.s. No. 183.

24. Small head, 2½" high. Forehead damaged. Persian headdress, with neck lappet covering ears. An admirable little head. **S**^{7}, west. 2′ b.s. No. 458.

25. Mask of miniature head, 2¼" high. Ornamental headdress: face in fair preservation. **S**^{8}, south. 3′ 6" b.s. No. 945.

26. Miniature head, 2⅛" high, with ornamental turban ending in knot over left ear. Right ear and tip of nose damaged. **S**^{8}, west. 3′ b.s. No. 829.

C.—Terracottas.

1. Lion's head from vessel, 1¾" high; surface débris. No. 1. (Pl. V; *l*).

2. Mask, 3¼" high; surface débris. No. 1070. (Pl. III, *d*).

3. Head of Bodhisattva (?), ht. 6¼". Hair arranged in strands passing from *ushṇīsha* to forehead and confined by band tied in front. Earlobes and left eyebrow damaged. Pronounced nose and lips. At back is veil (?) falling from *ushṇīsha*. Mon. **S**. 8′ b.s. No. 1195. (Pl. III *e*).

4. Upper part of head of Buddha (?). 5¾" high, with curly hair. Hood behind, passing over the *ushṇīsha*. Hole from neck to crown of head apparently for wooden support. Mon. **S**. 10′ b.s. No. 1202.

5. Bearded head, 7" high, with strongly pronounced features. Hair drawn back in coarse strands from forehead and knotted on crown of head. Mon. **S**. 8′ b.s. No. 950. (Pl. III *b*).

6. Female figure, 7⅜" high, carrying lamp. Base broken. Hollow inside; of ordinary earthenware. Mon. **S.** 4′ b.s. No. 1561. (Pl. V *a*.)

7. Spout (polished) of vessel in form of *makara* snout. 2¾" long, powdered with mica. Mon. **S.** 8′ b.s. No. 1538. (Pl. V *m*.)

8. Lion's head, 2" wide, apparently from a vessel. Solid. Mon. **S.** 7′ b.s. No. 1420.

9. Lion's head from vessel, 2⅝" wide, powdered with mica. Mon. $\mathbf{S}^2$. 6′ b.s. No. 1358. (Pl. V *g*.)

10. Toy tortoise rattle, 4" long. Mon. **S.** 10′ b.s. No. 1274.

11. Cover of an incense burner (?) diameter 3¾". Decorated with niches on the outside, each of which is pierced with a hole; powdered with mica. Mon. **S.** 3′ b.s. No. 1212. (Pl. V *i*.)

12. Spout of a vessel, 2¾" long, in form of *makara* snout. Mon. **S.** 7′ b.s. No. 472.

13. Lamp, 4¼" long. Of coarse clay. Mon. **S.** 6′ b.s. No. 431.

14. Miniature human head, 1" high, with conical cap; well modelled. Mon. **S.** 5′ b.s. No. 388.

15. Lion's head, 1½" high, from vessel. Mon. **E.** 2′ b.s. No. 155.

16. Toy bird rattle. 3¾" long. Headless and broken underneath. $\mathbf{M}^{10}$, north. 2′ b.s. No. 1100.

17. Head, 5" high. Mouth, chin and r. cheek damaged. Hair tied with ribbon, which is passed around head. Coarse workmanship; badly damaged and of little interest. $\mathbf{N}^4$, east; 5′ below top of stūpa. No. 1037.

18. Head, 7½" high, badly damaged. Ornamental turban. $\mathbf{S}^6$. 2′ 6" b.s. No. 321.

19. Spout, 3" long, of conventionalised animal head. $\mathbf{U}^1$, south; débris. No. 1439.

D.—Pottery.

1. Clay lamp, 6⅜" long. Mon. **S.** 8′ b.s. No. 1565.

2. Incense burner with handle. Ht. 3¼". Mon. **S.** 5′ b.s. No. 383.

3. Earthenware jar with lettering in ink  No. 1259.

4. Baked clay stamp, 1⅛" high, with circular face incised with geometric pattern and dots. $\mathbf{N}^4$, north. 3′ b.s. No. 513.

5. Incense burner, 4½" high. $\mathbf{T}^2$. 4′ b.s. No. 833.

E.—Metal Objects.

1. Betel leaf of copper. 2" long. $\mathbf{B}^{24}$. 1′ b.s. No. 1252.

2. Arrow-head, 2½" long, triangular with concave sides. $\mathbf{K}^4$, west. No. 400.

3. Copper antimony rod, 4⅞" long, with both ends rounded. Mon. **S.** 8′ b.s. No. 1555.

4. Copper antimony rod, 4⅞" long, plain. Mon. **S.** 5′ b.s. No. 810.

5. Copper pin, 4⅞" long with ornamental head. Mon. **S.** 5′ b.s. No. 811.

6. Silver bronze finger ring, diameter ¾". Mon. **S.** 10′ b. s. No. 1286.

7. Copper ear ring, diameter ⅞". Mon. **S.** 5′ 6" b.s. No. 528.

8. Copper ring, diameter $\frac{7}{8}$"; broken. Mon. S. 5′ b.s. No. 812.

9. Copper finger ring, diameter $\frac{3}{4}$", with diamond-shaped bezel. Mon. S. 8′ b.s. No. 984.

10. Copper ring, diameter $\frac{1}{2}$", with linear decoration on the outside. Mon. S. steps. No. 1058.

11. Copper bangle, diameter $1\frac{3}{4}$", with rope pattern. Mon. S. 4′ b.s. No. 775.

12. Iron arrow-head, $3\frac{1}{2}$" long. Triangular, damaged. Mon. S. 2′ 6" b.s. No. 128.

13. Double iron hook, $2\frac{3}{4}$" long, with staple attached. Mon. S. 5′ 6" b.s. No. 546.

14. Copper antimony rod, $4\frac{3}{4}$" long, twisted in middle; both ends bulbous. Mon. E. 2′ b.s. No. 276.

15. Copper finger ring, diameter $\frac{7}{8}$", broken. N^{17}. No. 1044.

16. Decorative fragment of copper in shape of arrow-head. $1\frac{1}{2}$" long. N^{17}. 2′ b.s. No. 676.

17. Bottom of silver casket enclosing one of gold. Rough geometric figure impressed on gold. Diameter $\frac{3}{4}$". N^{18}. No. 816.

18. Iron arrow-head, $2\frac{3}{4}$" long, triangular with concave sides, damaged. P^{9}. East, 3′ b.s. No. 827. (Pl. V *e*.)

19. Iron arrow-head, $2\frac{1}{4}$" long, triangular with concave sides, damaged. P^{12}, débris. No. 558.

20. Thin sharp-pointed copper pin. 4" long. T^{2}, 2′ b.s. No. 617.

21. Copper bangle, diameter 2", decorated with linear pattern on rim. T^{2}, 5′ 6" b.s. No. 926.

22. Copper hand, $1\frac{3}{4}$" long holding a bud; well modelled. T^{2}, 2′ b.s. No. 693.

23. Iron ring and staple, 8" long. T^{2}, 5′ b.s. No. 876. (Pl. V *d*.)

24. Iron bowl, diameter $4\frac{3}{4}$". Rim partially broken. T^{2}, 3′ b.s. No. 756.

25. Iron bell, $2\frac{3}{4}$" high, complete with tongue. T^{2}, 3′ b.s. No. 714.

26. Copper rod, $4\frac{1}{4}$" long twisted in the middle and bent. U^{1}, east; 8′ b.s. No. 1599.

27. Copper finger ring, diameter $\frac{3}{4}$", plain. U^{1}, east. 8′ b.s. No. 1514.

28. Copper object, 4" long crescent-shaped with rough edges; U^{1}, west, 6′ b.s. No. 1508.

29. Iron safety pin, $4\frac{7}{16}$" long, broken; Mon. S, 5′ b.s. No. 8766. (Pl. V *c*.)

30. Arrow-head, $3\frac{1}{8}$" long, double-edged; Mon. S, 5′ b.s. No. 1111. (Pl. V *h*.)

KUNĀLA MONASTERY.

In the description of the Kunāla Stūpa which I published in last year's Report I mentioned that a little to the west of the stūpa and on a slightly higher level there was an extensive block of buildings which General Cunningham had mistaken for a guardhouse, but which I assumed to be a monastery of the kind almost invariably found side by side with Buddhist stūpas in this part of

India. This season I have cleared the eastern side of the building and found my assumption to be correct. Both monastery and stūpa are set on an artificial plateau which was constructed by levelling up the rough, rocky ridge with débris, and which on its eastern side covers the remains of the old city wall. The monastery is of the same age and built in the same style as the stūpa to which it belongs, but it is devoid of the decorative features which distinguish the latter. The walls are standing to a height of between 13 and 14 feet at their highest point, and have a thickness varying from 5′ 0″ in the outer walls to 3′ 1″ in the inner. They are of semi-ashlar masonry once covered with mud plaster, and of singularly massive construction, some of the blocks of which they are composed measuring as much as 4′ by 2′ 6″ by 1′ 6″. It is noteworthy that, as a general rule, the bond is carefully broken both in the ashlar courses and in the alternate diaper courses. So far as can be seen at present, the monastery consists of a large rectangular court measuring 155′ 6″ along its eastern side, with a smaller court on its south, the two courts presenting a continuous frontage to the east of nearly 200 feet. A view of this front taken from the stūpa is reproduced in Pl. VI, *b*. The larger court is designed on the usual plan with an open quadrangle in the centre and a verandah and range of cells behind it on the four sides. Along the east side there are nine of these cells, the corner ones of which measure 11 feet deep by 20 feet wide, the remainder being of the same depth and just half as wide. According to the learned Secretary of the Mahābodhi Society these measurements still continue to be the orthodox measurements for such cells at the present day. In the cells are small niches closed over with a rounded or pointed arch and no doubt intended for the reception of lamps. The main entrance to the monastery is in the eastern wall, but not quite opposite to the middle of the quadrangle, since there are five cells to the north of it and only four to the south. Its width is 15′ 2″ and it is flanked by two massive pylons with a spacious threshold of heavy limestone flags in front. The verandah is 19′ 5″ wide and raised, like the cells, on a plinth about 3 feet above the level of the quadrangle, into which there are several small flights of steps descending. Judging from the accumulation of débris inside the building, from the charred remains of timber over the débris, and from the later additions and repairs, the monastery seems to have been in occupation for a considerable period and finally to have been burnt down. Two arrow heads discovered among the charcoal suggest that its destruction was due to a hostile invasion. Their description is as follows:—

(1) Iron arrow-head, 6¼″ long and exceptionally heavy; flat, with two barbs. 2′ b.s. Kunāla Mon., No. 9. (Pl. VII, *6*.)

(2) Similar, four-sided. 2¾″ long. 2′ 6″ b. s., Kunāla Mon., No. 10.

SIRKAP.

In the lower city of Sirkap there is still a large part of the strip of ground acquired by Government which has not yet been touched by the spade, and I decided that the most profitable course would be to drive trenches north and south at intervals through this unexcavated area, and so ascertain as soon as possible where the most promising remains were likely to be found. Several such trenches were dug on the east and west sides of the High Street extending to a length of nearly 1,200 yards in all, and within a very few days this trial digging enabled me to locate another very interesting stūpa court belonging to a complex of buildings which I have designated block **A**, immediately inside the north gate of the city and on the eastern side of the High Street. This court, of which a photo is reproduced in Pl. VI *a*, is much more spacious than the one in block **F**, and, in addition to several stūpas of varying sizes, contains a number of chambers ranged against its four walls. The whole of it has not yet been cleared, and for this reason I do not propose to publish a plan of it at this stage; but, so far as can be seen at present, it measures some 95 feet from east to west by 101 feet from north to south. On the side overlooking the High Street are the remains of what appears to have been a lofty terrace, which probably corresponded in height to the lowest storey and was intended for the support of projecting balconies above. It resembles the terrace in front of the Buddhist Apsidal Temple higher up the street; but in this case there are no traces either of steps or of an entrance opening on to the High Street, and it is likely, therefore, that access to the court was provided by a doorway leading from one of the side alleys. The chambers inside the court seem originally to have been confined to groups of two or three apartments of a fair size disposed in each of its corners[1]. Subsequently, however, these chambers were replaced by ranges of somewhat smaller apartments on all sides of the court. The masonry both in the earlier and later rooms is of the rough rubble variety approximating in appearance to the small diaper; but in the earlier walls limestone is generally used for the larger blocks as well as for the small sparls which fill the interstices between them, whereas in the later walls kañjūr and limestone are used indiscriminately. Pending, however, the more extended clearance of the building, the above observations regarding the plan and construction of these chambers must be regarded as tentative only.

Block A.

The largest of the stūpas in this court stands in its centre and has a base measurement of 32′ 9″ square. In appearance it resembles generally the shrine in block **F**, but it is less solidly built and, so far as can be judged from its remains, less ornate than the latter, and it differs from it, too, in that the flight of steps which gave access to the plinth is on the northern instead of the western side. The core of the structure is of rubble, and the facing, as usual, of kañjūr stone overspread with coarse stucco and finished with limewash, coats upon coats of which, added no doubt in the course of many decades, were found adhering to parts of the structure. Round the base runs a *torus* and *scotia* moulding surmounted by a series of pilasters, seven on each side; above which were a frieze and dentil cornice, similar to the corresponding members in the stūpa of block **F**. The frieze and the cornice are no longer *in situ*, but a multitude of carved blocks belonging to them were found amid the fallen débris. Round

[1] They have been traced hitherto only in the south-west and north-west corners.

the upper edge of the plinth ran a balustrade of the orthodox pattern, 3′ 8″ in height including a somewhat deep coping and base moulding. Fortunately, a very complete section of this balustrade, measuring 4′ 2″ in length and comprising three uprights, was lying on the south side of the structure and proves of special interest as demonstrating how this kind of balustrade was constructed. Hitherto, I have found only the detached members of such balustrades, and though it was clear enough that they could not have been constructed on the open principle, like those for example at Sāñchī, it was by no means clear how the interspaces between the crossbars and pillars were filled in. From the well preserved specimen that has now been recovered in this court, it turns out that the balustrade was first pieced together in stone, each of the members (pillars, cross-bars, coping, etc.) being cut independently as if they were intended for an open railing, but with this difference, that the back of the pillars and coping were not dressed or decorated, and that afterwards a thick layer of lime plaster was applied over the whole back of the balustrade, while the front was also finished off more carefully with the same plaster.

Of the superstructure of this stūpa nothing is left but some of the kañjūr blocks of the drum and three umbrellas[1] of the same material, the largest one of which has a diameter of 3′ 3″. The chamber containing the relics is in the centre of the plinth about 3′ 9″ below its upper surface. It is 7½″ square by 1′ 7″ deep and constructed of blocks of kañjūr with a heavy block of limestone as a cover. This block had been moved from its original position and was found lying at the side of the chamber which had apparently been rifled of some of its contents. The only articles that I found inside it were the following:—

A relic bone.
Three small pearls.
Two shell beads.
One cylindrical gold bead.
Eight small pieces of gold.
Three coins of Apollodotus and Azes I.
Five fragments of a crystal dish measuring, when intact, about 10½″ in diameter by 2$\frac{5}{16}$″ high.

The fragments of the crystal dish are very finely cut and polished and probably date from Maurya times. That the dish could not have been intact when placed in the relic chamber, is evident from their respective dimensions, the diameter of the dish being more than three inches in excess of the sides of the chamber. Accordingly I conclude that the crystal fragments were brought from some older stūpa, probably with the relic itself, and preserved here for the sake of their sanctity.

The smaller stūpas in the court are three in number, *viz.*, one in fairly good preservation on the south side of the main stūpa and two of smaller dimensions and in a more ruinous condition near its north-west corner. All three

---

[1] Seven umbrellas in all were found in this court, of which three probably belonged to the largest stūpa.

are built of rough rubble masonry faced with plaster, and the largest of the three, which is standing to a height of 3′ 7″, is adorned with the usual base moulding surmounted by three Corinthian pilasters on each side. Each of the pilasters is relieved by a depression sunk in its face with a 'bead and reel' moulding made out in stucco. No relic was found in any of the smaller stūpas, but the bottom of a small round steatite casket was recovered in the débris by the side of the largest one.

Among the other small antiquities found in this court are the following:—

1. Three small votive stūpas of kañjūr, of a height varying from 1′ to 1′ 6″.
2. Four bowl-shaped bells of copper from 4″ to 7″ in diameter, furnished with ring handles at the top and iron tongues inside, suspended from rings of the same metal. Nos. 631 *a* and *b* 1125 and 722. (Pl. IX, *9*).
3. Goldsmith's mould (?) of terracotta, 2¼″ long, No. 880. (Pl. IX, *14*).
4. Flesh-rubber of terracotta, 3½″ × 3¼″ × 1¼″, with incised linear and other patterns on all sides. No. 876. (Pl. VIII, *d*).
5. Votive tank of terracotta, 10½″ square and 2½″ deep, provided with chamber at one side and steps descending from it. By the side of the steps is a female figure and at each corner of the tank is a lamp. Three birds are perched on the walls and inside it are eels or snakes, a tortoise, and a frog (?), with a post near the centre. No. 718. (Pl. VIII, *a*).
6. Saucer of Gandhāra stone, 3″ diameter, No. 920.

Another spot in Sirkap which gives promise of interesting discoveries is the plot of ground on the west side of the High Street and opposite to the building P. Here my trial trenches are bringing to light the remains of another substantially built and apparently very extensive structure, which, to judge by the proportions of the walls and courts so far exposed, will probably be found to vie in size with the complex of buildings on the other side of the street, which I have tentatively designated the palace. This, however, is little more than a surmise; for the complex of rooms and courts so far unearthed cover an area of only 166′ from east to west and 156′ from north to south, and consists of hardly more than two rectangular courts with rooms ranged about them. The larger court, which lies to the north, is a rectangle measuring 40′ 0″ from north to south by 60′ 2″ from east to west. A noticeable feature of this court is a series of three square piers built against the eastern wall with intervals between them of approximately 4′ 9″. Four other piers of the same kind, but much smaller, occur in one of the chambers to the west of the court. What was the purpose of these piers, cannot be determined without the help of further evidence; but I am inclined to surmise that they were intended as supports for the timbers of a ceiling in the one case, and of a projecting balcony in the other, and that they were inserted when the superstructure was showing signs of decay. Building opposite block P.

I noticed above when describing the Stūpa Court A that two kinds of rubble masonry were employed in the construction of its chambers; an earlier in which limestone was almost exclusively used, and a later in which limestone and kañjūr were indiscriminately mixed together. In this building there are a few walls of limestone, but the majority of them correspond with the more modern of these two types, though in this case the kañjūr blocks and sparls considerably predominate over the limestone; and from this as well as from other facts it may safely be concluded that this is one of the latest buildings on the site.

In some of the chambers the old stucco is still adhering to the walls with traces here and there of red and black paint. The stucco is composed of coarse river *bajrī* and lime, and a curious feature, which I have not previously observed in other buildings, is that in some cases it is applied, not on the face of the walling itself, which by reason of its very roughness affords an excellent backing for it, but on a surface of mud used perhaps for the sake of economy to level up the inequalities in the walls before the plaster was applied. Probably the same method of application was adopted in other structures also, and this would explain why so much of the stucco has fallen from the walls. In cases where it is relatively well preserved, as for instance at the Moṛa Morādu Stūpa, it has been applied directly to the surface of the stone without any intervening layer of mud.

Of the minor antiquities recovered in this building the following are some selected examples.

1. Circular mirror of copper, 4⅝" diameter, with projection for handle. Socket and rim slightly raised on one face, but no engraving. 160 × 101′; 3′ b. s. No. 405. (Pl. IX, *10*).

2. Copper object, 3⅜" long. Purpose unknown. The metal is cast and finished by filing, presenting a modern appearance. (Pl. IX, *13*)[1].

3. Rectangular iron plate measuring 5¼" × 5⅛" with nail holes at the four corners and key-hole near the middle; apparently the front of a door lock. 167 × 105′; 7′ b.s. No. 668:

4. Iron knife blade with broad back, 9" long. 158 × 101′; 2′ b.s. No. 624. (Pl. VII, *11*).

5. Similar, slightly curved, 4" long. 158 × 101′; 2′ 6" b.s. No. 658.

6. Similar, 4⅛" long. 158 × 101′; 2′ 6" b.s. No. 658.

7. Iron axe-head, 6½" long, with crescentic cutting edge, 4½" broad. Broken. 158 × 101′; 2′ 6" b.s. No. 657.

8. Iron dagger, flat and double edged, 7⅞" long, handle broken. 162 × 113′; 1′ b.s. No. 287.

9. Small pick-hammer head, 3¼" long, pointed at both ends and with hole for handle in middle. Perhaps used for working kañjūr stone. 160 × 101′, 3′ 9" b.s. No. 512.

10. Limestone plaque, 4¾" diam. Inner face divided into four sunk compartments decorated with lotus petals and other floral and linear patterns. Beneath are outlines of lotus. 166 × 99′; 3′ b.s. No. 841. (Pl. VIII, *g*).

[1] The antiquity of this object is doubtful.

11. Capital of a miniature pillar of Persian design, of clay badly burnt, 3" long, composed of four humped bulls sitting back to back and pierced with a hole in centre. Three heads of the bulls are missing. 162 × 107'; 2' 9" b.s. Reg. No. 348. (Pl. VIII*e*). Similar to the capitals found in the early cave temples of Western India, etc. A capital of kañjūr stone of similar design was found at the Dharmarājikā Stūpa.

In other parts of the lower city and particularly to the west of block F' my previous excavations were extended for a considerable distance, but no further description of any other buildings is called for at the present stage, and I shall content myself therefore with noticing some of the smaller antiquities recovered in these buildings.

Copper or bronze objects.

1. Pan, $3\frac{3}{8}$" high, with a ring handle on one side only. 77 × 48'; 2' 2" b.s. No. 313.

2. Stand, pyramid-shaped, $1\frac{7}{8}$" high, furnished with 4 feet and decorated with oblong or triangular holes pierced in four sides near base. 125 × 68'; 2' 8" b.s. No. 470. (Pl. IX, *12*).

3. Lamp, $3\frac{1}{16}$" diameter, provided with serpentine handle, to which a stopper is attached by chain for closing wick hole. 126 × 67'; 2' 4" b.s. No. 734. (Pl. IX, *11*).

4. Saucer, $3\frac{3}{16}$" diameter, ornamented inside with "omphalos" in centre and two concentric incised circles. 125 × 68'; 3' 4" b.s. No. 517. (Pl. IX, *7*).

5. Ivory handle of mirror (Pl. IX, *3*), ornamented with incised linear patterns. 125 × 68'; 3' 4" b.s. No. 515.

6. Broken handle of spoon, 2" long, in the form of the *nandipada* symbol. 90 × 72'; 5' 5" b.s. No. 142.

7. Copper disc (? buckle), $1\frac{3}{8}$" diameter. 86 × 73'; 6' b.s. No. 90.

8. Copper spoon, $7\frac{3}{16}$" long. 35 × 53'; 2' b.s. No. 636. (Pl. IX, *6*).

9. Copper bangle, 2" diameter. 38 × 43'; 2' b.s. No. 940. (Pl. VIII, *c*).

Iron objects.

1. Folding chair, 2' 2" high, with 'hoof' feet of classical pattern. *Cf.* the curule chair depicted on coins of Kadphises I. Presumably the seat was of cloth or carpet. 134 × 53'; 2' 5" b.s. No. 218. (Pl. IX, *5*).

2. Knife, $3\frac{1}{16}$" long, with broad flat back. 32 × 44'; 4' 4" b.s. No. 807.

3. Saw, $4\frac{1}{4}$" long, broken; with single tooth edge. The saw is too corroded to determine which way the teeth point. 4' 3" b.s. No. 161. (Pl. VII, *9*).

4. Small pick, $5\frac{3}{4}$" long, with flat cutting edge. 125 × 67'; 2' 3" b.s. No. 732. (Pl. VII, *13*).

5. Chisel with broad crescentic edge, $6\frac{5}{8}$" long. 125 × 67'; 2' 3" b.s. No. 732. (Pl. VII, *12*).

6. Axe-head, $6\frac{3}{8}$" long. In this and some other specimens of axe-heads the hole for the handle is unduly small. 125 × 67′; 2′ 3″ b.s. No. 732.

7. Saucer, $4\frac{1}{8}$" diam. 125 × 68′; 3′ 4″ b.s. No. 579.

8. Bowl, 5″ diameter, with two spikes at one side for attachment of handle. 123 × 48′; 2′ b.s. No. 358.

9. Crescent, $9\frac{7}{8}$", between horns. Purpose uncertain. 125 × 67′; 2′ 3″ b.s. No. 680.

10. Chisel, $5\frac{7}{16}$" long, with flat cutting edge. 125 × 68′; 3′ 8″ b.s. No. 614.

11. Sword, 2′ $4\frac{3}{4}$" long. Broken, 125 × 68′; 2′ 3″ b.s. No. 473.

12. Casing of wooden handle, $3\frac{5}{8}$" long, with 3 bars between side pieces. 124 × 54′; 2′ b.s. No. 332. (Pl. VII, *4*).

13. Knife, $5\frac{5}{8}$" long, with broad back. 125 × 67′; 2′ 3″ b.s. No. 732.

14. Similar, $6\frac{3}{4}$" long. 135 × 55′; 1′ 6″ b.s. No. 215.

15. Similar, 5″ long. 133 × 54′; 2′ 5″ b.s. No. 294.

16. Arrow-head, $5\frac{5}{8}$" long, flat variety, with two flanges; the head is $2\frac{7}{8}$" long. 132 × 43′; 1′ 8″ b.s. No. 225. (Pl. VII, *5*).

17. Adze head, $5\frac{1}{4}$" long, made in two pieces and beaten together. The handle socket is provided with two cross bars. 134×54′; 1′ 4″ b.s. No. 221. (Pl. VII, *3*).

18. Chisel, $10\frac{1}{2}$" long; bent. 135 × 55′; 1′ 6″ b.s. No. 215.

19. Rod, 4′ $3\frac{1}{4}$" long, with a knob at one end, pierced with hole, perhaps belonging to a fire tripod. 134 × 54′; 6″ b.s. No. 216.

20. Stand of a vessel, $10\frac{5}{8}$" diameter, consisting of ring on three legs. 135× 54′; 1′ 6″ b.s. No. 215.

21. Saw-edged sickle, 5″ long. 134×55′; 6″ b.s. No. 216. (Pl. VII, *1*).

22. Side piece of horse's bridle. $3\frac{1}{2}$" long. 132×42′; 1′ 8″ b.s. No. 228.

23. Spear-head, $7\frac{1}{8}$" long, ribbed down centre on both sides. 114 × 49′; 2′ b.s. No. 487. (Pl. VII, *2*).

24. Chisel $3\frac{3}{4}$" long, crescentic edge at one end and spike for handle at other. 85 × 73′; 4′ b.s. No. 22. (Pl. VII, *8*).

25. Axe, $3\frac{9}{16}$" long, pierced with hole for handle. 88 × 74′; 9′ 6″ b.s. No. 156.

26. Rectangular iron plate with raised edges, $2\frac{13}{16}$" × $1\frac{5}{8}$". 86 × 73′; 7′ b.s. No. 156.

27. Dagger, $11\frac{1}{8}$" long, with bent hilt. The upper part of the hilt is rivetted on. 86 × 74′; 6′ 5″ b.s. No. 95. (Pl. VII, *14*).

28. Similar but with narrower blade, $7\frac{3}{4}$" long, hilt broken. 86 × 74′; 3′ 8″ b.s. No. 29.

29. Two pronged fork, $5\frac{5}{8}$" long, for gardening purposes. 97×48′. 1′ 3″ b.s. No. 570. (Pl. VII, *10*).

30. Axe, $3\frac{1}{4}$" long. 85 × 73′. 4′ b.s. No. 22 (*a*). (Pl. VII, *7*).

31. Pickaxe, $10\frac{1}{16}$" long. 85×73′. 4′ 8″ b.s. No. 215. (Pl. VII, *15*).

Miscellaneous objects.

1. Bone handle (?), $2\frac{7}{8}$" long. 45′ × 59; 2′ 6″ b.s. No. 813.

2. Ivory pin, $3\frac{11}{16}$" long, with carved head. 77 × 49′; 3′ 1″ b.s. No. 370 (Pl. IX, *8*).

3. Shell disc, $1\frac{9}{16}''$ diameter, with a hole in the centre. Decorated on the convex side with concentric circles. 134 × 55′; 2′ 4″ b.s. No. 377.

4. Female figurine in relief carved on bone, height $6\frac{1}{4}''$, nude but adorned with anklets, girdle, necklace and bracelets. Coarse workmanship. Face damaged. 72 × 75′; 5′ 4″ b.s. No. 37. (Pl. IX, *2*).

5. Steatite dish, $5\frac{1}{4}''$ diameter, covered inside with copper. The copper is decorated with border of raised dots round the rim. 125 × 68′; 3′ 4″ b.s. No. 525. (Pl. VIII *f*).

6. Top of stūpa of Gandhāra stone. $4\frac{1}{2}''$ high, comprising *harmikā* and five umbrellas. The stone was finely turned on lathe and covered with gold leat, of which traces remain. Broken at base. 137 × 53′; 2′ 11″ b.s. No. 782. (Pl. VIII *b*).

7. Horn, $8\frac{1}{2}''$ long, with two tines and pierced with two holes at $2\frac{1}{4}''$ and $3\frac{1}{2}''$ from the base. Decorated with three incised lines at base. Side piece of horse's bridle. 90 × 79′; 7′ b.s. No. 166. (Pl. IX, *4*).

8. Earthen bowl, $7\frac{1}{2}''$ diameter, with almost straight sides, ornamented with incised lines in centre. Unusual shape. 85 × 73′. 4′ b.s. No. 23.

9. Bone object, $2\frac{15}{16}''$ long. 45 × 59′. 2′ 6″ b.s. No. 813. (Pl. IX, *1*).

SIRSUKH.

In connexion with the topography of Taxila which I discussed in my first report on the exploration of the site, I stated[1] that the latest of the three cities was that of Sirsukh, and that there was reason to believe that it had been built by the Kushāns, probably during the reign of Kanishka. This deduction regarding the date of the city was based partly on such remains of the fortifications and interior buildings as were then exposed to view, partly on the finds of coins which had been made from time to time by the peasants digging in their fields, but it has now been fully confirmed by two excavations that have been carried out during the past winter. The first of these, which like all Fortifications.
the other diggings in this quarter of the site, was under the immediate supervision of Mr. V. Natesa Aiyar,[2] the Officiating Superintendent in the North-West Frontier, was directed to laying bare a section of the fortifications on the eastern side of the city near its south-east corner, where the height of the mounds gave promise of the buried walls being in a better state of preservation than in other parts of the site. The nature of these fortifications will be clear to the reader from the plan, section and elevation of them on Pl. X, *a*, as well as from the photograph on Pl. XI, *a*, which has been taken from outside the defences. The wall, which is constructed of rough rubble faced with neatly fitting limestone masonry of the large diaper type, is 18′ 6″ in thickness and is provided at the base, both at its inner and outer face, with a heavy roll plinth, which was added after the wall itself had been completed, in order apparently

[1] *A. S. R.*, 1912-13, Pt. II, p. 4.

[2] I cannot allow this opportunity to pass without saying how much indebted I am to Mr. Natesa Aiyar for the energy and care which he has displayed in the excavation work at Sirsukh and Mora Morādu.

to strengthen its foundations. On the outer face of the wall and separated from each other by intervals of about 90 feet are semi-circular bastions, access to the interior of which is provided by a narrow passage carried through the thickness of the wall. Both the bastions and the wall itself were furnished with loopholes, which are placed immediately above the plinth referred to, at a height of 4 feet 10 inches from what I judge to have been the floor level. In the case of the bastions these loopholes widen towards the outside and are closed on both faces of the wall with triangular arches which give them a singularly western appearance. Beneath them, in the interior of the bastions, is a hollow horizontal chase in the wall, now filled with earth, which marks where timbers were once let into the masonry. Still lower down (on a level, that is to say, with the old floor) and opposite the entrance of the bastions, is an aperture 1′ 8″ high and 7″ broad, which no doubt served the purpose of a drain.

The foundations of the wall proper and of the bastions descend about 2′ 6″ below the floor level and are provided, inside the bastions, with a single footing about 6″ in width. The floors of the bastions were composed of lime concrete containing a large admixture of river sand.

If we compare these fortifications of Sirsukh with those of Sirkap, we shall find that they differ from the latter in several essential features. In the first place, they are faced with the large diaper masonry characteristic of the early Kushān period instead of the rubble masonry characteristic of the Greek and Scytho-Parthian periods. Secondly, they are pierced with loopholes for the use of defenders standing on the ground floor. Thirdly, the bastions are semi-circular in plan instead of rectangular, and are hollow within instead of solid. In the case both of Sirkap and of Sirsukh it may be assumed that the bastions were divided, like the bastions of later Indian fortresses, into two or more storeys, and that the upper storeys were hollow like the lowest storey at Sirsukh. In both cases, too, it may be taken for granted that the wall was provided with an upper terrace (possibly with two such terraces) and with lines of loopholes corresponding with the terraces, from which the defenders could shoot down on an attacking force.

Two other striking features in which the city of Sirsukh differs from its predecessor, are its symmetrical and almost rectangular plan and its situation in the open valley,[1] its builders having manifestly placed more reliance on their artificial defences than on any natural advantages which the hills could afford them. Whether these new features were the outcome of developments in military engineering in India itself, or whether they were introduced by the foreign invaders—the Kushāns—from Central Asia or elsewhere, is a question which we have not as yet enough data, either monumental or literary, for determining.

The minor finds from the bastions of Sirsukh include two copper coins of Hermaeus and Kadphises I, which were recovered on the floor level, an ivory handle, presumably of a mirror, 3¼″ long, and decorated with raised bands and hatchings (Pl. XV *n*) and a deposit of 59 copper coins of Akbar the Great, which were unearthed near the surface.

[1] For the situation and shape of Sirsukh see the plan on Plate I of my Annual Report, Pt. II, for 1914-15.

My second excavation at Sirsukh was carried out in the interior of the old city. Conditions here are less favourable for digging than in Sirkap; for, on the one hand, nearly all the area enclosed within the walls is low lying and abundantly irrigated, with the result that the ancient remains are buried deeper beneath the alluvial soil than in Sirkap; on the other hand, the few mounds which rise here and there among the cultivated fields and which doubtless mark the sites of relatively important structures, are now occupied by graves and ziārats or modern villages, such as those of Piṇḍ Gākhṛā and Piṇḍorā, and, while any disturbance of the graves or ziārats is, of course, out of the question, the removal of the modern dwellings could only be effected at an inordinate cost. As, therefore, excavation on any of the rising ground was precluded, a plot was selected between the village of Tofkiāñ[1] and the mound of Piṇḍorā, where dressed stones and pottery had often been turned out by the plough and where there was promise of ancient structures being found relatively near the surface. This promise was not falsified; for the two cross trenches which were first opened, led immediately to the disclosure of several walls of semi-ashlar masonry at a depth of between 3′ and 5′ below the crops, and, as the digging proceeded, a complex of buildings was revealed, which is likely to prove of considerable interest. A general view of these remains taken from the south-east is reproduced on Pl. XI, *b*, and a plan of them on Pl. X, *b*. From the latter it will be observed that they comprise parts of two courts, a larger one to the west and a smaller one to the east, with a series of chambers disposed around them and a connecting passage between. Obviously it would be idle at the present stage of digging to speculate on the extent or plan of this building: all that can be said, is that the principle on which it is designed, namely, the principle of the open court flanked by rows of chambers, is the same as that followed in the older structures of Sirkap; and, judging by the dimensions and structural character of what has been exposed, it may be surmised that the whole will prove to be an elaborate and extensive building, not unlike the one which I have designated the "palace" in the earlier city. In one respect, however, there is a noticeable difference between these two structures. In contradistinction to the other buildings in that city, the palace of Sirkap is provided with doorways leading from the courtyard to the ground floor chambers as well as from one chamber to another; here, in Sirsukh, there is no evidence of any such openings in the walls, and we are left to infer that access to the ground floor chambers was provided, as it was provided also in the ordinary houses of Sirkap, by steps descending from the first floor rooms. Tofkiāñ.

It remains to add that the wall stretching across the northern side of the Court A appears to be the foundation of a raised plinth, which probably supported a

[1] In *A. S. R.*, Vol. II, p. 133, and Vol. V, p. 67, Cunningham describes the find in one of the mounds near this village of a copper plate inscription dated in the year 78. But Cunningham himself is in doubt as to where precisely the inscription came from. In one place, he says that its find-spot is situated nearly a thousand yards to the south-west of Sirsukh, while in another he speaks of its having come from the village of Tofkiāñ inside the city, the reason for these conflicting statements being that the copper plate in question was discovered, not by Cunningham himself but by a *bhishti*, named Nur, who gave different accounts at different times and whose versions, therefore, are altogether unreliable. The remains which I have so far excavated near the village belong to a much later date than this inscription.

pillared verandah ; that, below the ground level, the foundations of the walls are rubble rather than semi-ashlar in character ; and that in the chambers C^{34} and D^{33} there were found three large earthenware jars, two in the former and one in the latter, of the type usually employed for the storage of grain, oil or water. Among the other minor antiquities recovered from this site may be mentioned the following :—

1. 50 copper coins attributable to Kadphises II, Kanishka and Vāsudeva.

2. Copper bowl, 9¼" diameter. Damaged. Four copper nails at rim for attachment of two handles. Found 2′ 6″ below surface. (Pl. XV *b.*)

3. Copper hair-pin with knob at one end, 5" long. Found 1′ 6″ below surface. No. 27.

4. Iron frying pan with handle, in two pieces, 19½" long. In good preservation. Found 4′ below surface. No. 21. (Pl. XVI *b.*)

5. Iron *kaucha* for making sweetmeats, 3¾" long. Handle missing. Found 2′ below surface. No. 49.

6. Bracket of Gandhāra stone, 12½" long and 4¼" high. The bracket is serpentine in form with Corinthian cap. Behind it, on one side, is the bust of a male figure crudely executed. Between the figure and bracket is a depression 2¾" wide by 2" deep. Dowel-hole below bust. Found 4′ below surface. No. 21. (Pl. XV, *e.*)

7. Cornelian intaglio, oval shape, ½" long. One side convex and the other flat. On the flat side, engraved figure of Nike (?) holding wreath in right hand and cornucopia or palm in left. Decadent type. Circa 3rd century A.D. Found 3′ 6″ below surface. No. 95.

8. Two *stili*, 3¾" and 3⅜" long, respectively. Found 2′ 6″ below surface. No. 74.

9. Bone die, 1¾" long. Nos. 1-4 indicated by concentric circles on the sides. Burnt to ashy grey colour. Found 4′ below surface. No. 57.

10. Shell hoop finger ring, 1⅛" diam. Incised petals on rim. Found 5′ below surface. No. 41. (Pl. XV *l.*)

11. Earthenware *surāhi* with handle, 9¾" high. Flat bottom. Wheel-turned. Red slip. In very good preservation. Found 2′ 6″ below surface. No. 70. (Pl. XV *a.*)

12. Earthen cup, 4½" across. Reddish clay with no slip or paint. Found 4′ 6″ below surface. (Pl. XV *c.*)

13. Miniature earthen bowl, 3¼" high. Buff-red clay, unevenly baked. No slip or paint. (Pl. XV *j.*)

14. Earthen *chirāgh* 4" diam. Raised handle in centre. Found 4′ 6″ below surface. (Pl. XV *d.*)

15. Miniature vase (*ḍoli*), 3¼" high. Coarse buff-red clay. Unevenly baked. No slip or paint. Found 2′ 6″ below surface. (Pl. XV *f.*)

16. Ditto, 3¼" high. No slip or paint. Found 6" below surface. (Pl. XV, *g.*)

17. Ditto, 3¼" high. No slip or paint. Rim damaged. Found 4′ 6″ below surface. (Pl. XV *h.*)

18. Ditto, 3" high. Reddish clay. No slip or paint. Found 3′ 6″ below surface. (Pl. XV *i.*)

19. Steatite slab (*āyāgapaṭa ?*), 4½" × 3¼". Circular depression in the middle of upper face, 2¼" diam. and figures of *śaṅkha*, *matsya*, *svastika*, lotus bud and *nīlotpala* on the edges. Found 2′ 6″ below surface. No. 65. (Pl. XVI *g.*)

LĀLCHAK.

Buddhist stūpa and monastery.

If the reader will refer to the map which I published in my last year's report,[1] he will find, between one and two hundred yards from the north-east corner of Sirsukh and on the pathway to the village of Gaṛhī Sayyadān, a group of four small mounds which are known locally as Lālchak.[2] These four mounds cover the remains of a Buddhist settlement containing stūpas, shrines and monasteries, which appear to date from about the year 300 A.D. Most striking among them is a small monastery in the northern part of the site (Pls. XII and XIV). It is standing to a height of between seven and eight feet above the ground level and contains a vestibule in front, four chambers for habitation leading off from it, and a small apartment on the west side, which probably served as a godown. The entrance is in the middle of the southern side and is approached by a flight of four stone steps. A second stairway, also of stone, led from the vestibule to the upper storey, which has now perished (Pl. XIV *b*.) The foundations of the walls descend to a depth of 3′ 6″ below the interior floor level, and starting from the top of the plinth are splayed slightly on the outside. They were strengthened both inside and outside the building by a packing of gravel, river sand and clay, with a small admixture of lime, which may, however, have been accidental. Both the foundations and the superstructure are constructed of heavy limestone blocks in the later semi-ashlar style. No doubt, the walls of the upper storey were of similar construction, but to judge by the large quantities of ashes, burnt earth, iron nails, clamps and the like, which were found in the débris, the fittings and upper floor must have been of timber and the roof of the same material with the usual covering of earth. The date—end of third or beginning of fourth century A.D.—which I have assigned above to this monastery, is based upon the style of its masonry; for no minor antiquities to which a definite date can be assigned, were found associated with its foundations or walls. On the other hand, in the débris a few feet below the surface of the mound there came to light four silver coins belonging to the White Huns, which suggest, though they do not prove, that the building had been burnt out and buried from view before the sixth or seventh century of our era. Indeed, it is quite possible that it was not in occupation for more than a few decades; for, though the stairway is worn and smoothed by the passage of many feet, fifty years would, I think, be quite enough time to account for this.

Among the minor antiquities recovered from this site the following are the most interesting:—

1. Copper *triśūla*, 5″ long. Gilt on both sides and with two iron rings at back, of which one is broken. Found 6′ below surface. No. 52. (Pl. XVI *a*.)

2. Two copper rosettes, gilt on one side, 2¾″ diam., with hole in centre bearing traces of iron nails. Probably served as bosses on a wooden door. Found 6′ below surface. No. 40.

---

[1] *A. S. R.*, 1914-15, Pl. I.

[2] Cunningham does not appear to have noticed the remains at this place, as there is no reference to them in his reports.

3. Bronze finger ring with flat bezel and knobs at either end, $\frac{13}{16}$" diam. Found 3' below surface. No. 3.

4. Iron pickaxe, 6½" long. Hole for handle broken. Found 8' below surface. No. 6.

5. Iron arrow-head, 2½" long, with triple flange but no barbs. Found 3' below surface.

6. 150 beads, perhaps belonging to a necklace, of cornelian, garnet, calcedony, crystal, malachite, lapis-lazuli, gold, pearl, and shell. Found 6' below surface. No. 36. (Pl. XVI *d.*)

Stūpa I. The stūpa numbered I in the plan on Pl. XII, of which photographs are reproduced in Pl. XIII, *b* and *c*, is situated to the south-east of the monastery just described and about forty yards distant from it. It stood in the middle of a rectangular compound belonging apparently to a monastery,[1] and was square in plan with a broad flight of steps projecting on its northern side. As usual, its core is of rubble, and its facing of neatly dressed semi-ashlar masonry with kañjūr let into the limestone for all decorative features, both limestone and kañjūr being finished with a coating of stucco. The mouldings at the base are the familiar *torus* and *scotia*, the former being bevelled in three facets, as is generally the case in the later structures at Taxila. The pilasters which adorn the plinth, are of the Corinthian order, but very stunted and decadent, and surmounted, as is also usual in late structures, by Hindu brackets.

Inside the court of this stūpa, to the right and left of the entrance, are the remains of two small chapels of which the one to the east consisted of a square sanctum for the image with a portico in front, paved with stone slabs. What is left of the other is too fragmentary to be made out with certainty. The design no less than the construction of this and the following building indicate that they were coeval with the neighbouring monastery described above, and it is therefore interesting to record that a pit sunk into the rubble core of this stūpa yielded 140 tokens and coins of various issues, including those of Taxila, of Antialcidas, Kadphises II, Indo-Sasanian kings and Sāmantadeva. It is very unlikely that these coins, lying haphazard in the earth, were intentionally deposited there when the stūpa was erected. Their presence may be accounted for on the assumption that the débris used for the core of the stūpa was brought from one of the ancient city sites where such coins are found in abundance.

Stūpa II. The second stūpa[2] illustrated on Pl. XII lies between Stūpa I and the monastery, but in this case nothing is now left standing except its semi-ashlar foundations. Fortunately, however, the relic-deposit in the centre of the stūpa and at a depth of three feet below the surface had not been disturbed. The earthenware pot in which it reposed had been broken by the weight of the superincumbent débris, but the deposit itself was intact and proved to consist of thirty beads of gold, garnet, ruby, jasper and shell. The relic bone, which had presumably accompanied them, had crumbled to dust.

---

[1] Traces of cells were observed around the limits of this court but were not excavated, and are not therefore shown on the plan.

[2] The remains of this stūpa have been covered in again since excavation.

MOṚA MORĀDU.

There remains, finally, to be described a group of Buddhist monuments which in some respects, perhaps, is more interesting than any group of such monuments hitherto discovered in this part of India. They lie about a mile to the south-east of the city of Sirsukh, and are situated in a small glen at the back of the village of Moṛa Morādu. Here, as one goes eastward, the slopes grow noticeably greener; for the wild olive and *sonattha* shrub flourish freely among the rocks, and the rugged gorge of Meṛi, through which the pathway ascends to the monuments, is singularly picturesque. Inside the glen —or I might better, perhaps, term it a cup in the hills—an oblong terrace was constructed by the Buddhist builders, and side by side on this terrace were erected a stūpa and a monastery of commanding size—the former at its western, the latter at its eastern end. When first discovered, both monastery and stūpa were buried in a deep accumulation of débris and detritus from the surrounding hills, the only part of the structures visible to the eye being about five feet of the ruined dome of the stūpa, Pl. XVIII, *a*, which in years gone by had been cut in twain by treasure hunters in search of the relics, and, like the Dharmarājikā stūpa, had been sadly damaged in the process. Beneath this accumulation, however, both buildings proved to be remarkably well preserved, standing actually to a height of between fifteen and thirty feet and still retaining many admirably executed reliefs in stucco on their walls. The design of the stūpa and its decoration will be clear to the reader from the plan, section and details on Pl. XVII, as well as from the photographs in the three following plates: and there is little for me to add by way of further explanation. Its core, as usual, is rubble and its facings semi-ashlar masonry of limestone, kañjūr being used only for the mouldings, pilasters and other decorative features, and the whole finished with a coat of lime plaster. The pilasters between the bays round the plinth of the stūpa are of conspicuously slender proportions and are composed not, as might have been expected, of long perpendicular blocks of kañjūr let into the limestone walls, but of piles of small and neatly dressed pieces measuring about 9" × 3½" on the face, and presenting almost the appearance of bricks. In the base moulding (*torus* and *scotia*) only the stucco facing was rounded off, the core of kañjūr being merely bevelled off in flat facets and provided with channels to which the stucco could better adhere. The berm, which is placed at a height of sixteen feet above the ground level, was covered with a layer of concrete about one inch in thickness composed of river *bajrī* and lime. No trace of any relic chamber was found in the drum or plinth, and if such a chamber ever existed, it must have been placed high up in the dome, which is now destroyed.

In point of architectural design there is nothing specially remarkable about this stūpa, nothing to distinguish it from other memorials of a like character, such as the Bhallaṛ and Kunāla stūpas, which were erected in the third and fourth centuries of our era. Thanks, however, to its protected position in the hills and other fortunate circumstances, many of the stucco reliefs with which its walls were decorated and which in other cases have almost entirely perished, are here tolerably well preserved; and, though their colouring has mostly disappeared, they suffice to give us a much better idea than we could otherwise have got, of how these monuments looked when they first emerged from the hands of their builders. Apparently, the whole surface of the structure up to the top of the drum was covered with figures; for there are groups of Buddhas and Bodhisattvas both standing and seated in the bays between the pilasters; on the face of the pilasters themselves there are series of Buddhas ranged one above the other; on the drum, again, above the berm the same figures are repeated on a smaller scale; and on each side of the steps was a continuous row of figures disposed in decreasing sizes beneath the raking cornice, just as they might have been in pedimental groups. Some examples of these reliefs are figured in Pls. XIX and XX, and it will easily be understood from these illustrations to what a relatively high standard both their style and their technique attained. What strikes one most, perhaps, about them, and particularly about those in the bays on the south side of the plinth, is the life and movement combined with the dignified composure of the figures. This life and movement is specially evident in some of the attendant Bodhisattvas, the swish of whose robes, with the limbs delicately contoured beneath them, is wonderfully true and convincing. Delicate, too, and singularly effective are the hovering figures which emerge from the background to the sides of the Buddhas, as if they were emerging from the clouds. Yet another point that arrests the attention, is the highly successful manner of portraying the folds of the drapery, the technical treatment of which points to Hellenistic tradition and to accurate observation on the part of the artists.[1]

A number of heads, needless to say, were found detached from the figures around the base of the stūpa. Some examples of these heads are figured in Pl. XX and are described in the following list:—

1. Buddha head, 15" high. Ears and nose damaged. *Ūrṇā* missing. Hair treated in conventional curls. Of solid stucco throughout. Traces of red paint on hair. No. 232. (Pl. XX *c*).

2. Ditto, 7" high. In splendid preservation. Only ear-lobes damaged. Small but prominent *ūrṇā*. Hair waved back from forehead. No moustache. Traces of crimson paint on lips, eye-lids, forehead and neck. No. 297 (Pl. XX *d*). This head affords a good opportunity of studying the technique of these figures. Over the plaster is a fine slip apparently applied before the final definition was given to the features. The face is left white, but the lips, edges of nostrils, edges and folds of eye-lids, edge of hair, folds of neck and ear-lobes are picked out in red and the hair itself is coloured grey-black.

3. Bodhisattva head, 5" high. Ears and headdress damaged. No *ūrṇā*. Traces of crimson paint on lips. Hair grey-black; roughened with age. No. 292. (Pl. XX *e*.)

[1] In Greek sculpture of the good period, the mass of the material was chiselled away and the folds left, as it were, in relief; in Roman and decadent Greek work, labour was saved at the expense of truth by merely grooving out the folds from the mass of the material.

4. Ditto, 4¼" high. R. ear and side of throat missing and headdress damaged. Wears ear-rings and ornamental headdress with fillet across forehead. No *ūrṇā* or moustache. Sharp, clear-cut features. No. 305. (Pl. XX, *f*.)

5. Ditto, 3¼" high. Slightly damaged. No *ūrṇā* or moustache. Headdress in form of crown with twisted band round forehead. Wears ear-rings. No. 296. (Pl. XX *g*.)

6. Buddha head, 6¼" high. Ear-lobes, nose, chin and forehead damaged. *Ūrṇā* missing. Traces of red paint on lips and neck. No. 285. (Pl. XX, *h*.)

Stūpa II. On the south side of the steps of this stūpa is a smaller monument of the same kind, a plan and section of which are shown on Pl. XVII. It is of the same date and constructed and decorated in much the same manner as the larger edifice, but only a few fragments of the stucco reliefs have survived on the south and west sides.

Monastery. The monastery connected with these stūpas is as interesting as the stūpas themselves. From the plan of it reproduced on Pl. XXI it will be seen that, in addition to the usual open rectangular court, it comprises an extension containing several chambers at its eastern side. The entrance to the rectangular court is on the north, and access to it is provided by a broad flight of steps with a landing at the top (Pl. XXII *c*). The steps, which are built of limestone and are much worn, are 9′ 9″ in width, with treads 1′ 2″ broad and risers 10½″ in height. Originally, the doorway leading into the portico was 10′ 8″ in width, but some alterations and additions seem to have been made at a later date, which had the effect of reducing its width by about six feet. On the west wall of the portico and at a height of 3′ 4″ from the floor is a niche containing a remarkably well preserved group of figures in high relief, namely: Buddha in the centre and four attendant worshippers on either side. The niche is 4′ in height by 1′ 8″ in depth and is closed above by a pointed Gandhāra arch.

Passing from the portico into the interior of the monastery we find ourselves in a spacious court with 27 cells ranged on its four sides (Pl. XXII *a*). In the middle of the court is a depression about 2′ 0″ deep with steps descending into it on each of its four sides, and, at its south-east corner, a square platform which once supported the walls of a chamber. Near the edge of this depression and at intervals of about five feet from each other, is a series of stone slabs, the upper surface of which is level with the rest of the court. These slabs acted as bases to the pillars of a broad verandah which appears to have been constructed of wood [1] and which, besides shading the fronts of the cells, served also to provide communication with the cells on the upper floor. The eaves of the verandah no doubt projected beyond the pillars which supported it, so as to discharge the rain water into the depression in the middle of the court, whence it could be carried off by a covered drain. The height of the lower storey was about twelve feet, as is proved by the ledge and row of socket holes, evidently intended for the timbers of the first floor, in the back walls of the cells on the south side. Access to the upper floor was obtained, not, as might have been expected, near the entrance portico but by way of two flights of steps in cell

[1] The wood construction is evidenced by the mass of charcoal, iron fittings, etc., found in the débris.

No. 15 on the south side of the building. On the western and southern sides of the court all the cells are provided with windows; on the northern side they were not perhaps so necessary, as the light admitted through the cell doors would be brighter; and on the eastern side they were impracticable, inasmuch as there were other chambers at the back of the cells. The windows are placed at a height of about eight feet from the ground, are somewhat narrower at the top than at the bottom, and contract considerably towards the outside. In some of the cells, but not in all, are small niches apparently for lamps, like those in the monastery at Lālchak and in the one adjoining the Kunāla stūpa.

The interior of the chambers occupied by the monks were covered, like the rest of the monastery, with a coating of plaster, in this case of mud, but were probably destitute of any decoration. In the verandahs, on the other hand, the walls appear to have been relieved with colours, and the wood-work was no doubt carved and painted or gilded, while the courtyard was further beautified by effigies of the Buddha of superhuman size set on pedestals in front of the cells or by groups of sacred figures in little niches in the walls (Pl. XXII *b*). Of the larger effigies remains of seven have survived round about the quadrangle, namely, in front of the cells 1, 2, 5, 7, 11, 12 and 23; but only the first three of these are even tolerably well preserved. In each of these cases there is a particular interest attaching to the smaller reliefs on the front of the pedestals, from the fact that they illustrate the dresses worn by lay-worshippers at the time they were set up, namely about the fourth or fifth century A.D. (Pl. XXIII *b*). Of the groups in the niches, the one illustrated in plate XXIII *a* depicts the Buddha seated in the *dhyāna-mudrā* with attendant figures to the right and left.

A still more valuable discovery than these statues or reliefs, is a stūpa almost complete in every detail which was found inside the cell No. 9 (Pl. XXIV *f*). It is standing to a height of twelve feet and is circular in plan with a plinth divided into five tiers, with elephants and Atlantes alternating in the lowest tier, and Buddhas seated in niches alternating with pilasters in the tiers above. The core of the stūpa is of kañjūr, and the mouldings and decorations are of stucco once decorated with colours, *viz.*, crimson, blue and yellow. The umbrella was constructed in sections threaded on to a central shaft of iron, but in the course of ages this shaft had decayed, and the umbrella was found lying at the side of the stūpa. The edges of the umbrellas are pierced with holes intended apparently for streamers or garlands. This stūpa is, I believe, the most perfect one of its kind yet discovered in Northern India and as such possesses a very exceptional antiquarian value.

The plan of the monastery on Pl. XXI was drawn out before the clearance of the extension on the east had been finished, and consequently it fails to show the interior walls to the full extent to which they have now been exposed. As a fact, the extension, as originally designed, comprised four spacious chambers, the largest of which, on the northern side, is distinguished by the presence of four kañjūr columns, and presumably served as the 'conference hall' of the community. To what use the other three chambers were intended by their original builders to be put, there are not yet sufficient data for determining, but it may be surmised that one of them, probably the middle one, was used as a refectory. At a later date—that is, some two centuries after the building of the monastery—this part of it was considerably altered by adding two small closets in the middle chamber and by raising the floor of the chamber in the south-east corner by some eight feet and constructing therein a reservoir, meant apparently for a bath, with a water channel leading down into the middle chamber. The two closets referred to are of unusual form, one being a sort of small *rotunda* with an entrance on its western side, the other rectangular in plan with raised benches on two of its sides. In appearance the *rotunda* looks more like a well than anything else; but its walls are carried down no deeper than the foundations of the monastery, and beneath them there is nothing but solid rock. Possibly this and the other closet adjoining formed part of the baths of the monastery and served as hot or cold chambers.

It remains to add that the original walls of this monastery are in a rather late variety of the large diaper style and may be assigned both on this and other evidence to about the close of the 2nd century A.D. The additions and repairs were in the late semi-ashlar style and were executed, as I have indicated above, about two hundred years later. Many coins of the Kushān Kings, Huvishka and Vāsudeva, were found on the floor of the monastery.

The following is a list of the principal antiquities recovered from this monastery :—

1. Copper lamp, in several pieces, made of thin metal. The cup is detachable. 1¼" diameter, with hole in centre for wick. 3′ b.s. No. 61. (Pl. XV, *k*.)

2. Bronze bracelet, 2" diameter. Notched rim. 8′ b.s. No. 41. (Pl. XV, *o*.)

3. Copper gilt *triśūla*, 6¾" long, surmounted by circular disc, apparently a *chakra*. Four holes for attachment. No. 244. (Pl. XVI *c*.)

4. Copper rosette, 4½" diameter. Iron nail in centre. Probably served as a boss on a wooden door-frame. 1′ 6" b.s. No. 31. (Pl. XVI *e*.)

5. Lamp of Gandhāra stone, leaf-shaped, 5" long. Carved with lotus petals on the outer surface and bead ornament along the rim, which is damaged. A slight projection on each side. 1′ 6" b.s. (Pl. XV *m*.)

6. *Harmikā* of kañjūr, coated with stucco, 1′ 10½" wide and 10" high. Much damaged. Traces of blue and red paint. The crowning member of a miniature stūpa. (Pl. XVI *f*.)

7. Terracotta[1] head of Buddha, 8" high; earlobes broken and *ushṇisha* damaged. Small *ūrṇā*. Hair treated in small conventional curls. Lime slip, but no paint visible. 4′ 2" b.s. No. 149. (Pl. XXIII *d*.)

8. Terracotta Bodhisattva (?) head, 4¾" high. Lobe of r. ear and top of head damaged. Fairly well baked. Red ware. Traces of lime slip. 4′ 6" b.s. No. 73. (Pl. XXIII *g*.)

[1] It is not certain whether the clay of these and other terracottas was burnt intentionally or merely resulted from a conflagration in the monastery. The surface was rendered smooth with a clay wash and afterwards coated with a lime slip, to which colours or gold leaf were applied. In one specimen the face is coloured pink, in another gilded.

9. Terracotta Buddha head, 12" high. Ears and forehead with *ūrṇā* damaged. Circular depression in centre of upper lip. Traces of lime slip. No. 168. (Pl. XXIV *b*.)

10. Terracotta image of Buddha, 1' 8" high, seated cross-legged in the *dhyāna-mudrā*. *Saṅghāṭī* covering both shoulders. Small *ūrṇā*. Curly hair taken back in waves from the forehead and prominent *ushṇīsha*. Made of buff red clay but badly baked. Formerly occupied one of the niches in front of the cells of the monastery. No. 21. (Pl. XXIV *e*.)

11. Figure of Bodhisattva Gautama (?) of Gāndhāra stone, standing on rectangular pedestal carved with lotus rosettes. Height, including pedestal, 3' 4". Part of halo missing. Prominent *ūrṇā* and *ushṇīsha*. *Saṅghāṭī* covers only left shoulder. Wears ear-pendants in form of lions, perhaps to indicate that he represents Śākya-Siṁha. Elaborate necklace with numerous amulets. Bracelets on upper right arm. Headdress of beaded netting. Sandals on feet. Moustache. Hair waved from forehead and falling in corkscrew curls down back. Fore-arms, which were separate pieces dowelled on to upper arms, are missing. Part of pedestal beneath left foot cracked. Found in cell No. 8. No. 121. (Pl. XXIV *a*.)

12. Figure of Bodhisattva Maitreya, of Gāndhāra stone. Height 2' 10". Right hand, feet and pedestal damaged. Holds flask in left hand, while the right hand is raised in *abhaya-mudrā*. Wears two necklaces and tasseled ear-rings. Plain halo. No *ūrṇā*. Hair treated in conventional curls. Socket-hole above *ushṇīsha*. *Saṅghāṭī* covers only left shoulder. Found in room No. 8. No. 118. (Pl. XXIV *d*.)

13. Decorative fragment of Gāndhāra stone. Divided horizontally into three compartments and closed above by trefoil niche. In the upper compartment, Buddha standing in the centre in *abhaya-mudrā*, attended by *Vajrapāṇi* on the proper right and surrounded by five lay worshippers, of whom one appears to be Indra. In the central compartment is the scene representing the offering of the bowls by the four Lokapālas. In the lowermost panel, which is almost completely defaced, is Buddha under the Bodhi tree with worshippers on either side. Found in room No. 8. No. 111. (Pl. XXIV *c*.)

14. Soapstone seal, 2¾" square and ¾" thick, carved on both sides. Deep groove on the rim all round and hole running through two sides for attachment. On obverse, conventional *garuḍa* (?) standing l. with a branch in its beak and trampling on a serpent. In front of it, a coiled serpent with raised hood, and behind it, a rampant lion. In exergue, an inscription in Gupta Brahmī characters of about the beginning of the 5th century A.D., which reads *Hariśchandrasya* "of Hariśchandra." (Pl. XXIII *e*.) On reverse, figure of wind god (?) blowing horn. In field to l., foliage; to r., figure holding offering (?) in l. hand and uncertain object in right. Below, two *gaṇas* in violent motion, one holding water pot. Found in room No. 3 on the floor level. (Pl. XXIII *f*.)

15. Bronze cylinder seal, ⅝" long, with a hole through centre engraved on four sides with following designs:—(a) Male figure seated cross-legged in niche, (b) Draped female figure with cap, holding indistinct object. In front

of her, and apparently held by l. hand, a serpent, (c) and (d) obscene figures. Carving crude and coarse. Found in room No. 3 on the floor level. No. 21. (Pl. XIII X c.)

List of rare and unique coins found at Taxila during 1915-16,[1] (Pls. XXV and XXVI.)

No.	Metal and size.	Obverse.	Reverse.	Reg. No. and Find-spot.	Remarks.
			Local Taxilan.		
			Single die.		
1	Æ ·55	Bull to l., couched .	Blank	Sk. 882. 156×102′; 3′ b.s.	Much defaced. Not represented in the Indian collections.
2	Æ ·6	*Svastika*, with taurine symbol between each arm in incuse circle.	Blank	Dh. 1597. East of U 1.	Ditto.
			Heliocles.		
3	Æ ·8× ·75	Diademed bust of king to r. Greek legend :— [B]ΑΣΙΛΕΩΣ ΔΙΚΑΙΟΥ ΗΛΙΟΚΛΕΟΥ[Σ]	Elephant standing to l. Kh. legend : *Maharajasa dhramikasa Heliyakreyasa*. In exergue, mon. Σ	Sk. 1070. 88×72′; 6′ 9″ b.s.	Rare. Cf. *P.M. Cat.*, Pl. III, *148*.
			Apollodotus.		
4	Æ 1·×·9	Apollo standing r., helmeted, clad in chlamys and boots ; holding out an arrow in both hands : quiver at his back. Greek legend on three sides : ΒΑΣΙΛΕΩΣ ΣΩΤΗΡΟΣ ΑΠΟΛΛΟΔΟΤΟΥ	Tripod lebes. Kh. legend : *Maharajasa tratarasa Apaladatasa*. In r. field, Kh. *ge*. In l. field, Kh. *ji*.	Sk. 971. 89 ×72′; 5′ 6″ b. s.	Cf. *P. M. Cat.*, Pl. V, *344*.
			Menander.		
5	Æ ·65× ·65	Elephant's head with bell round neck. Greek legend : ΒΑΣΙΛΕΩΣ ΣΩΤΗΡΟΣ ΜΕΝΑΝΔΡΟΥ	Club of Herakles. Kh. legend....... *tratarasa Menadrasa*. To r., M. 70.[2]	Sk. 148. 86×73′; 7′ b. s.	

[1] Again I have to thank my friend Mr. R. B. Whitehead, I.C.S., for the valuable help he has given in the listing of these coins.

[2] The monogram references are to the Plate of monograms and marks in Mr. Whitehead's *Punjab Museum Coin Catalogue*, Vol. I (1914). It is necessary to differentiate between Bactrian, Indo-Scythian and other monograms.

No.	Metal and size.	Obverse.	Reverse.	Reg. No. and Find-spot.	Remarks.
			Theophilus.		
6	Æ ·8× ·75	Bust of Herakles to r., with club over l shoulder. Greek legend : [B]ΑΣΙΛΕΩΣ ΔΙΚΑΙΟΥ ΘΕΟΦΙΛΟΥ	Cornucopiæ. Kh. legend : *maharajasa dhramiasa . . philasa.* To l., mon indistinct.	Sk. 855. 21×67'; 2' b. s.	Very rare. Cf. *P M. Cat.*, Pl. VIII, 632 ; *B. M. Cat.*, Pl. XXXI, 4 (supplement.)
			Hermæus.		
7	Æ ·65	Diademed bust of the young king to r. Greek legend indistinct.	Winged Nike to l. with palm and wreath. Kh. legend indistinct. To r., M. 94.	Sk. 978. 88×71'; 5' 10" b. s.	
8	Æ ·7	Diademed bust of the young king to r. Greek legend indistinct.	Winged Nike to l., with palm and wreath.	Sk. 672. 125×68'; 4' 9" b. s.	
9	Æ ·65	Diademed bust of the bearded king to r. Greek legend indistinct.	Winged Nike to l. with palm and wreath. Kh. legend indistinct. In l. field, Kh. *pra.* In r. field, indistinct mon.	Sk. 651. 125×68'; 4' 9" b. s.	
			Idharasa.		
10	Æ ·5	King on horseback to r. Greek legend indistinct. In front Kh. *ya.*	Pallas, armed, to r. Kh. legend : *Idha (?) rasasa . . . pra . . . . sa.* In r. field, Kh. *pra.*	Sk. 612. 125×68'; 4' b.s.	Cf. Annual Report for 1912-13, Pt. II, p. 49.
			Aśpavarma.		
11	Æ ·5	King on horseback to r. Greek legend indistinct. In front, Kh. *ra.*	Pallas, armed, to r. Kh. legend : *Aśpavarmasa strategasa Indravarmaputrasa.* In l. field, mon. ·ꝫ . In r. field Kh. *sa.*	Sk. 1035. 87×72'; 6' 6" b. s.	A new type of Aśpavarma. The two types hitherto known are described on pp. 130 and 150 of the *P. M. Cat.* See also Annual Report for 1912-13, pp. 49 and 50, Coins 27-34.

No.	Metal and size.	Obverse.	Reverse.	Reg. No. and Find-spot.	Remarks.
			Aśpavarma—*contd.*		
12	Æ ·45	King on horseback to r. In front mon. ⊙ and Kh. *ya*. Greek legend indistinct.	Pallas, armed, to r. Kh. legend.....*śpa*..... In r. field Kh. *pri*.	Sk. 620. 125×68′; 3′ 8″ b. s.	This coin is of the type published as No. 28 in the Annual Report for 1914-15. The attribution to Aśpavarma is not certain.
			Abdagases.		
13	Æ ·9	King on horseback to l. In front, symbol of Gondopharnes. Greek legend corrupt : ΒΑΣΙΛΕΟΝΤΟ ... ...ΕΩΝ.....	Zeus standing to r. with long sceptre in l. hand and r. arm extended. Kh. legend :.......... *bhrataputra*......To r. Kh. *pra*. To l., M. 2.	Sk. 651. 125×68′; 4′ 9″ b. s.	
			Soter Megas.		
14	Æ ·45	Erect nude figure with long sceptre in r. hand and drapery over l. arm. To l., M. 9. To r., Kh. *ri*.	Draped figure standing to r., holding *cornucopia*. To l., M. 2.	Dh. 1466. E. gate of main stūpa ; 2′ b. s.	Rare. Cf. *P. M. Cat.*, Pl. XVI, *113*.
			Rājūvula.		
15	Lead ·8	Lion to r. Corrupt Greek legend. Above, tree-shaped mon.	Herakles standing to front. Kh. legend : ......*trapasa apa*.....	Sk. 309 ; spoil earth.	Rare. Cf. *P. M. Cat.*, p. 166, No. 133.
			Hermæus and Kadphises I.		
16	Æ ·8	Crude bust of Hermæus, diademed, to r. Gk. legend obliterated.	Herakles facing, with lion's skin on l. arm ; club resting on ground in r. hand. Kh. legend : ....*Kujula*.	Ss. 3 ; 3′ b. s.	Decadent type.
17	Æ ·65	Crude bust of Hermæus, diademed to r. Gk. legend obliterated.	Herakles facing, with lion's skin on l. arm ; club resting on ground in r. hand. Kh. legend defaced.	Ss. 5 ; 9′ b. s.	Ditto.

No.	Metal and size.	Obverse.	Reverse.	Reg. No. and Find-spot.	REMARKS.
			Kadphises I.		
18	Æ ·7	Buddha seated in conventional attitude with uncertain object in r. hand. Kh. legend illegible.	Zeus, wearing diadem, standing to r., with r. arm extended and long sceptre in l. hand. Corrupt Greek legend. To l., Kh. *pu*.	Sk. 554. 125×68'; 3' 5" b. s.	Rare. Cf. *P. M. Cat.*, Pl. XVII, *29*.
19	Æ ·65	Buddha seated in conventional attitude with uncertain object in r. hand. Kh. legend: ·····*kada[pha]sa khu* ·······	Zeus wearing diadem, standing to r., with r. arm extended and long sceptre in l. hand. Gk. legend corrupt. In l. field, Kh. *pu*.	Sk. 612. 125×68'; 4' b. s.	Ditto.
			Kanishka.		
20	Æ 1·05	King standing at altar. Greek legend defaced.	Buddha seated facing, cross-legged; arms in posture of benediction. Greek legend defaced.	Dh. 94. R³; 4' b. s.	Very rare. Cf. Cunningham, *Coins of the Kushans*. Pl. XVIII, *12*.
			Kushān Coin.		
21	Æ ·9	King facing, diademed and radiate, reclining on a low couch.	Two armed Śiva to l., with long trident in r. hand and gourd in l. To l., M. 4.	Dh.1601. Débris; south quadrant of Stūpa I.	Debased Huvishka type.
			Sasanian.		
22	Æ ·65× ·6	Bust of king to r., no legend.	Altar with heavy base and top; symbol on shaft. No legend, rude square piece.	M. M. Mon. 253; 6' b. s.	Cf. *I. M. Cat.*, Pl. XXIV, *5* and *7*.
23	Æ ·65× ·65	Ditto . . .	Altar with heavy base and top. No legend; rude polygonal piece.	M. M. Mon. 181.	Ditto.
24	Æ ·55× ·55	Ditto . . .	Defaced	M M. Mon. 268; 3' b. s.	Ditto.
25	Æ ·55× 45	Ditto . . .	Defaced	M. M. stūpa 271; 4' b. s.	Ditto.

No.	Metal and size.	Obverse.	Reverse.	Reg. No. and Find-spot.	Remarks.
			Uncertain.		
26	Æ ·5	Crude figure standing in incuse	Thick lines . . .	Dh. 1303. P⁴; 1′ b. s.	These uncertain coins are all probably of debased Indo-Sasanian types and were current in mediæval times. See Cunningham's *Coins of Mediæval India*, pp. 46 to 52.
27	Æ ·5	Crude fish (?) within incuse.	Four thick lines . .	Dh. 1303. P⁴; 1′ b. s.	
28	Æ ·45	Crude figure standing within incuse.	Thick lines . . .	Dh. 1303. P⁴; 1′ b. s.	
29	Æ ·45	Crude figure standing .	Four thick lines . .	Dh. 619. T⁸; 2′ b. s.	
30	Æ ·5× ·45	Crude human figure standing.	Three parallel lines .	Tofkiāñ 44; 5′ 3″ b. s.	
31	Æ ·45	Ditto . . .	Four parallel lines .	Tofkiāñ 35; 4′ b. s.	
32	Æ ·5× ·45	Ditto . . .	Two thick lines . .	M. M. Mon. 17; 2′ b. s.	
33	Æ ·6× ·55	Ditto . . .	Four parallel lines .	Tofkiāñ 43; 4′ 3″ b. s.	
34	Æ ·55× ·45	Crude human figure seated (?)	A symbol within dots .	Lc. stūpa 13; 11′ b. s.	
35	Æ ·5× ·45	Solar symbol . .	Solar symbol . .	Lc. stūpa 19; 10′ b. s.	

No.	Metal and size.	Obverse.	Reverse.	Reg. No. and Find-spot.	REMARKS.
			Uncertain—*contd.*		
36	Æ ·45× ·4	Fire altar . . .	Defaced . . .	Lc. stūpa 68; 11′ b. s.	
37	Æ ·45× ·4	Crude figure standing .	Crude figure standing .	M. M. Mon. 100; 7′ 6″ b. s.	
38	Æ ·6×·5	Crude design . .	Defaced . . .	Lc. Mon. 20; 2′ 6″ b. s.	
39	Æ ·5× ·45	Fire altar . . .	Defaced . . .	Lc. stūpa 48; 12′ 6″ b. s.	
40	Æ ·55× ·55	Crude elephant(?) within incuse square.	Defaced . . .	Dh. 880 T²; 5′ b. s.	
41	Æ ·9	Crude figure standing .	Indistinct object . .	Dh. 916 T²; 5′ 6″ b. s.	
42	Æ ·9	Ditto . . .	Defaced . . .	Dh. 861 T²; 4′ b. s.	
43	Æ ·55× ·5	Crude figure standing within incuse.	Crude figure of a tree(?)	Dh. 1303 P⁴; 1′ b. s.	
44	Æ ·8	Tree in railing . .	Indistinct . . .	M. M. stūpa 230; 3′ 6″ b. s.	
			Kidār Shāhi.		
45	AR 1·1	Bust of king to the front with bushy hair on both sides of the face; crown with triple ornament. Legend in Gupta letters: Kidāra *Kushān shā*.	Fire altar, with two attendants carrying drawn swords. Below the altar are three characters. Sir Alexandar Cunningham took these to be numerals.	M. M. stūpa 309; 10′ 6″ b. s.	Rare. Cf. Cunningham, *Coins of the Later Indo-Scythians*, Pl. VI, *1*.

No.	Metal and size.	Obverse.	Reverse.	Reg. No. and Find-spot.	Remarks
			White Huns.		
46	AR 1·2	Beardless head of king to r., diademed, with crescent on helmet; large crescent behind shoulders; club in front of face; Huna symbol behind head. Legend in Brāhmī letters behind head, *shāhi*; in front, *Jabula*.	Part of fire-altar with attendant presenting sword. Rest indistinct, the coin being repoussé.	Lc. Mon. 16; 3′ 6″ b. s.	Restruck. Rare. Cf. Cunningham, *Coins of the Later Indo-Scythians*. Pl. VII. *13*.
47	AR 1·25	Ditto . . .	Indistinct . . .	Lc. Mon. 16 a; 3′ 6″ b. s.	Ditto.
48	AR 1·2	Beardless head of king to r., diademed with crescent on helmet; large crescent behind shoulders; club in front of face; Huna symbol behind. Legend in Brāhmī characters behind head, *shāhi*; in front *Jubula*.	Fire-altar with attendants.	Lc. Mon. 16 b; 3′ 6″ b. s.	Ditto.
49	AR 1·15	Ditto . . .	Traces of fire-altar. Rest indistinct.	Lc. Mon. 16 d; 3′ 6″ b. s.	Ditto.
50	AR 1·15	Ditto . . .	Traces of fire altar with attendants.	Lc. Mon. 16 c; 3′ 6″ b. s.	Ditto.
51	Æ ·65	Sasanian bust to r. To r., legend possibly meant to be *shaonano shao*......	Fire altar . . .	Dh. Relic vase in stūpa N[11].	
52	Æ ·65	Ditto . . .	Ditto . . .	Ditto .	
			Medal.		
	Æ 1·1 × ·7	Bust of king to r., no legend.	Blank . . .	M. M. Mon. 267; 2′ 6″ b. s.	Unique. Broken.

Seals.

1. Bronze seal. ·55″ across ; oval. Deity standing. Ring at back. Sk. 972. 89 × 72′ ; 5′ 6″ b. s.

2. Bronze seal, ½″ across ; oval. Lion (?) standing to r. Rings at back. Sk. 652. 125 × 68′ ; 4′ 9″ b. s.

3. Copper seal, ·65″ across ; oval. Flying swan (?) within an oval border. Mark of rings at back. Dh. 1522 ; 9′ b. s.

JOHN MARSHALL.

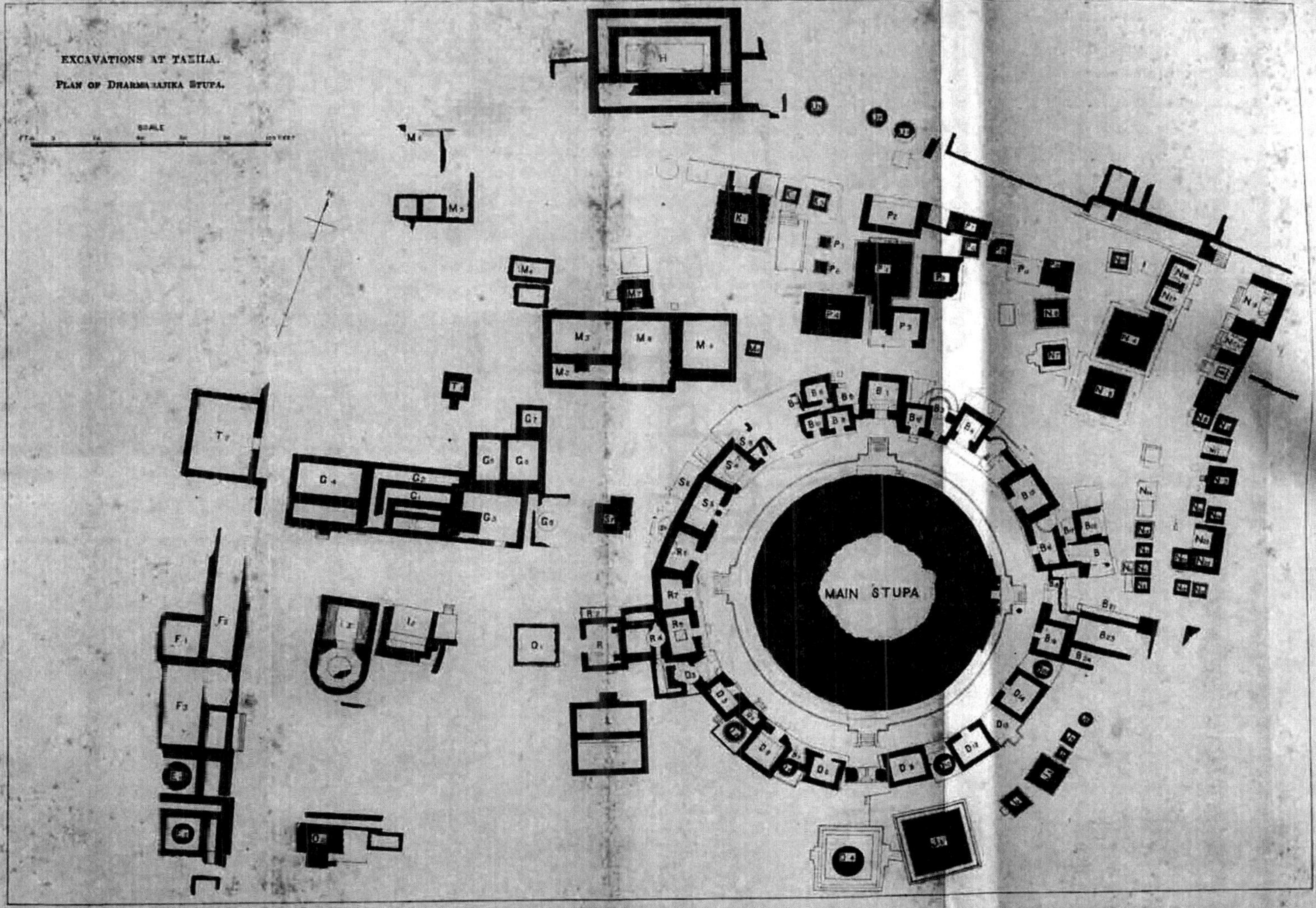
EXCAVATIONS AT TAXILA.
PLAN OF DHARMARAJIKA STUPA.
SCALE
MAIN STUPA

EXCAVATIONS AT TAXILA: DHARMARAJIKA STUPA.

a. THE MAIN STUPA FROM N.-E.

b. CHAPEL N18 FROM WEST.

EXCAVATIONS AT TAXILA: DHARMARAJIKA STUPA.

a

b

c

d

e

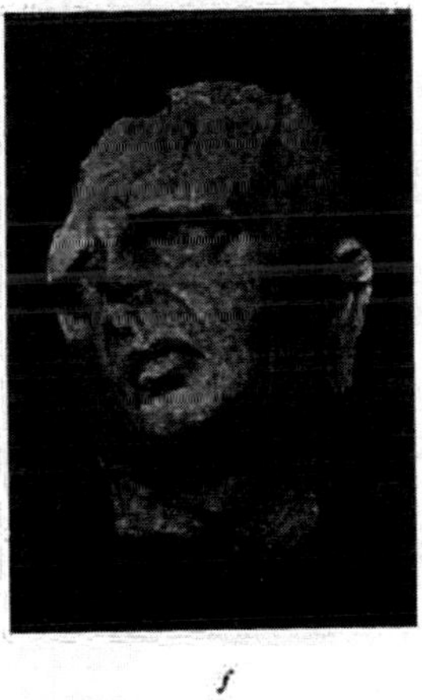

f

g

TERRACOTTA AND STUCCO OBJECTS.

Photo-engraved & printed at the Offices of the Survey of India, Calcutta, 1917.

EXCAVATIONS AT TAXILA: DHARMARAJIKA STUPA.

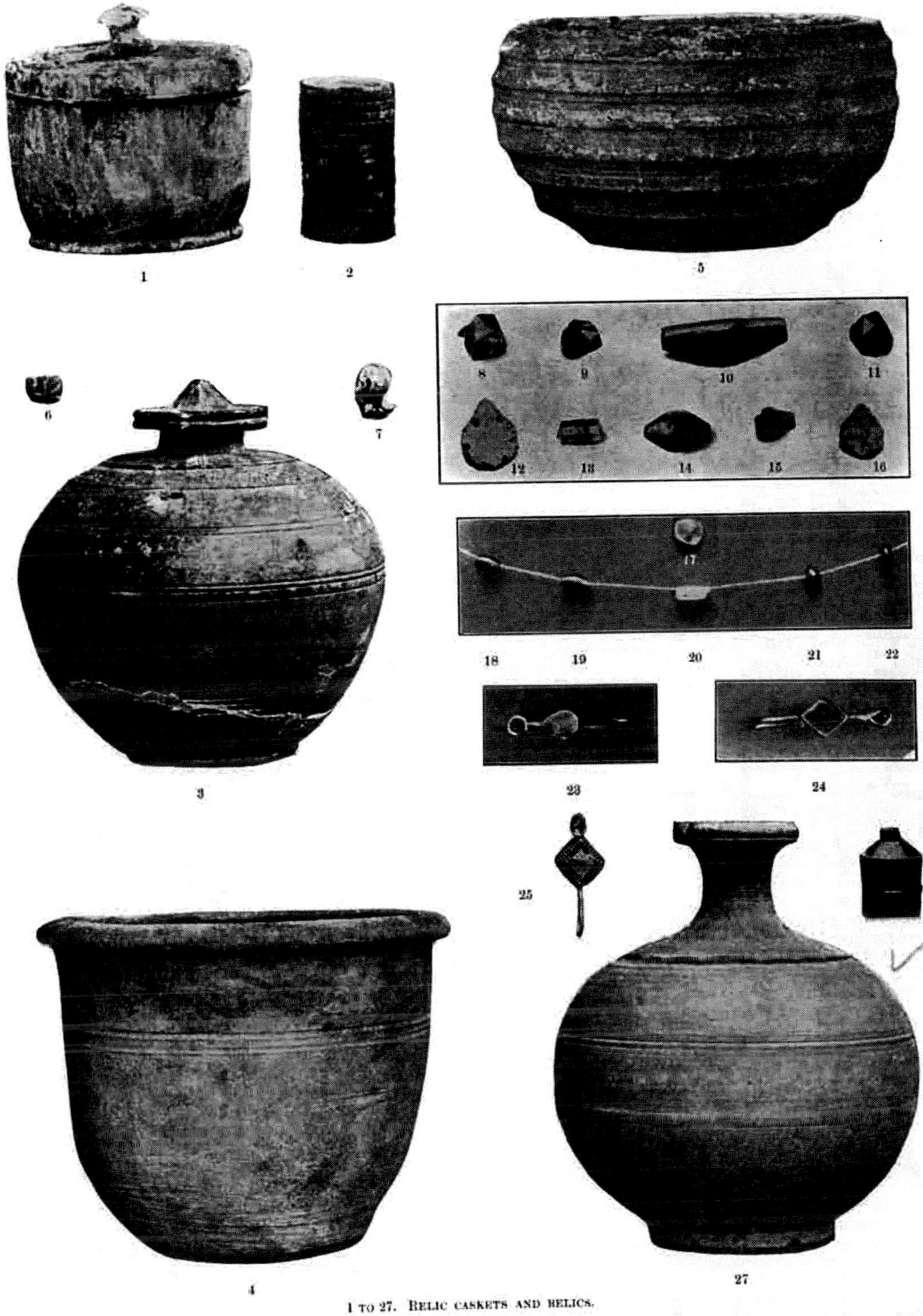

1 TO 27. RELIC CASKETS AND RELICS.

Photo-engraved & printed at the Offices of the Survey of India, Calcutta, [illegible]

PLATE V.

EXCAVATIONS AT TAXILA: DHARMARAJIKA STUPA.

MISCELLANEOUS OBJECTS.

Photo-engraved & printed at the Offices of the Survey of India, Calcutta, 1917

EXCAVATIONS AT TAXILA: SIRKAP.

a. SHRINE IN BLOCK A FROM S.E.

b. KUNALA MONASTERY FROM EAST.

Photo-engraved & printed at the Offices of the Survey of India, Calcutta, 1917.

EXCAVATIONS AT TAXILA: SIRKAP.

IRON OBJECTS.

Photo-engraved & printed at the Offices of the Survey of India, Calcutta, [illegible]

EXCAVATIONS AT TAXILA: SIRKAP.

MISCELLANEOUS OBJECTS.

Photo-engraved & printed at the Offices of the Survey of India, Calcutta, [illegible]

PLATE IX.

MISCELLANEOUS OBJECTS.

Photo-engraved & printed at the Offices of the Survey of India, Calcutta, 1917.

EXCAVATIONS AT TAXILA.

a. SIRSUKH FORTIFICATIONS: SOUTH-EAST CORNER.

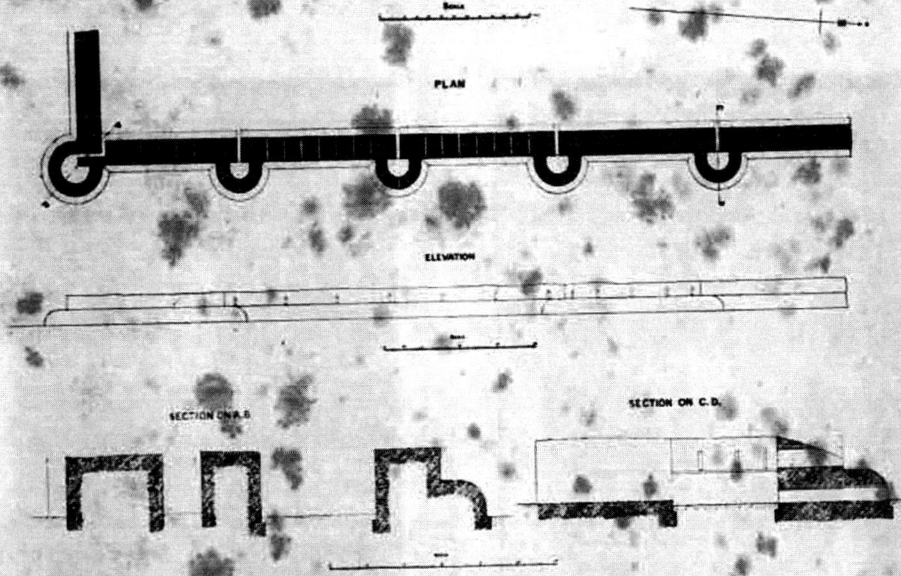

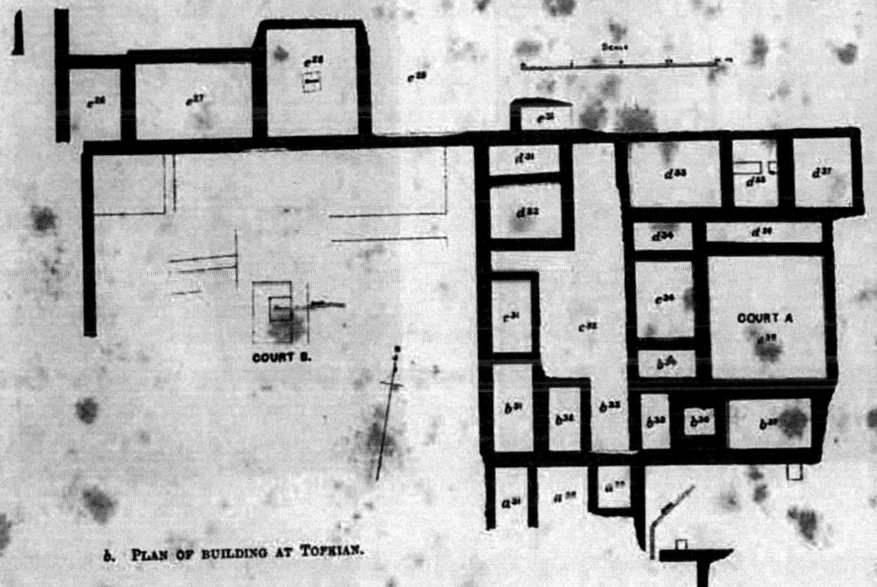

b. PLAN OF BUILDING AT TOFKIAN.

EXCAVATIONS AT TAXILA.

a. SIRSUKH FORTIFICATIONS: VIEW FROM EAST.

b. TOFKIAN: VIEW OF EXCAVATIONS FROM S.-E.

Photo-engraved & printed at the Offices of the Survey of India, Calcutta, 1917.

EXCAVATIONS AT TAXILA.

BUILDINGS AT LALCHAK.

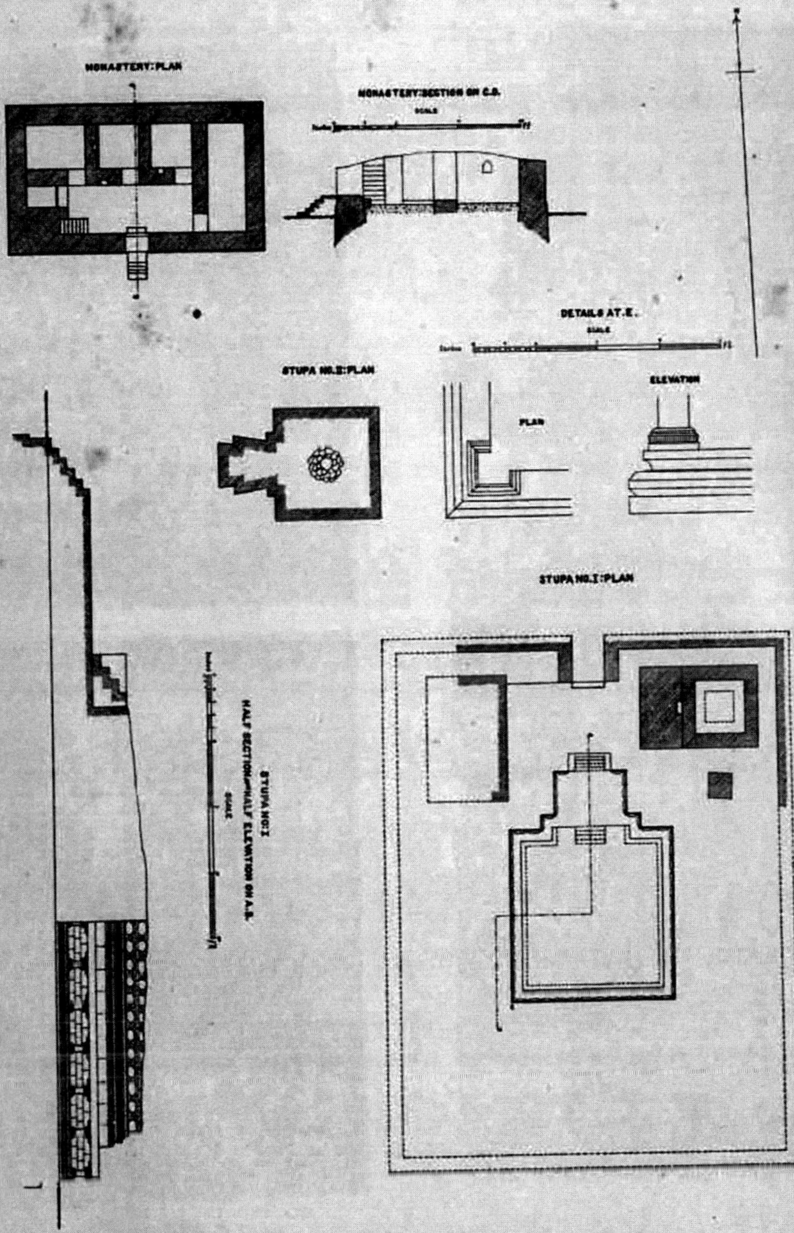

a. SIRSUKH FORTIFICATIONS: VIEW FROM EAST.

b. LALCHAK: VIEW OF THE STUPA PARTIALLY EXCAVATED.

c. LALCHAK: GENERAL VIEW OF THE STUPA AFTER EXCAVATION.

Photo-engraved & printed at the Offices of the Survey of India, Calcutta, [illegible].

a. Monastery from S.W.

b. Interior view of Monastery from East.

Photo-engraved & printed at the Offices of the Survey of India, Calcutta, 1917.

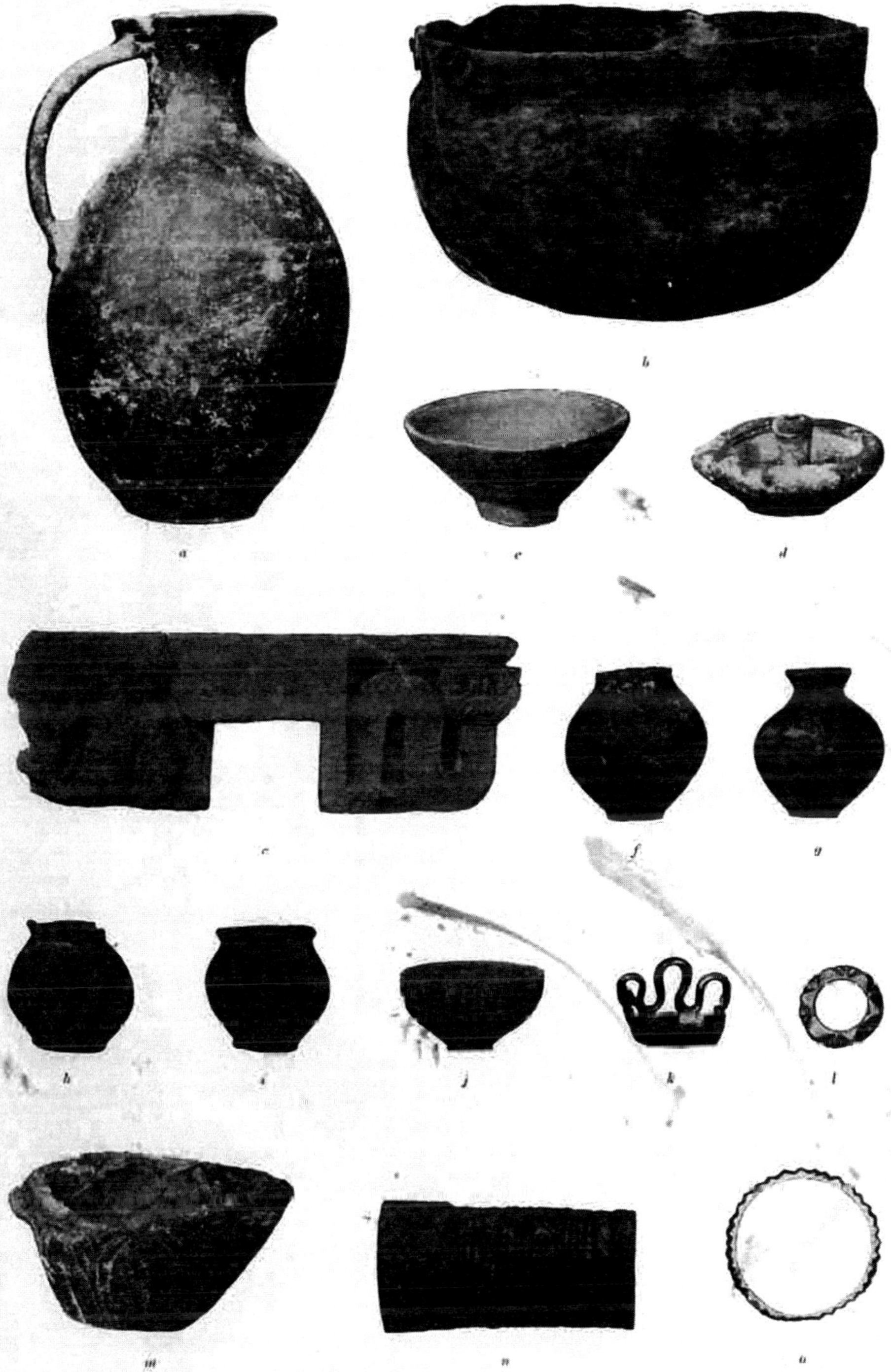

MINOR ANTIQUITIES FROM SIRSUKH FORTIFICATIONS, TOFKIAN AND MORA MORADU.

PLATE XVI.

a

b

c

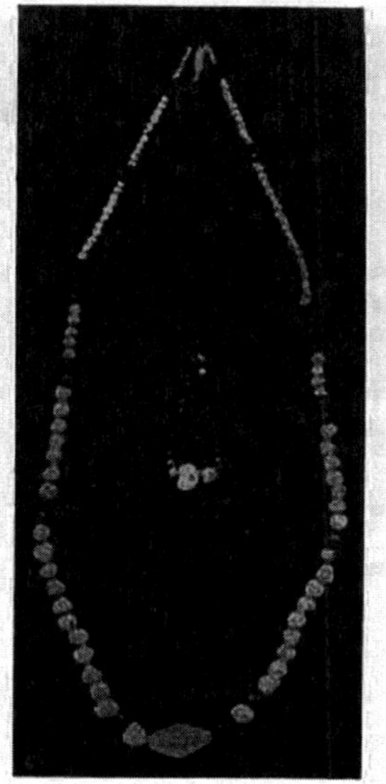

d

e

f

g

MINOR ANTIQUITIES FROM TOPKIAN, LALCHAK AND MORA MORADU.

Photo-engraved & printed at the Offices of the Survey of India, Calcutta, 1917

EXCAVATIONS AT TAXILA: MORA MORADU.

PLAN, SECTION AND DETAILS OF STUPA.

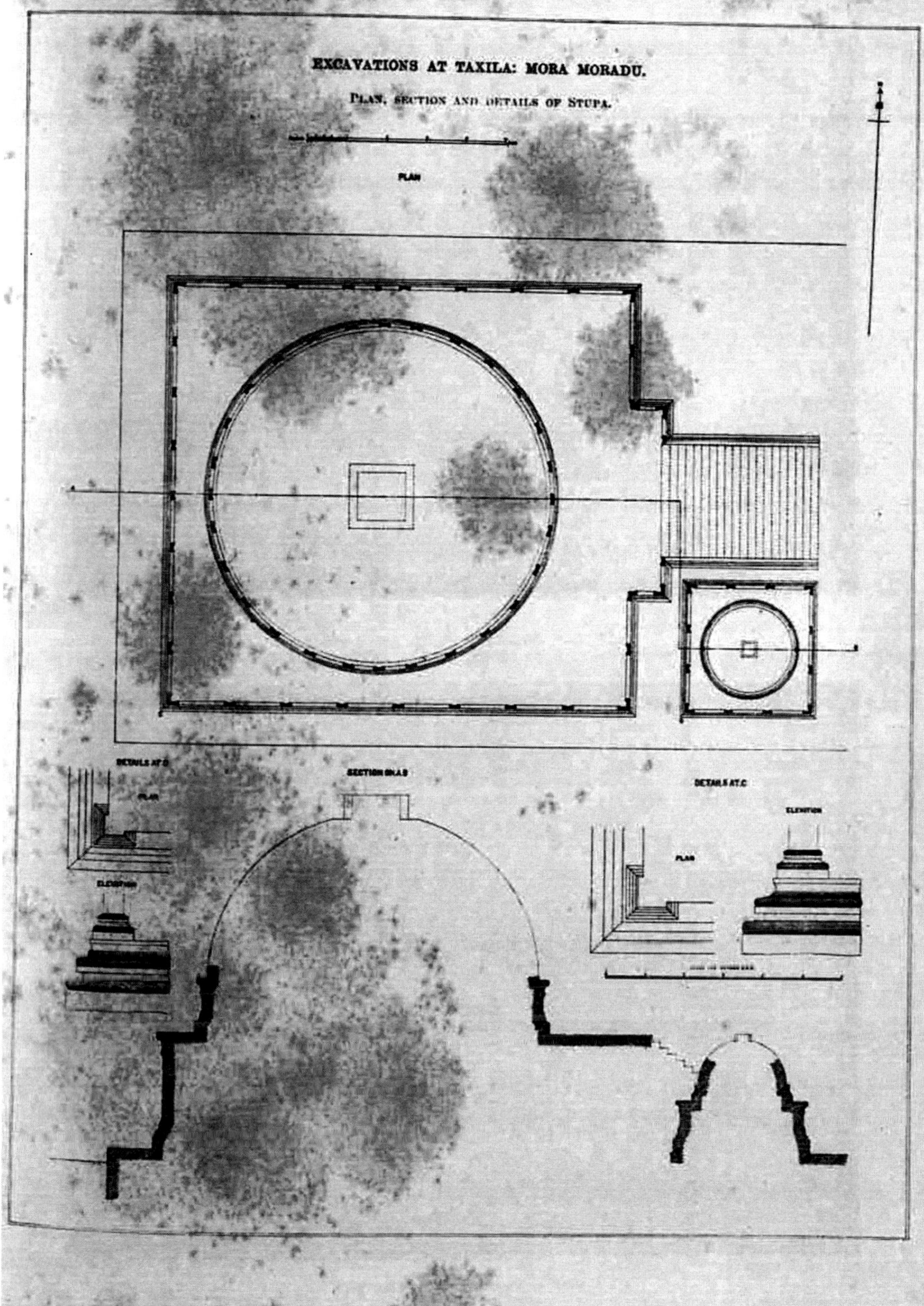

EXCAVATIONS AT TAXILA: MORA MORADU.

a. MAIN STUPA, BEFORE EXCAVATION, FROM WEST.

b. THE SAME, AFTER EXCAVATION, FROM S.-E.

Photo-engraved & printed at the Offices of the Survey of India, Calcutta, 1917.

PLATE XIX.

a

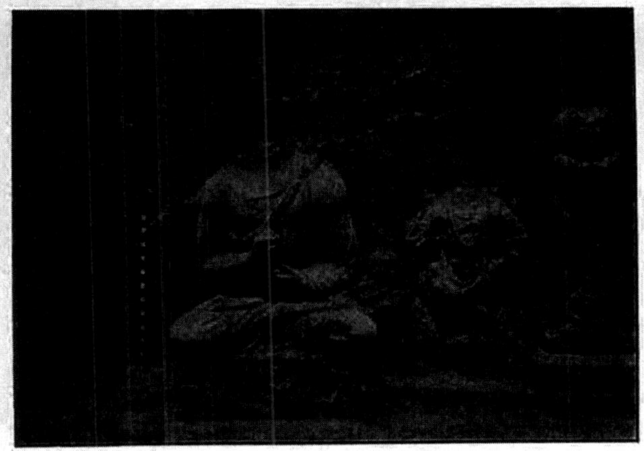

b

c

d

STUCCO RELIEFS ON SOUTH FACE OF MAIN STUPA

Photo-engraved & printed at the Offices of the Survey of India, Calcutta, [illegible]

a

b

c

d

e

f

g

h

STUCCO RELIEFS ON SOUTH FACE OF MAIN STUPA AND LOOSE STUCCO HEADS.

Photo-engraved & printed at the Offices of the Survey of India, Calcutta, 1917.

EXCAVATIONS AT TAXILA: MORA MORADU.

PLAN AND SECTION OF MONASTERY.

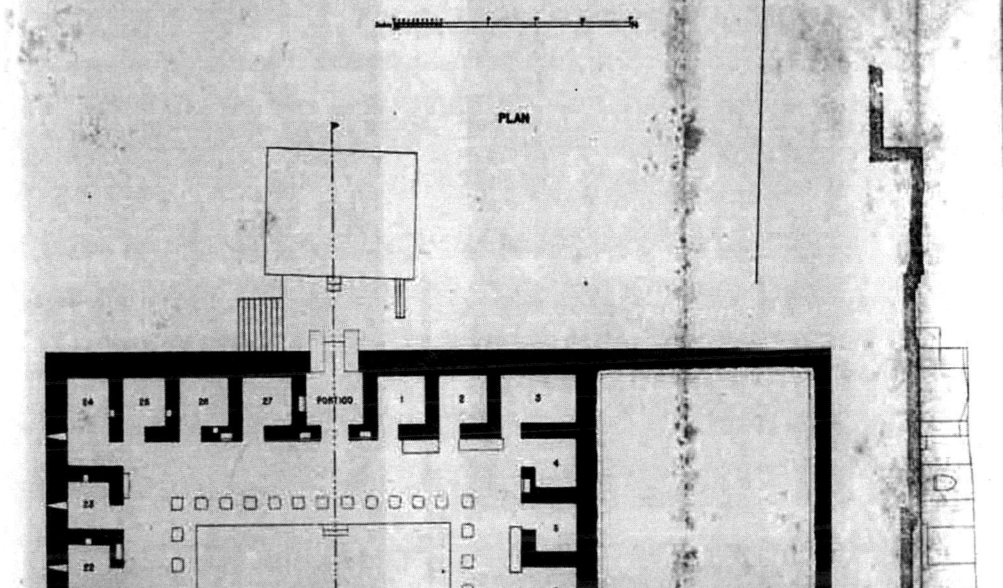

a. PANORAMIC VIEW OF EXCAVATIONS FROM NORTH.

b. INTERIOR VIEW OF MONASTERY, AFTER EXCAVATION, FROM S.-W.

c. MONASTERY, AFTER EXCAVATION, FROM WEST.

Photo-engraved & printed at the Offices of the Survey of India, Calcutta, 1917

a. STUCCO RELIEF IN NICHE IN FRONT OF CELL.

b. STUCCO RELIEFS IN FRONT OF CELL.

c. BRONZE CYLINDER SEAL.

d. TERRACOTTA HEAD.

e

f

e-f. STEATITE SEAL.

g. TERRACOTTA HEAD.

Photo-engraved & printed at the Offices of the Survey of India, Calcutta, 1917

EXCAVATIONS AT TAXILA: MORA MORADU MONASTERY.

a. STONE BODHISATTVA.

b. TERRACOTTA HEAD.

c. STONE RELIEVO PANEL.

d. STONE BODHISATTVA.

e. TERRACOTTA BUDDHA.

f. SMALL STUPA IN CELL.

Photo-engraved & printed at the Offices of the Survey of India, Calcutta, 1917

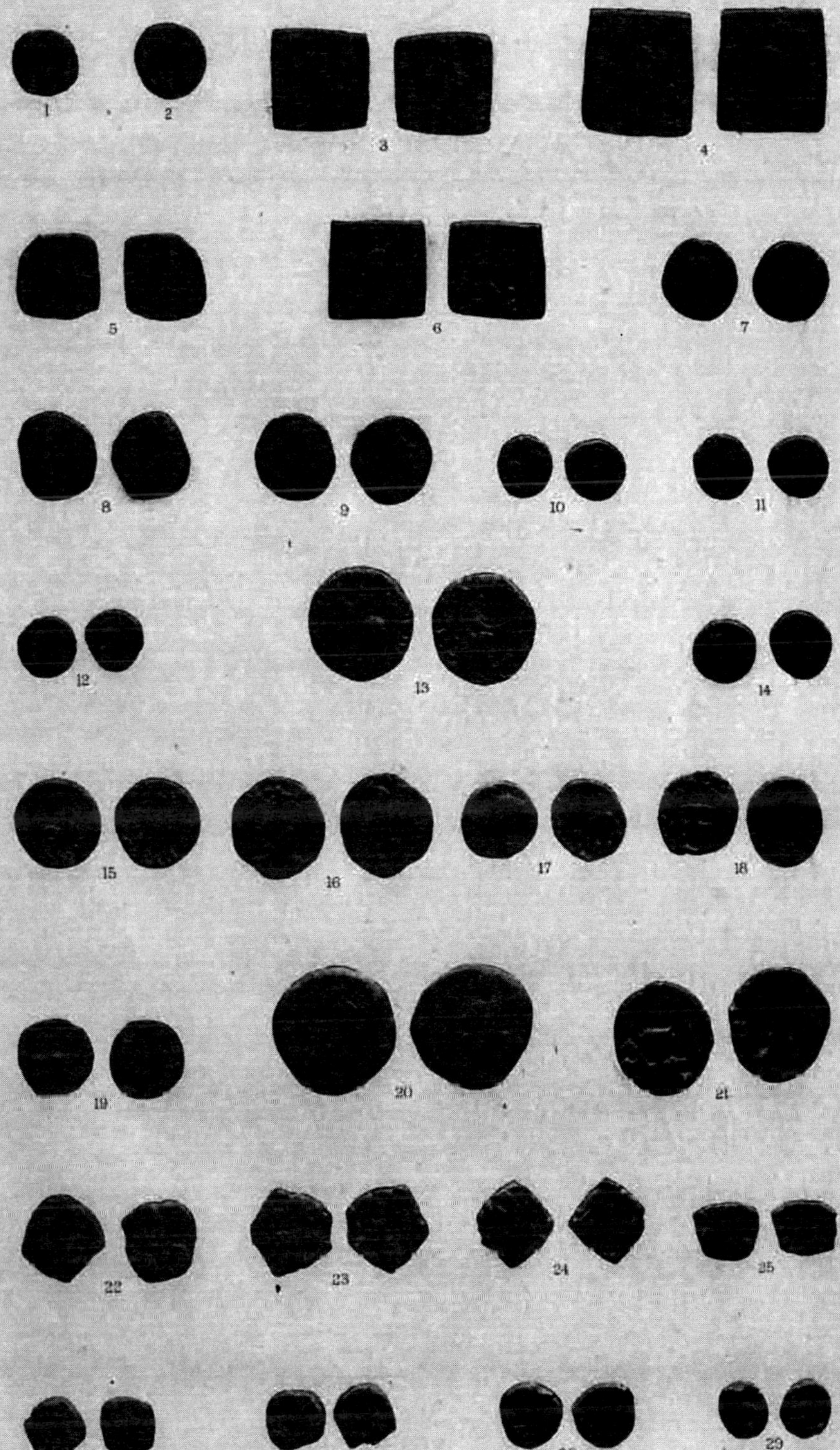

Photogravure

Survey of India Offices, Calcutta

COINS.

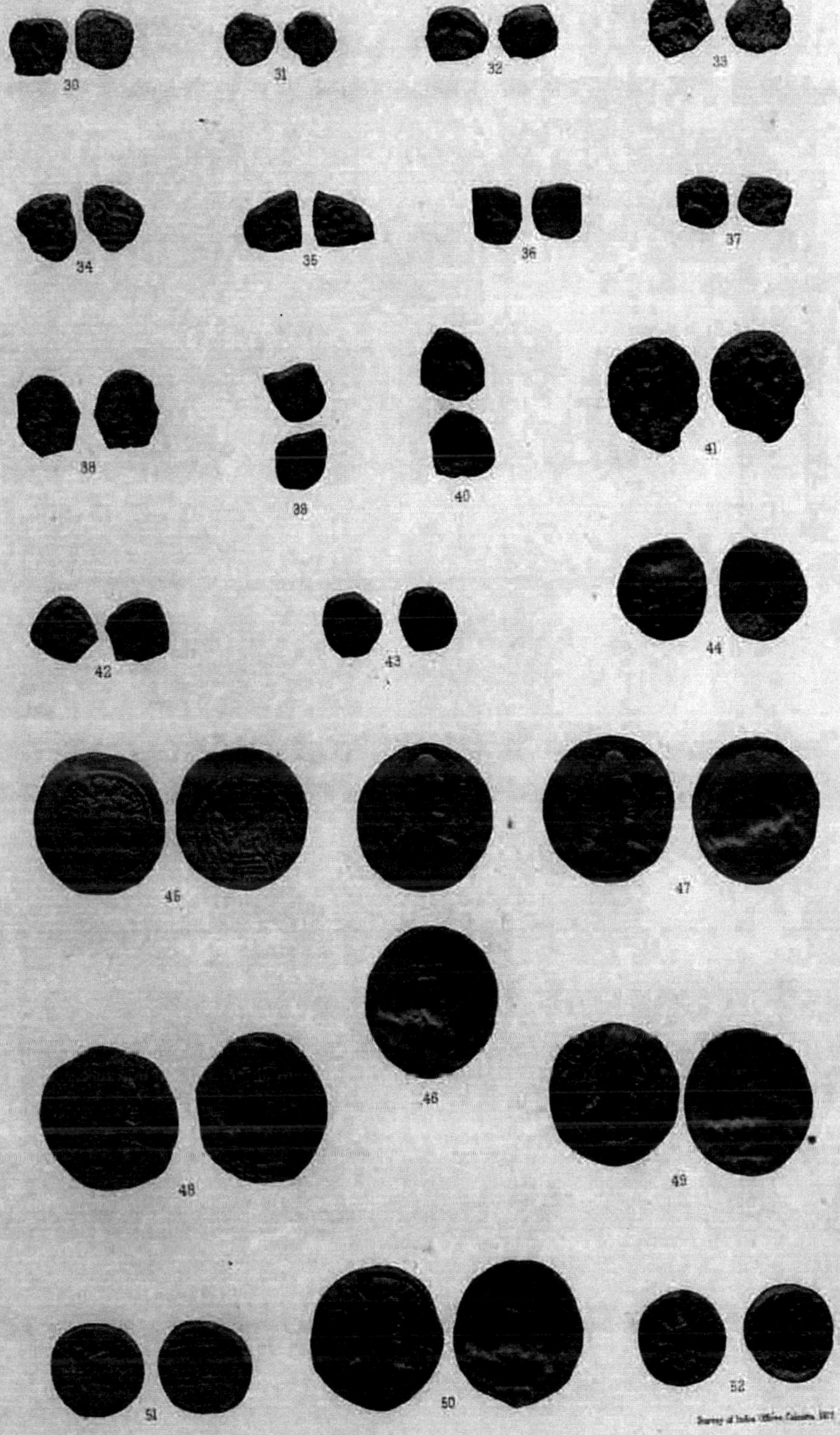

COINS

THE MONOLITHIC TEMPLES OF MASRUR.

EIGHT miles as the crow flies west-south-west of Kangra, and some fourteen by rough jungle paths, lies the hamlet of Masrur in the Dera Tehsil of the Kangra District of the Punjab. To the north-east of the village rises a rocky ridge, the main axis of which, like that of most of the lower ranges in this corner of the district runs from north-west to south-east. The crest of the hill is accentuated by an outcrop of sandstone rock, the highest and central portion of which has been separated from the rest by two transverse and more or less parallel cuttings, each varying from eleven to eighteen feet in width. The intervening portion of the living rock, some 160 feet in length and not less than 105 feet in width[1], has been excavated and sculptured into a series of temples unique in the Himalayan region and of a type rare in Hindustan. Standing some 2,500 feet above sea-level and commanding, as they do, a magnificent view over a beautiful, well-watered and fertile tract, their situation, though remote, is singularly pleasing. In front, to the north-east, towers the lofty, grey mountain wall of Chamba with Dharmsala seemingly nestling at its foot, while in the opposite direction over a low range of hills lies the valley of the Beas, whose wide sandy bed forms at all seasons of the year a conspicuous feature of the landscape. Immediately in front of the monument lies a large tank, 155 feet in length and 85 feet wide. Although perched almost on the hill top and apparently fed from an exceedingly small catchment area, it is reputed to contain water even in the driest seasons. The presence of this tank is a fortunate circumstance; for it has prevented any accumulation of buildings in front of the temples, and, now that certain modern additions and some trees have been removed, a comprehensive view of the monument is obtainable from its eastern side. (Pl. XXVII *a*.)

The remote situation and general inaccessibility of the temples have been at once the cause of their neglect and of their fortunate escape from the destroying hand of the various Muhammadan invaders of the valley, while to their monolithic character may be attributed their survival amid the devastation which in 1905 overtook so many of the ancient monuments of this region. No travel-

[1] The back of the monument is now destroyed, so that it is impossible to state with certainty its original width.

lers who have passed through the Kangra valley have left any account of the monument, and, while, of course, its existence must have been known to the various settlement officers, it is not referred to in their published reports or in the *Gazetteer of the Kangra District*. Nevertheless it was not entirely unknown, and the first traceable reference to it is to be found in the list of archæological monuments prepared in 1875[1], where it is described as follows:

24. *Ṭhākurdvāra Temple in the village of Masrur, Tehsil Dehra. In good order. Not photographed. Said to have been built in the time of the giants.*

In the revised list of 1891[2] it is thus described:

"12. Masrur, 20 miles north-west by north of Dehra, rock cut temples. The ridge of the hill has been cut through in two places and the intervening ridge has been cut into nine temples. Only one was excavated but nine towers were cut out and sculptured on the outside. Some door frames, too, were sculptured in bands but no further progress was made. It is undoubtedly a very ancient place but it has no inscriptions. It is in possession of attendants who cannot, however, preserve the temples from the effects of the weather by which the southern and exposed portions of the pile have been entirely destroyed."

Unfortunately, in this account of the monument no emphasis was laid upon its unique character and no information given that the monument had ever been surveyed. The senior draftsman now attached to my office, and to whom I am indebted for the excellent drawings which illustrate this article, was a member of the staff of the short-lived office of the first Archæological Surveyor in the Punjab, and in 1887 assisted in the preparation of certain sketches of details of the temple. Of these drawings only two sheets have been preserved and were made over by the Public Works Department to the Superintendent, Archæological Survey, Lahore, when that appointment was revived in 1902.

Thus, from a variety of causes, one of the most important monuments in the Punjab disappeared from notice and remained unvisited by any archæological officer for a quarter of a century. It was inspected in 1912 by the Assistant Surveyor and by myself in October 1913, when plans and photographs were obtained and proposals for the protection and conservation of the monument drawn up and submitted to the Government of the Punjab, whose interest and liberality have rendered possible the excavation and conservation of the existing remains.

If the report of 1875 correctly described the monument, then the intervening forty years have dealt more hardly with it than the preceding ten centuries; for by no stretch of imagination can it now be said to be "in good preservation." That the hand of man, in the way of ignorant *pujāris*, has been responsible for some injury in recent years is certain, while the disintegrating effects of *pipal* roots are but too clearly marked. Nevertheless, it is more than probable that to one whose imagination failed to conjure up the former glories of the shrines and the missing members, the existing monolithic spires might, by com-

[1] *Objects of antiquarian interest in the Punjab and its dependencies*, Lahore 1875. p. 6.
[2] *Revised List of Objects of Archæological Interest in the Punjab*, Lahore 1891. p. 41.

parison [illegible] ancient structural remains, have appeared to be in better preservation than was actually the case. Be that as it may, at the time of my first visit the whole of the front of the temple area to the right was under cultivation, while to the left of the entrance to the main shrine was an enclosure bounded by the temple, a large cowshed, a *dharmaśālā* and the *pujārī's* residence and kitchen. In this courtyard were kept the *pujārī's* cattle, some dozen cows and goats. (Pl. XXVII *c*). Agricultural and pastoral occupations engage the greater part of the *pujārī's* time, and, as worshippers at the shrine are but few and the offerings consequently small, it was but natural that the cowhouse was more imposing than the *dharmaśālā* and that the conveniently hollowed out verandahs of the corner shrines should be used as storehouses for fuel and fodder; also that portions of the monument suffered when more space was required or structural alterations became necessary. Moreover, the front of the temple to a height of some eight feet was buried under an accumulation of earth, while modern erections were built over the remains of some of the shrines. In these circumstances it was imperative, if the shrines were to receive adequate protection, that from the temple area, that is, between the face of the monument and the edge of the tank, all secular buildings should be removed without delay. This has accordingly been done, the *pujārī* being accommodated in new buildings on a purchased site clear of the monument, where he can carry on his agricultural operations without hindrance and still conveniently celebrate the simple temple service.

While rock-cut caves are numerous in various parts of India, only three[1] series of free standing rock-cut shrines have hitherto been noted, namely the raths of Mamallapuram (the so-called Seven Pagodas), the two Kailas shrines at Ellora, and the temple at Dhamnar in Rājputānā. Of these the two former are Dravidian in style, the Dhamnar temple being the only example where the Indo-Aryan architect has attempted to rival the Dravidian in producing a monolithic exterior. In point of style, therefore, the Masrur monument has only one rival,[2] but one it entirely outclasses. The Dhamnar shrine, like the more magnificent Kailas, has the defect of lying in a pit-like hollow, which is, as Fergusson justly remarks, a test few buildings can stand and to which none ought to be exposed. The Masrur monument, on the other hand, is not only free from this imperfection, but, standing on the highest point of the hill, occupies a position of peculiar architectural advantage. In point of size, too, the Masrur temple concedes nothing to its rival, being three times its length, while in beauty of ornament and boldness of conception its superiority is equally marked.[3]

At Masrur, the main monument is a complex of shrines, the arrangement of which may be best realized by reference to the plans and section (Pls. XXVIII

---

[1] The *nandī* pavilion of the Pañchāleśvara Temple near Poona being only an adjunct of a shrine has naturally been omitted from the list.

[2] Since writing the above I have received information from H. A. Lomas, Esq., I.C.S., regarding a small rock-cut shrine at Thal in the Almora District, United Provinces. No photograph of this interesting monument, which has yet to be surveyed, has been obtained. Another similar shrine is rumoured to exist near Lohaghat in the same district but awaits inspection.

[3] Cf. *A.S.R.* 1905-06, Pl. XLII (*b*).

—XXX). The centre is occupied by the principal shrine which faces a little north of east.[1] Almost in line with this and on either side are two subsidiary shrines of decreasing size, the smaller and more distant one occupying the outer angle. A similar arrangement of these secondary shrines appears to have formed the back of the monument (Pl. XXVII *b*) so that the principal temple stood in the centre of eight smaller ones, the whole hewn in the base of a more or less rectangular mass of rock, the thresholds of all the shrines, therefore, on one level.[2] Above the cella of the main shrine, and level with the now lost roof of the *maṇḍapa*, the rock is cut as a flat roof broken only by the main spire and the *śikharas* which mark the sanctum of each of the eight smaller shrines. (Pl. XXXI *b*). There is, however, a most marked difference between the height of the main pinnacle and the *śikharas* of the surrounding shrines (Pl. XXVII *a*), and the defect of such a design, whereby the principal spire would so overtower and stand aloof from the adjoining *śikharas*, had apparently been realized by the architect who, to lead the eye gradually upward from the outer edges of the monument to the crowning glory of the main *śikhara*, placed on either side of it what appears at first sight a *śikhara* of intermediate size, but which is, in reality, a complete shrine with cella and spire, the doorways only partially excavated, level with the flat roof. (Pls. XXVII *a*, and XXXI *a*). Access to the main shrine was through a small portico and larger *maṇḍapa* but of these but little remains. On either side of the *maṇḍapa* rose a *śikhara* which did not, however, mark the sanctum of a shrine but masked the stairs leading to the level of the flat roof (XXVII *c* and *d*). Similarly flanking the portico were two monolithic shrines each with a false door opening as it were, into the portico (Pl. XXXIII *b*).

The thirteen shrines and two staircases already enumerated are still part of the same rock, but in front of this complex and in line with the portico rises on either side a cruciform monolithic temple, a square cella, with a porch on each face, the spire a sixteen sided polygon, the tapering faces of which are ornamented with the effective horse-shoe diaper which formerly beautified the now destroyed Jamadagni Temple at Baijnāth[3] some forty miles further up the valley.

The material in which the monument is excavated, is a sandstone of varying fineness and strength. In some places it is so hard and well preserved that the ornamentation might but yesterday have left the master's hand while adjoining portions have so weathered as to preserve but the faintest outlines (Pl. XXXII, *b* and *c*). This unevenness of texture must have constantly hindered the progress of the work, and in more than one place, where the material was so friable as to render ornamentation impossible, stone of better quality was substituted. Thus, the lintel of the angle shrine on the south-east (Pl. XXVII *d*) is an inserted slab and all the portico pillars, save the bases, are structural, while

[1] The doorway faces almost exactly E. N. E., this orientation being necessitated by the axis of the rocky ridge.

[2] See Fergusson, *History of Indian and Eastern Architecture*, Vol. I, fig. 190, Vol. II, fig. 332 for the arrangement of subsidiary shrines at the Kailas and Dhamnar Temple respectively.

[3] Fergusson. *History of Indian and Eastern Architecture*, Vol. I, p. 299, Fig. 165.

numerous fragments recovered in the excavations bear evidence to the fact that the craftsmen did not hesitate to substitute better material when necessity demanded it (Pl. XXXIV). And that necessity must have been very real and apparently made itself felt early in the operations, possibly accounting for the fact that only the principal shrine and its adjuncts were completely excavated, though some progress had been made in the clearing of the common verandah of the angle shrines (Pl. XXVII *b*), and several doorways show that the original .ntention was more ambitious than the actual achievement. (Pls. XXVII, *d* and XXXIII, *a*). The staircases had necessarily to be excavated and with disastrous results; one has almost entirely disappeared, the other is but precariously preserved.

The entrance to the Main Shrine on the occasion of my first visit was a narrow passage bounded on the right by a rough stone wall and on the left by a thatched shed which was the *pujārī's* kitchen (Pl. XXXII, *a*). Since its excavation one now enters, between the projecting porches of the two flanking shrines (Pl. XXXII, *b*), a small portico by ascending two steps. Here two broad and parallel stylobate-like plinths of original rock, 2′ 6″ in width, 9″ high and 4′ 11″ apart, carry the square bases of the pillars and pilasters which supported the now lost roof of the portico. **Main Shrine.**

In view of the fact that of the few preserved fragments of these portico pillars only the bases are cut from the living rock, the roof may possibly have been structural.[1] The pillars were circular shafted and 5′ 0¼″ in circumference, with a slightly larger octagonal necking and pot and foliage capital; when complete, they cannot have been less than 11′ 6″ in height. On either side of the portico is seen the false door of the flanking shrine. Of that to the left the greater portion is still preserved and shows two parallel and vertical series of square panels, each with a circular conventional floral design. The false door to the right has completely disappeared. On the right side of the portico is a small covered drain which carries off the water from the *maṇḍapa*. This *maṇḍapa*, which is 28′ wide, 26′ 7″ in length and 19′ 9″ in height, has in the centre a platform of original rock (Pl. XXXII *b*). The solid stone roof, 1′ 6″ in thickness, has now fallen, but was formerly supported by four massive columns, of which only a portion of the one to the left remains (Pl. XXXII *a* and *b*). This fragment is 16′ in height, the circular shaft 8′ 9½″ in circumference, and, like the portico pillar, has an octagonal necking. The capital is lost but the base of this column, as well as that of the corresponding one on the same side, is still preserved and consists of a square plinth surmounted by a heavy torus and two other series of mouldings. Both the torus and the face of the plinth are beautifully ornamented, the former with floral forms, the latter with conventional designs in diamond shaped lozenges (Pl. XXXI, *d*). The walls of the *maṇḍapa* are quite plain, but the still preserved fragments of the roof show graceful ornamentation resembling that of the plinth of the columns which supported it. The entrance to the sanctum lies in a recess 5′ 4″ deep (Pl. XXXII *b*). Originally, no door was required to protect the cella, as in front lay the *maṇḍapa* and portico. Now that these are destroyed, a door

[1] Cf. p. 45 *infra*, regarding roof of common verandah to north.

is required to keep out wandering cattle and to guard the images. A wooden door of Hindu design based on the model of the false doorway of the flanking shrine will, therefore, be provided.[1] The ornamentation and technique of the pilasters, door-jambs and lintel of this recessed entrance are of peculiar beauty and excellence (Pls. XXXII *b* and XXXI *c*). The sanctum itself is a perfectly plain chamber, 13′ square, 16′ high, the flat roof adorned with a large conventional lotus in the centre and smaller ones around. In the centre of the floor is a platform of original rock, on which the *pujārī* has erected a roughly built wall to form a throne for his images.

The solid roof of the *maṇḍapa* has fallen, but its thickness and form can be ascertained by a reference to Pl. XXXII *b*. Now level with the top of the *maṇḍapa* roof and over the sanctum, but necessarily springing from a base greatly exceeding that of the cella it marks, rises the principal spire, its base 27′ 10″ square (Pls. XXVII and XXXI *a*). Huge masses of the rock having fallen away owing to the angle of cleavage, the ornamentation of the east and west faces is almost entirely lost, but the side faces cutting across this angle are, fortunately, better preserved and clearly indicate the original form. Representations of five small *śikhara* shrines form the lowest and most noticeable feature, while above rise three successive and receding trefoil pediments, each with a sunk medallion containing a large head shown facing and a face in profile on either side, the latter but rarely preserved (Pl. XXXI *a*, *b*). The upper part of the spire, the *āmalaka* and *kalaśa* are now missing, but, nevertheless it still rises 39′ 6″ above the flat roof and from the base of the *maṇḍapa* to its present summit measures no less than 65 feet. When complete with finial it cannot have been much less than 80′ in height.[2] It is worthy of notice that on the main *śikhara*, and on the miniature representations in the centre of each face, the usual *āmalaka* string course is not shown as the edge of a rectangular slab but as a circular *āmalaka*, such as would form one of the crowning members of an actual shrine, so that the edge of the spire appears as though composed of a series of superposed *śikhara* shrines.

Roof Shrines. The roof shrines, which have been already referred to as standing on either side of the main spire, are, from their position, incapable of marking any shrine whose cella could be indicated below, while their doorways, but partly excavated, prove that they were meant to represent simple but complete shrines (Pl. XXXI *b*). Like the main *śikhara*, and for the same reason, the east faces have suffered considerable damage, and it is noticeable also that only the upper portions of the shrines have been completely finished, that is, those parts of the monuments which would be visible from below, a fact which supports the suggestion already advanced regarding the architectural necessity which dictated their presence.

---

[1] To assist in meeting the cost of this door H. L. Shuttleworth, Esq., I.C.S., some time Settlement Officer in this corner of the Kangra District has generously offered to contribute Rs. 300. Mr. Shuttleworth who has taken much interest in the monument has himself published a brief account of it in the *Ind. Ant. Vol. XLIV, Jan.* 1915, under the title of *Note on the Rock-hewn-Vaishnava Temple at Masrur, Dehra Tahsil, Kangra District, Punjab.*

[2] Compare with the Kailas at Ellora, which is stated to be 96 feet in height, Fergusson *loc. cit.* Vol. I. p. 343.

Of the four original shrines which stood at the corners of the monument only one, namely: that at the south-east angle, exists in any perfection; of the others but traces remain. (Pl. XXVII *b*). Each had a porch facing the narrow cutting which divides the monument from the rocky ridge, while a verandah of noble proportions joined each pair. This common verandah is, in each case, only roughly excavated and the roof of the one to the north has fallen. This verandah roof was supported by two pillars, but not one has survived in its entirety, though their bases and a capital have been preserved. That these verandah roofs were original rock, is undoubted; but the existing remains of the pillars in the north verandah are *structural*. The spires were of the usual form, with horse-shoe diaper ornaments, and the existing one is preserved to the height of the *āmalaka* (Pl. XXVII *d*). **Angle Shrines.**

On each face of the monument and on either side of the main shrine, but separated, on the front of the monument at least, by the spire of the staircase, is a subsidiary shrine. Of the four which originally existed only one to the south of the main shrine is comparatively well preserved (Pl. XXVII *d*), though remains of the spires of those at the back of the monument still exist and the fallen mass of the one to the north bears pathetic witness to its former beauty (Pl. XXVII *a*). Now, the face of the existing shrine is 13′ 7″, which would, therefore, have given to the base of its spire, had it remained square in plan, an area which would have brought it into contact with the roof shrines already described and, moreover, partially hidden both that and one face of the *śikhara* of the angle shrine. This has, however, been avoided by reducing the side of the spire to 7′ 8″. Springing, therefore, from an oblong base the spire is suggestive of a Dravidian *gopura* rather than an Indo-Aryan *śikhara*, a resemblance intensified by the loss of the finials, which were probably two or three *āmalakas* with *kalaśas* placed on the long roof ridge.[1] **Shrines Flanking Main Temple.**

Reference has already been made to the two monolithic cruciform shrines standing in front of the angle shrines of the main monument on the east face (Pl. XXVIII). Whether similar shrines originally stood behind the monument, that is, on the west side, it is impossible to state, but from the conformation of the ground it does not appear probable. When first inspected the bases of both the shrines were buried under several feet of earth; indeed, of the one to the south only the merest trace was visible, as the *pujārī's* cowshed was built over it, but excavation has revealed most of the plinth (Pl. XXVII *a*). Of the one to the north sufficient remains to indicate its original form and the beauty of its ornamentation. No less than five of the images in the niches are recognizable and three are of Śiva (Pl. XXXII *d*). The lintels of the porches are of peculiar excellence (Pl. XXXIII *a*) and the plain pointed ridge roofs are of unusual type. **Cruciform Shrines.**

On either side of the *maṇḍapa*, stairs led to the flat roof. How the masking spire gave to the whole the semblance of a shrine—an appearance strengthened by **Stairs to Roof.**

[1] Cf., Fergusson, *loc. cit.* Vol. II, p. 140. Fergusson's belief that this form was once common is borne out by the fact that miniature shrines recovered at Sārnāth and elsewhere frequently have this form of spire. A structural example with long ridge roof is found at Yāgeśvar in the Almora District. See *A. P. R. of Supt. Hindu and Buddhist Monuments* 1913-14, p. 9.

doorway, porch, niches on the outer face and spire itself—has already been remarked (Pl. XXVII *d*). But this *śikhara* is of special interest, as, unlike the usual curvilinear spire, it is star-shaped in plan (Pl. XXIX) and, when complete, must, like that of the cruciform temple, have resembled more nearly the pointed spires of Europe rather than the Indian *śikhara*. On the right of the *maṇḍapa* it has been found impossible to excavate and reveal either the remains of the entrance to the second staircase or the pillar bases of the *maṇḍapa* columns owing to the existence on this side of a number of graves (*samādhi*) marking the places of interment of former *pujāris* (Pls. XXVII *d* and XXXII *b*).[1] Nevertheless, traces of the upper steps of the other staircase are to be found near the yet unremoved roots of the former huge *pīpal* tree on the left of the *maṇḍapa* (Pl. XXXII *a*).

Shrines Flanking Portico.

Little remains of the two shrines flanking the portico, but their plan is plain. The false door opening into the portico was supposedly the entrance to the shrine (Pl. XXXIII *b*), but doorways are also indicated in the projections on the outer and front faces. Only a portion of the spire of the shrine to the right still exists.

The local name of the shrine is *Ṭhākurdvāra*, the shrine of Vishṇu, and it is so designated on the survey map. At present three gaily robed modern stone images, identified by the *pujārī* as Rāma, Lakshmaṇa and Sītā, are enshrined in the sanctum (Pl. XXXII *a* and *b*). These are recent introductions, as twenty-six years ago a small metal image alone was the object of devotion. Before excavation there was an astonishing lack of images and reliefs, the only iconographical data being furnished by the carved lintels. That of the main shrine shows nine seated divine figures between *chaurī*-bearing attendants. The central figure, over whose head flying *gaṇas* hold a jewelled crown, is Śiva, but the following deities are also represented, Vishṇu, Indra, Gaṇēśa, Skanda and Durgā. On the lintel of the east porch of the cruciform shrine are seven deities, Śiva again occupying the position of honour (Pl. XXXIII *a*). Five *śaktis* are depicted over the doorway of the angle shrine at the south-east corner, among whom Māhēśvarī, Aindrī, and the three-headed Vajra-Varāhī are still recognizable. The lintel of the porch of this same shrine shows five seated gods, the centre one apparently Gaṇēśa. There is no lack of variety for the only remaining lintel, that of the north porch of the cruciform shrine (Pl. XXXII *d*), displays the remains of five seated female deities, Lakshmī occupying the post of honour. Excavation has now, however, revealed many of the original images in the niches of the various shrines, most of them carved in the rock, but some few on separate slabs. In these niches images of Śiva occur thrice, of Indra and Sūrya twice, of Kārttikēya (Pl. XXXII *c*) and Gaṇēśa once. . Vishṇu is identifiable with certainty once only (Pl. XXXIV *c*), but two somewhat defaced figures in small panels are probably representations of the three-headed form, a human face in the centre and a lion's head on one side and a boar's head on the other, indicative of the Narasiṁha and Varāha *avatāras*. On a separate slab, now broken

[1] The most that has been possible has been the replacement of the rubble wall by one of roughly dressed ashlar.

is an image, possibly intended for Varuṇa,[1] if one may judge simply from the *vāhana*, a *makara* (Pl. XXXIV *a*). There is thus nothing in the monument itself pointing to its dedication in the first place to Vishṇu, and the little *garuḍa* figure, which formerly stood on the fragment of one of the columns of the portico is undoubtedly later work. To attempt, as has been done, to count the shrines as ten in number and indicative of the incarnations of Vishṇu, is entirely to misread the plan. On the other hand the presence of the figure of Śiva, in the centre of the lintel of the main shrine, is a strong presumption that the temple was dedicated to Mahādēva. While[2] the Hindu pantheon is well represented, it is noticeable that neither images of Brahmā nor reliefs of the Navagraha and the incarnations of Vishṇu, such favourite subjects for the chisels of the mediæval sculptors, have been recovered in the excavations.

As to the date of this monument, local tradition assigns it, as usual, to the Pāṇḍavas, who are said to have executed the work during a night of six months' duration, which so tried the patience of a *tēlin* busy at the oil press, that lighting her lamp she went out to discover the cause of the seeming endless night, and thus interrupted the work, the Pāṇḍavas fleeing away as recognition would have entailed a prolongation of their exile. For her temerity and impatience she was turned to stone and her head (from one of the sunk medallions adorning the spires) is still shown to visitors by the *pujārī*. It is a pity, perhaps, that the simple faith of the *pujārī* in his own story has been considerably shaken by the recovery, in the recent clearance, of several similar heads from other medallions, but the legend is too edifying and interesting to be forgotten, and, with a little good-will on the part of the pilgrims, it is likely to be preserved for many years to come. There are, unfortunately, no inscriptions to lend their aid in dating the monument, and considerations of style alone remain. The dangers attending chronology based merely on such data are only too well realized; for variations may be due as much to difference of locality, material, ability of workmen and wealth and taste of the founder as to differences of time. But even lacking the pleasing certainty of dated epigraphs, there still remain certain broad bases on which an approximate date can be advanced. The monument being a reproduction of a structural design must necessarily be later than the earliest of structural monuments of similar type, and it possesses all the features of the Indo-Aryan style perfected as if they had been practised for centuries. There is in this monument no appearance of hesitation, no copying of wooden forms, nothing tentative, nothing archaic. The columns, it is true, are almost classical in form and the foliated torus of the pilasters and capitals are reminiscent of the Gandhāra school, but the beautiful pot and foliage capitals are of a type unlikely to have been evolved at a very early date (Pl. XXXII *b*). There are, it must be admitted, certain features, such as rosettes on the lintel faintly recalling Gupta technique (Pl. XXXIII *a*), but the limits of the persistence of certain

[1] The two pieces of this image do not fit together with such accuracy as to afford *absolute certainty* that they are parts of one and the same image. Nevertheless, from a careful examination it appears as if the two fragments are correctly restored.

[2] In the adjoining tract of Kulu the introduction of Rāma and Kṛishṇa worship can be referred to the 16th Century. See Vogel, *Triloknāth*, *J. A. S. B.* Vol. LXXI, p. 39.

forms of ornament are so wide as to render them useless for chronological purposes. On the other hand, however, the treatment of floral ornament, which is distinguished by marked characteristics in almost every period of Indian art comes to our aid. Lacking the naturalistic treatment of the Gupta age, it is yet far removed from the flat conventional treatment of the later mediæval period (*c.* 11th century). It, therefore, appears that the monument can hardly be assigned to an earlier date than the 8th Century of our era and may probably be somewhat later. One of the most striking impressions produced by monolithic structures, is that of eternal durability and immeasurable might; and shattered and weather-worn as the Masrur monument is[1], one realizes, in its presence, that, after all, in the first list of ancient monuments it was not entirely inappropriately assigned to *the time of giants.*

H. Hargreaves.

[1] A final estimate has been framed to meet the cost of conservation measures which should preserve for many years the existing remains.

MONOLITHIC TEMPLES, MASRUR.

a. GENERAL VIEW AFTER CLEARANCE.

b. VIEW OF TEMPLES FROM S.W.

c. VIEW OF S.E. CORNER BEFORE CLEARANCE.

d. VIEW OF S.E. CORNER AFTER CLEARANCE.

Photo-engraved & printed at the Offices of the Survey of India, Calcutta, 1917.

MONOLITHIC TEMPLES, MASRUR.

GROUND PLAN OF BRAHMANICAL ROCK-CUT TEMPLES.

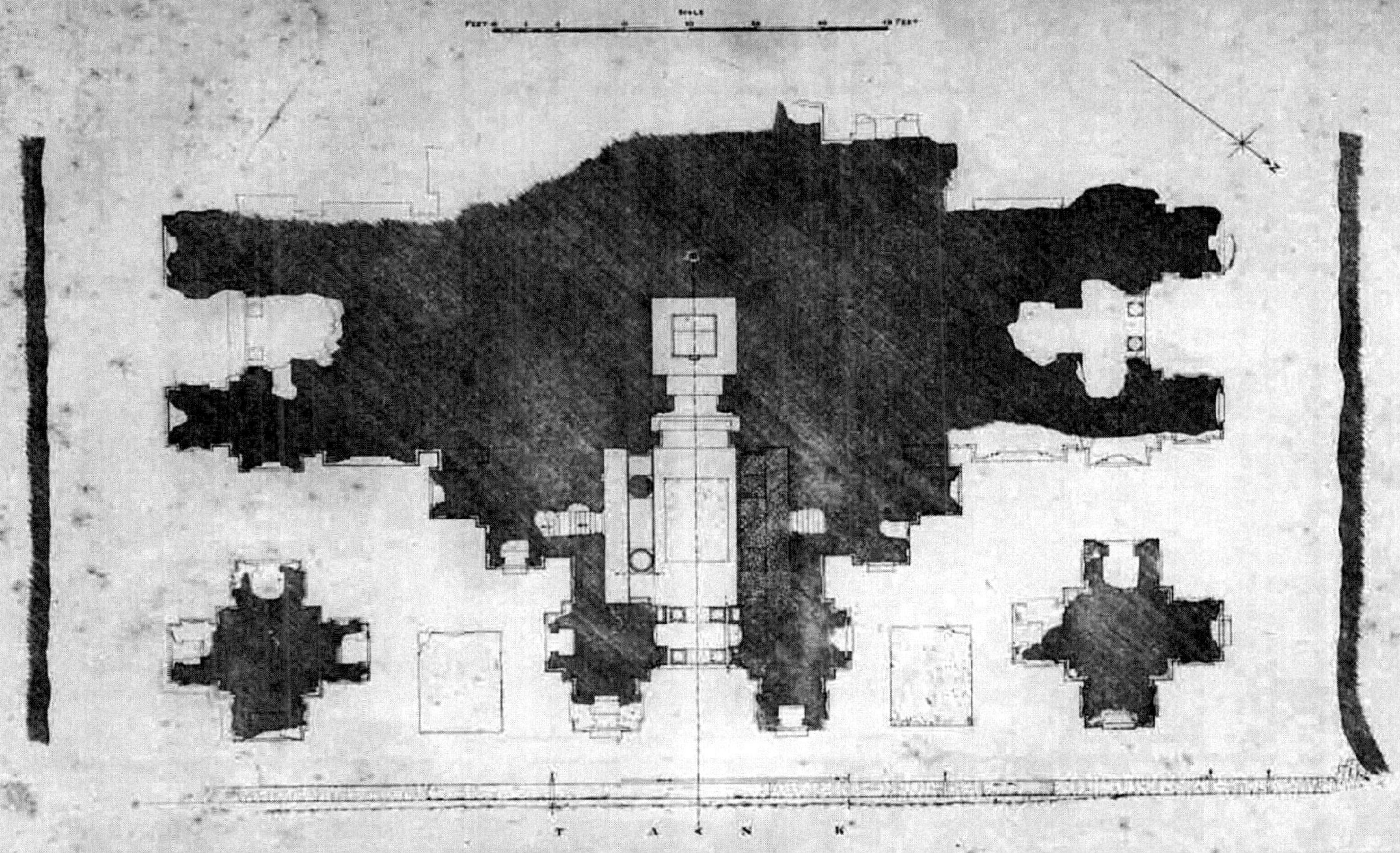

MONOLITHIC TEMPLES, MASRUR.

ROOF PLAN OF BRAHMANICAL ROCK CUT TEMPLES.

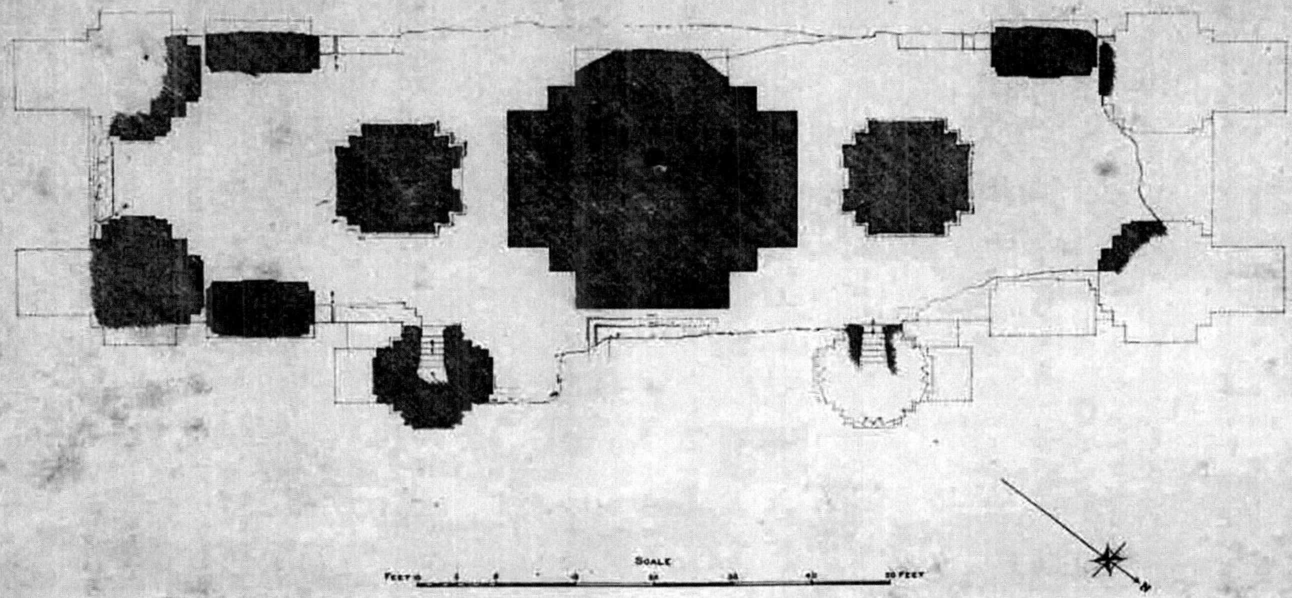

MONOLITHIC TEMPLES, MASRUR.

SECTION OF ROCK CUT TEMPLES.

SECTION ON LINE A.B.

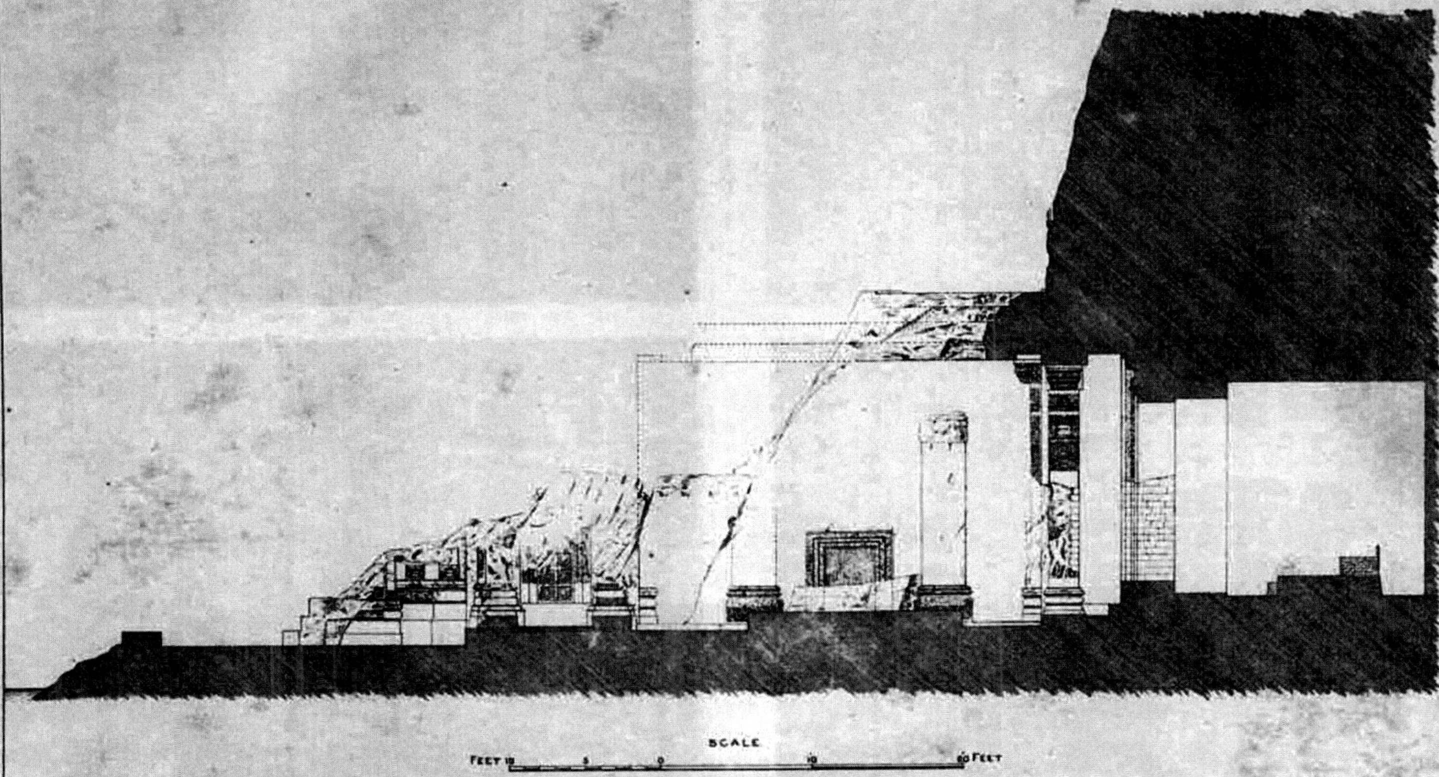

a. NORTH FACE OF MAIN SPIRE.

b. ROOF FROM NORTH.

c. PILASTER IN MANDAPA.

d. BASE OF MANDAPA PILLAR.

a. Mandapa before clearance.

b. Mandapa after partial clearance.

c. Karttikeya in Southern shrine.

d. Northern Cruciform shrine.

MONOLITHIC TEMPLES, MASRUR.

a. LINTEL OF CRUCIFORM SHRINE.

b. SHRINE FLANKING PORTICO.

a. IMAGE OF VARUNA.

b. STRUCTURAL CAPITAL.

c. VISHNU AND ATTENDANTS IN RELIEF.

Photo-engraved & printed at the Offices of the Survey of India, Calcutta, 1917.

PRE-MUHAMMADAN MONUMENTS OF KASHMIR.

WHEN I was deputed to Kashmir in the spring of 1913, I was urged by the Director General of Archæology in India to make a special effort to compile a detailed and up-to-date account of the pre-Muhammadan monuments of the State, and I was asked particularly to illustrate my account with really accurate drawings of, at any rate, the principal buildings, inasmuch as those published by Gen. Cunningham and Lieut. Cole were very imperfect and often incorrect. This behest I have since tried to carry out and the results of my efforts are contained in the present article. In my remarks on the origin and history of the Kashmir style, as well as in my description of the individual buildings, I have made full use of an unpublished note which Sir John Marshall himself wrote in Kashmir in 1907, when I had the privilege of accompanying him during a tour of inspection in the Srinagar valley; and, needless to say, I have made use of whatever other literature exists on the subject, notably of Sir Alexander Cunningham's *Essay on the Arian order of architecture*, together with Mr. Cowie's supplementary notes[1]; of Lieut. Cole's work entitled *Illustrations of ancient buildings in Kashmir*; of Sir James Fergusson's chapter in his *History of Indian and Eastern Architecture;* and of Sir Aurel Stein's monumental edition of the *Rāja-taraṅgiṇī* of Kalhaṇa.

The additions made to our knowledge since Gen. Cunningham and Mr. Fergusson wrote about the monuments of Kashmir are many and of a varied nature. Foremost among our new sources of information is Sir Aurel Stein's work referred to above, which now enables us to identify and date many sites and buildings about which nothing was known before. In the course of his researches, Sir Aurel Stein himself succeeded in identifying a large number of interesting spots. Among those were the famous city of Parihāsapura built by the great Lalitāditya as his favourite residence and the capital of Kashmir, which Gen. Cunningham wrongly located near Sambal; Shaḍarhadvana (modern Hārvan), where the great Buddhist teacher Nāgārjuna is reputed to have lived and where an interesting group of prehistoric monoliths still exists; the temples of Śiva-Bhūtēśa and Śiva-Jyēshṭhēśa situated near the hamlet of Vāngath (Vasishṭhāś-

[1] *J. A. S. B.*, 1848, pp. 241-327 and Pls. VI to XXII; and Vol. XXXV. pp. 91-123.

rama ?) ; Kapaṭēśvara (modern Kōṭhēr) with its two temples of the eleventh century A.D. ; and Māmalaka (modern Māmal) near Pahlgām with its little shrine of Mammēśvara-Śiva, which presumably dates from the time of Jayasiṁha (A.D. 1128-49). Sir Aurel Stein's suggestion that the ruined temple now converted into the tomb of Pīr Ḥājī Muḥammad in the city of Śrīnagar probably represents the temple of Raṇasvāmi attributed to Raṇāditya[1] does not seem to rest on sufficiently strong evidence. The identification of the ancient city of Jayapura-Dvāravatī founded by Jayāpīḍa-Vinayāditya, grandson of Muktāpīḍa-Lalitāditya, towards the end of the 8th century A.D. with the extensive remains near the village of Andᵊrkōṭh, is due to Dr. Bühler.[2] Dr Vogel made known the remains of the basement of what seems to have been a Buddhist *stūpa* near a village called Malangpura, three miles south-west of Avantipura,[3] and Dr. Sten Konow observed, for the first time, the temple in the Fīrozpur Nāla below Gulmarg. Neither of these two places has yet been identified.

The antiquities recently unearthed by me will be discussed in their proper places. The chief interest of my own excavations centres in the discovery of a number of interesting Buddhist monuments at Parihāsapura, Purāṇādhishṭhāna (modern Pāndrēṭhan) and Hushkapura, and of a large collection of sculptures, which reveal the existence of an important local school of art in Kashmir in the mediæval period.

A notable fact, which I have brought to light in connection with the monuments of Kashmir, is the discovery of at least two representations of Lakulīśa, or Lakuṭa-pāṇi, on the doorways of the well-preserved temples at Purāṇādhishṭhāna and Pāyar. Mr. Bhandarkar has shown[4] that this form of Śiva was widely worshipped in ancient times in the plains of India, and it is interesting to find that it was not unknown in Kashmir, though it seems probable that the Rājataraṅgiṇī of Kalhaṇa does not record the erection of any temple or image of this deity ; nor does the name of Lakulīśa seem to figure in the later Sanskrit chronicles of Kashmir. This, however, is not to be wondered at. The usual designation of the followers of Lakulīśa in the inscriptions published by Mr. Bhandarkar is Pāśupata, and the Rājataraṅgiṇī of Kalhaṇa makes several references to the existence of Pāśupatas in Kashmir at least from the time of Mātṛigupta, king of Kashmir, who was ruling about the 6th century A.D.[5] The immediate value of this discovery lies in the fact that it enables us to determine the true character of the temple of Purāṇādhishṭhāna. Gen. Cunningham recognized in it the temple of Mēruvardhanasvāmi-Vishṇu erected by a minister of Pārtha (906-921 A. D.). But the presence of a figure of Lakulīśa over the northern entrance of this temple, coupled with other considerations, which will presently be discussed in connection with this temple, proves that the building was a Śaiva fane ; and accordingly we shall now be safe in discarding Gen. Cunningham's identification.

The general character of the Kashmiri style of architecture has been dis-

[1] Kalhaṇa, *Rājat.*, trans. by Stein, book III, vv. 453-54 and note.

[2] *Detailed Report of a tour in search of Sanskrit Mss. made in Kashmir, etc.*, p. 13.

[3] *Progress Report, Archæological Survey, N. C.*, for the year ending 31st March 1904, p. 44.

[4] *Annual Report of the Archæological Survey of India*, Pt. II, for 1906-07, pp. 179 sq.

[5] *Kalhaṇa, Rājat.*, trans. by Stein, bk. III v. 267.

cussed at length by Gen. Cunningham, who concludes[1] that while several of the Kashmiri forms and many of the details were borrowed from the Greeks, the arrangement of the interior and the relative proportions of the different parts were of Hindu origin. Mr. Smith[2] also appears to be of the same opinion, inasmuch as he states that no building yet examined anywhere in India was designed on a Greek plan or with an elevation exhibiting one or other of the Greek orders, Doric, Ionic or Corinthian. He is aware of the existence of Doric columns in Kashmir and the few Ionic capitals in the plains of India, but believes that these and similar architectural features of Greek origin were used by Indian architects merely for decorative purposes. Mr. Fergusson[3] holds the same opinion and adds that this Greek influence must have been introduced through the country of Gandhāra.[4] The precise date of its introduction into the Kashmir valley can not be definitely determined, until remains of a much earlier date than those that now exist above the surface are discovered. The principal Greek forms so far noticed in Kashmir are pediments, which, however, are much more highly pitched than the Greek examples, and fluted columns. All authorities on Indian architecture agree that the columns used in Kashmir are of the Doric order, though it was hitherto believed that they differed to this extent that, whereas Doric columns have twenty flutes, the columns of Kashmir have only sixteen. It is noteworthy, however, that my excavations at the Avantisvāmi temple at Avantipura and the Sugandhēśvara temple at Paṭan have brought to light twenty-four-sided and twenty-sided columns, while the pillars in the Buniār temple are only 12-sided. Similarly, we notice that the bases and capitals of the Kashmiri columns are much more elaborate than those of the purely Greek orders; and the Avantisvāmi and Sugandhēśa temples have also yielded bracket capitals with spiral volutes at the sides which must be traced ultimately to Ionic models. From these circumstances we may infer that the Kashmiri architects, at any rate during the mediæval period, did not adhere to any particular Greek order, any more than did the artists of Gandhāra, where Ionic and Corinthian forms may be found carved side by side with Persepolitan.

The trefoiled arch, which is such a common feature of the Kashmiri buildings of the Hindu period and is noticed in some later examples of the Muhammadan period also, is frequently met with in niches for sculptures on the walls of Gandhāra stūpas and other shrines. Mr. Fergusson conjectures that the outline of this trefoil arch of Kashmir was suggested by a section of the ancient cave temples, such as the *chaitya* halls at Ajaṇṭā. Mr. Havell[5] on the other hand believes that the trefoil arch had its origin in ancient Indian symbolism and was a compound aureole, or nimbus, made up of a combination of the lotus and *pīpal* or *banyan* leaf. He believes that the trefoil arch of the Græco-Roman artists of Gandhāra is only a late imitation of the earlier Indian prototype which

[1] *J. A. S. B.*, 1848, p. 326.

[2] *Fine Art in India and Ceylon*, p. 101.

[3] *History of Indian and Eastern architecture*, 1910, Vol. I, p. 257.

[4] In this article, the term "Gandhāra" is used to connote the semi-classical school of the north-west in the old region of Gandhāra which included Taxila as well as the Peshawar valley.

[5] *Indian architecture*, pp. 81 seq.

should be sought for in Magadha. No such early examples, however, have yet been found anywhere in India and the only instances known in Bengal are of the mediæval period, such as those at Konārak and in the Mānbhūm district.

It is to Gandhāra also that we must trace a large number of detail ornaments found in the architecture of Kashmir. Among them are to be noticed the chequer pattern of the kind used in the spandrils of arches on the walls of the gateway of the Avantisvāmi temple; the string course of lions and atlantes, such as is found round the lower part of the Mārtaṇḍa temple and its side chapels; and the zigzag pattern on the pilasters of the porches of the Śaṅkaragaurīśvara temple at Paṭan. The ornaments which Gen. Cunningham describes as dentils in the Kashmiri cornices are in reality the upright sides of miniature trefoils, quite unlike the tooth-like ornaments in the Ionic and Corinthian cornices, and are frequently adorned with lions' heads and other devices. Some interesting examples of these were found in the monuments at Avantipura and Parihāsapura. It is noteworthy that none of the most typical Greek ornaments such as honeysuckle, acanthus, bead and reel, leaf and dart, etc., which are so common in Gandhāra, have yet been traced anywhere in Kashmir. Ornamental motifs of a purely Indian origin are naturally more numerous. Among them may be mentioned the water-pot with many modifications, the lotus flower as on the central stone of the ceiling and on modillions, and lotus petals on cornices of capitals, etc., geese with foliated tails, parrots and other animals in cornices, supporting figures of the class of Yakshas on capitals, figures of Garuḍa on imposts of pilasters, leogryphs with human riders, amorous human couples, gandharvas in spandrils of arches, and others too numerous to mention.

It has been stated above that the inner arrangement of the Kashmir monuments is essentially Indian. This applies to the Buddhist as well as to the Brahmanical buildings. The only Buddhist buildings at present known in Kashmir are those brought to view by my excavations at Parihāsapura and Purāṇādhishṭhāna. The structures unearthed at the former place were erected by Muktāpīḍa-Lalitāditya in the middle of the 8th century A.D. and those exposed at Purāṇādhishṭhāna, to judge from their style, are assignable to the same period. The Buddhists of Kashmir were conversant with every kind of sacred building erected by their co-religionists in the plains of India. Consequently, there is no essential difference between the plan and design followed in Kashmir and those followed in India proper, except that the only Kashmiri example of *chaitya* which has yet been found at Parihāsapura has no apse, which is an unfailing peculiarity of the chapels of India. Some of the Mediæval Buddhist stūpas of Kashmir must have been relic-towers, as Sikandar Shāh, who destroyed the temples of Kashmir, is said by Muhammadan historians to have discovered a vase containing some liquid (آب حیات) and a copper plate with an inscription which could not be deciphered, in one of the structures he demolished at Parihāsapura. The interior of the big stūpa exposed at this place still awaits exploration. The ruined stūpas of Purāṇādhishṭhāna revealed small hemispheric objects of stone, presumably intended for small model stūpas in the same way as little clay stūpas are found in the stūpas of Gupta and later periods at Sārnāth and other Buddhist sites of the Indian plains. A noteworthy feature of the Buddhist structures of Kashmir are the figures of Atlantes which appear on the front of the stair walls similar to those frequently noticed in Gandhāra art.[1] We shall see that in Brahmanical temples of Kashmir, Vaishṇava and Śaiva scenes take the place of these Atlantes on the stairs.

Turning to the Brahmanical temples we find that they differ from the temples of the plains of India in several respects. They have neither the stepped roof of the South nor the curved spire (*śikhara*) and typical Hindu columns of the north, nor yet the exuberance of decorative detail which characterizes architecture alike in the north and south. Save in the temple of Mārtāṇḍa, the central shrine of the Kashmir temple is a single apartment, while those of India proper consist of two to four chambers. Here it may be noted that as Sir John Marshall has shown,[2] the bracket capital of the Hindus, far from being absent in Kashmir, is fairly common, as this form is preferred for supporting architraves of colonnades, porches, etc. As in the plains of India, the compounds of Brahmanical temples frequently hold shrines of subsidiary deities, and while figures of doorkeepers (*dvārapāla*) and the river goddesses are generally carved on stairs and jambs of gateways, distinctive cognisances of Vaishṇava or Śaiva cults are engraved on lintels or over the doorways and stairs. Figures of the vehicles of the deities worshipped in the temples were also placed mounted either upon pillars (*dhvaja*) or platforms in front of the shrines.

The temples of Kashmir are either square or oblong, subdivided into closed (*vimāna*) or open (*maṇḍapa*) types. Gen. Cunningham speaks of another kind, the octagonal, but the so-called temple of Śaṅkarāchārya on the Ta<u>kh</u>t, which he considered to belong to this category is in reality square in plan with recessed corners. The doorways are everywhere rectangular, the height being equal to twice the width, and the doors two-leafed as laid down by ancient Hindu architects.[3] In *vimāna* temples, the closed sides have rectangular niches or chambers for images, of the same dimensions as the entrance and preceded, like them, by bold trefoiled arches, which in their turn are enclosed in high-pitched pediments. The doorways of the Brahmanical temples of Kashmir face in all directions, but care is everywhere taken to place the water-spout invariably to the left of the image.[4] The former practice is also at variance with the rule that Vishṇu temples should always face towards the east. **Types of temples.**

The straight-sided pyramidal roof of the Kashmiri temples, which Gen. Cunningham rightly suggests is a reproduction of the usual wooden roof of Kashmiri dwelling houses, is, with the single exception of the Bum.* zu cave temple, two storied; but Gen. Cunningham's suggestion that, like the monolithic shrine standing to the west of the Jāmi' Masjid in Śrinagar, some of the structural temples had three and more stories, seems to be unfounded.[5] The ceiling is, as in India, constructed of overlapping stones, the interior of the pyramid above being left hollow for considerations of weight and the economy of material.

[1] Slab from Muhammad Nari in Smith, *Fine Art in India and Ceylon*, Pl. XXIV.
[2] *Note on Archæological work in Kashmir*, p. 6.
[3] Rām Rāz, *Hindu Architecture*, p. 47.
[4] Cf. *ibid*, p. 45.
[5] *Cf.* Sir John Marshall's *note*, p. 16.

There is, however, another form of ceiling, the dome-shaped, of which Gen. Cunningham was unaware, but which is noticed by Mr. Cowie in connection with the temples near Vāngath. These domes, which are such a remarkable feature of some of the temples of Kashmir, are nearly hemispheric in shape. In mode of construction, they differ fundamentally from the radiating domes of the Muhammadans, inasmuch as they are constructed of concentric horizontal courses, each circle projecting beyond the one below it, the opening at the top being closed with a single slab generally engraved with a lotus pattern. Where the cella is square, the plan is first reduced to the circle by filling in the corners with light pendentives before the dome is laid on it. The crowning feature of the Kashmiri temples is invariably a conventionalised kind of water-pot, sometimes ribbed in the body, which Gen. Cunningham erroneously describes as a "melon-like fruit".[1] Lieutenant Cole's assumption that similar ornaments adorned the top of pediments of the Pāndrēṭhan temple must be accepted as correct; for one of the pediments of Pāyar still possesses such an ornament.

The basements of the Kashmiri temples, consist of a single or double platform, thus affording a single or double[2] *pradakshiṇā* passage. Their core is composed of stone rubble, and the walls of the shrine which start from it have no foundation. This defect has proved the cause of the early decay of many an otherwise strong structure, such as the temple near Uri. The hollow construction, such as was used in the Greek entablatures, is unknown in Kashmir.

Most of the temples of Kashmir stand in the centre of an open courtyard surrounded by ranges of cells on all sides, which rest on moulded basements; and the same arrangement is also found at some Jaina temples, as for example at Girnār and Khajurāho.[3] In Kashmir the cellular quadrangles may have been suggested by Buddhist monasteries of an earlier date, though the only one yet unearthed is one of the eighth century at Parihāsapura. The cells of the Brahmanical temples, however, seem to have been mostly used for holding small images. Some temples are made *pañchāyatana* by the erection of smaller shrines in the corners of the courtyard.

The peristyles are in many cases preceded by lines of fluted columns which support a shallow portico in front of the cells, the entrances to which are closed above with trefoil arches. The exact form of the roof of the peristyles cannot be ascertained with certainty. Mr. Fergusson believed that it was flat and constructed of stone. It is possible that he was led to this view by Mr. Moorcroft who says that the colonnade of the Mārtaṇḍa temple, where remaining, was "of large flat slabs of stone."[4] In a snowy country like Kashmir such roofs would be out of the question, and Gen. Cunningham's opinion that the roof of the colonnades was triangular in section, like the coping of the walls of the temple on the Takht, seems more plausible, all the more, as I believe that the enclosure wall of this temple represents a decadent form of the cellular peristyle.

The gateways of the Kashmiri temples like the *gōpuras* of the south were imposing structures alike in point of size and in their architectural grandeur.

---

[1] *J. A. S. B.*, 1848, p. 306.

[2] *Cf.* the basements of some of the later stūpas of Taxila, such as the Bhallaṛ Tope.

[3] Fergusson, *ibid.* 1910, Vol. II, pp. 32 and 51. [4] *Travels*, Vol. II, p. 256.

Unfortunately, no complete example has survived and it is now difficult to ascertain the exact form of its roof. To judge, however, by the best preserved gateway at Buniār, it seems probable that it was triangular in section, the pediments on the front and on the rear coinciding with it in outline. In plan, the gateway is a rectangle divided into two chambers of equal dimensions by a cross wall in which the entrance is set. In some cases the gateway is emphasised by porticoes supported on advanced columns.

Gen. Cunningham's theory that the interior of the temples of Kashmir was kept filled up with water up to a fixed level, access to the temples being obtained by causeways similar to those in Mughal gardens, has already been proved untenable by Sir John Marshall.[1] The recent excavations have supplied conclusive evidence against that theory in the shape of stone reservoirs bedded in the paved floors of the courtyards for receiving the washings of the images worshipped in the temples, and of steps leading up to the shrines right from the floor of the courtyard. These would be superfluous if Gen. Cunningham's idea were correct. Nor have any raised pathways or remnants of canals, which could have supplied water to the courtyard, been found in any of the temples which have been completely excavated. To Gen. Cunningham's argument that the tanks were essential for the protection of the temples by Nāgas, it is hardly necessary to refer, since no Nāga images have been found in any of them.

There are a few temples in Kashmir which do not follow the usual plan and design set forth in the preceding paragraphs, and about the date and character of these temples there has been a great deal of diversity of opinion. One of them is the temple generally known as the Śaṅkarāchārya temple on the Takht-i-Sulaimān hill and the remains of another have survived in the enclosure wall of the tomb of Zainu-l-'ābidīn below the Zaina Kadal of Śrīnagar. In the enclosure wall of the former structure Gen. Cunningham[2] sought to trace the earliest model (220 B.C.), which by gradual improvements and additions had expanded into the noble peristyle of the mediæval period. The enclosure of the tomb of Zainu-l-'ābidīn he believed to be somewhat later, and following his suggestion Lt. Cole dated it about 400 or 500 A. D. Mr. Fergusson, on the other hand, on account of the slightly pointed form of the arches in these enclosure walls and the semi-circular arch of the doorway to the stairs of the Śaṅkarāchārya temple assigned the latter structure to the reign of Jahāngīr. He believed that the enclosure wall of Zainu-l-'ābidīn's tomb was built by that prince himself. Sir John Marshall has shown that both these views[3] are unsatisfactory, and has concluded that these structures belong to the same mediæval period as all the other buildings of this class. In support of Sir John Marshall's view some further evidence has come to light which will be noticed later on.

The only other form of ground plan exhibited by the Kashmiri temples is the square with rectangular projections at each angle. Of this plan two examples are known to us, namely: the temple basement on which the brick mausoleum of

[1] *Note*, p. 27.
[2] *J. A. S. B.*, 1848, p. 311 seq.
[3] *Note*, pp. 32 and 14.

Zainu-l-'ābidīn's mother rests and the temple now doing duty for the tomb of Pīr Ḥājī Muḥammad.

Materials. The temples of Kashmir are without exception what Rām Rāz[1] designates as Śuddha edifices, *i.e.*, composed of one kind of material from the base to the summit. The material employed in them is limestone of a somewhat bluish colour, fine-grained and susceptible of receiving a high polish. Only one temple, that of Buniār, is built in granite stone of a whitish colour. A porous kind of stone, locally known as Kanaiṭ and similar to the *Kañjūr* of Taxila, is used for ceilings of the dome-shaped type and sometimes also for foundations of cells, as in the temple near Uri. As far as I am aware, brick has never yet been found in actual use as a material for ancient religious buildings[2] in Kashmir and is only mentioned in a Śāradā inscription of Rāmadēva, which was discovered by Dr. Konow at the village of Ār'gōm (Skt. Hāḍigrāma).[3] As regards the size of stone blocks employed in the construction of these temples, it is to be observed that some of them compare very favourably with those of the Egyptian pyramids. One block for example, which forms the floor of *Chaitya* C at Parihāsapura measures 14' × 12' 6" × 5' 2", which should be roughly equivalent to 64 tons in weight. The principal means of transport in Kashmir must have been strong boats and bullock carts. Most probably earthen ramps were used for raising heavy blocks to the required height.

Gen. Cunningham's idea,[4] which has been freely adopted by writers on Kashmir, that no cement whatever was used in the construction of these temples is wrong. So far as my own experience goes, I have not come across any structural temple in which lime mortar is not employed. If we are to believe Kalhaṇa,[5] lime mortar (*sudhā*) must have been in common use in Kashmir before the time of Aśōka. It may be noted that Mr. Vigne[6] was aware of the use of lime mortar in these temples.

The destruction of the temples of Kashmir is attributed by historians, both Hindu and Muhammadan, to Sikandar named Butshikan, assisted by a Hindu convert named Sūha. Gen. Cunningham has expressed the opinion that these temples must have been blown up with gunpowder, a specimen of which Sikandar might have obtained from Timūr, who invaded India about the same time. I am unable to find any evidence for the use of gunpowder anywhere. The more probable mode of destruction was by timber fire, and I am glad to find corroboration of this view in the Persian manuscript history of Bīrbal Kāṭsar who says that Sikandar destroyed these temples by piling heaps of wood in them and setting fire to them.

History. The ancient monuments of Kashmir, so far known to us, range in date from about the middle of the eighth to about the 12th century A.D , the only examples

[1] *Hindu Architecture*, p. 49.

[2] There are probably some brick ruins in the neighbourhood of Hārvan, but they have not yet been examined.

[3] *Ep. Ind., Vol. IX*, p. 300 seq.

[4] *J. A. S. B.*, 1848, p. 301.

[5] *Rājat.* ed. Stein, B. I, v. 105.

[6] *Travels*, Vol. I, p. 386.

of a later period being small shrines of no architectural value. Mr. Fergusson was not aware of any temples of a later date than 1000 A.D. but Sir Aurel Stein has shown that the temples of Kōṭhēr and Māmal belong to the 11th and 12th centuries, and there are some other structures also which belong to the same period.

The beginnings of the Kashmir style of architecture are shrouded in darkness. The Rājataraṅgiṇī records the erection in Kashmir of Buddhist and Brahmanical buildings by the Maurya Kings Aśōka and Jalauka, and Gen. Cunningham thought he could recognize one of these primitive buildings in the so-called Sankarāchārya temple, which, however, has no claim to any such antiquity. Nor have any elements of the Maurya style of architecture been noticed in any of the extant remains of Kashmir. The part played by the art of Gandhāra in the growth of the architecture of Kashmir has been indicated above. Kashmir was under the sway of the Indo-Scythian Kings of Gandhāra during the early centuries of the Christian era, when buildings may have been erected in the valley under the direct supervision of Gandhāra architects. Hence came the quasi-Greek forms and details which were incorporated into the architecture of Kashmir and which have persisted till very modern times. With the help of the many Gandhāra monasteries and other Buddhist buildings unearthed at Taxila and in the valley of Peshawar we can reconstruct a fairly complete picture of the architecture of Kashmir of that period. Unhappily, no buildings of that age have survived in Kashmir above the ground, and we infer from Kalhaṇa's chronicle that, even in the days of Lalitāditya, earlier buildings had become scarce. Kalhaṇa describes at length how this king discovered by excavation, deep under the ground, two ancient temples with closed doors containing images of Kēśava, which, on the grounds of inscriptions engraved on their bases, were interpreted as having been put up by Rāma and Lakshmaṇa the heroes of the Rāmāyaṇa, a story which serves to show that the script of the inscriptions was not known to the Pandits of Lalitāditya's time. The two images in question are stated in the Rājataraṅgiṇī to have been re-installed in new temples at Parihāsapura. Beyond this vague information there is no evidence of the existence of antiquities of that age in Kashmir. It is possible that future explorations may bring to light such antiquities, though at present it seems hardly likely.[1] Sir John Marshall was the first to discern the influence of Gupta art in the sculptures of Mārtāṇḍa, and his view is corroborated by the many mediæval sculptures which have now been excavated. In this connexion it is interesting to note that according to Kalhaṇa, Lalitāditya imported into Kashmir a Buddha image from the country of Magadha.[2]

The dedicatory inscriptions which most of the temples of Kashmir are said to have contained are lost, but the Rājataraṅgiṇī has supplied the dates of many of them, and, for the rest, a chronological arrangement is rendered possible by considerations of style, which despite its well-known conservative character shows in certain features definite progress and evolution. The features in question are

[1] Since writing this article, I have unearthed at Hushkapura a collection of terracotta figures which are assignable to the Kushāna period.

[2] *Rājat.*, ed., Stein Bk. IV, v. 259.

the shape and character of some of the principal architectural forms, such as the peristyle, which is an important feature in the temples of the eighth and ninth centuries and which gradually loses its grandeur and finally, as in the temples of Pāyar, Māmal and Kōṭhēr, disappears. A similar process is observed in the form of the trefoil arch, which gradually merges into the round arch, and of the pediment, which dwindles into a mere decorative ornament. The porticoes in the side walls of the sanctum, which in the early mediæval examples are equal in dimensions to that on the entrance side, degenerate in later examples into small-sized niches such as we notice in some of the later temples near Vāngath. It is to be noticed that much of this decay in the style of architecture must have been also due to the weakness and comparative resourcelessness of the later Hindu rulers of Kashmir, a few of whom were even driven to the necessity of robbing the valuable property of temples and other religious institutions.

The most prosperous period of the architecture of Kashmir coincided with the eighth and ninth centuries A.D., from which period date the majority of the principal temples that have come down to us. For about three quarters of the 8th century, Kashmir was administered by two kings, Lalitāditya and his grandson Vinayāditya, who may well be considered the most powerful rulers the country has had in the past. The former of these kings is credited with having founded a large number of towns and religious edifices. Those of them that have been identified entitle him to a place among the greatest builders of India.

Buddhist Monuments.

The Rājataraṅgiṇī records the erection of many Buddhist edifices from the time of Aśōka to the late mediæval period. Among the Maurya stūpas there were four in the capital city, which according to Hiuen Tsang contained each a measure of the relics of the Tathāgata. A tooth of the Buddha, 1½" in length, is stated to have been enshrined in a stūpa attached to the Jayēndravihāra in the same city, in which Hiuen Tsang spent the greater part of his sojourn in Kashmir. In another stūpa, which Kanishka erected at some place in Kashmir, he deposited sheets of red copper, engraved with a commentary on the three Piṭakas. Unfortunately, there is no means of localising this stūpa. From the evidence of inscriptions it appears that Buddhist religious structures continued to be built in Kashmir until the end of the 12th century A.D. One of these was a *vihāra* erected at Hāḍigrāma (modern Āṛ'gōm) in honour of the Bōdhisattva Avalōkitēśvara.[1] In the 7th and 8th centuries A.D. when Hiuen Tsang and Oukong visited Kashmir, the Buddhist faith was in a most prosperous condition. The only Buddhist structures that are now visible above the ground are those excavated by myself at Parihāsapura and Pāṇḍrēṭhan which are described below.

Parihāsapura. Parihāsapura was the name of an ancient city founded by Lalitāditya in the first half of the 8th century A.D. Already in the time of Kalhaṇa, the city

[1] *Ep. Ind.* IX. p. 300.

was in ruins and the historian relates that the temples of Paṭan were partly built with the materials carried away from this city. Gen. Cunningham proposed to locate its ancient site near the village of Sambal.[1] The correct identification of the city with the ancient remains on the plateau between Shād'pūr and the Baramula road, we owe to Sir Aurel Stein.[2] The Brahmanical structures erected at this place by Lalitāditya will be described later on.

Of the Buddhist edifices constructed at Parihāsapura, remains of three buildings have been unearthed in the mounds marked A, B, C in Sir Aurel Stein's plan. Sir Aurel Stein and Sir John Marshall recognised in Mound B, the monastery built by Lalitāditya and named Rājavihāra. The structure unearthed in this mound is in reality a monastery of the usual type of India proper and probably also the same as the Rājavihāra. It must be noticed, however, that there was another monastery at Parihāsapura built by Lalitāditya's minister Chaṅkuṇa, and, as no inscriptions have been found in it, it is difficult to be sure as to which of the two monasteries this one is. The mound marked C in Sir Aurel Stein's plan has revealed a structure which I believe to be a *chaitya* hall. The only *chaitya* whose erection at Parihāsapura is recorded in the Rājataraṅgiṇī was the one built by the king himself. Consequently there is no doubt as to the identification of this structure. The third mound (A in Sir Aurel Stein's plan) has revealed the basement of a large stūpa, which must have been a lofty structure. This I believe to be the lofty stūpa erected by Chaṅkuṇa[3], as Lalitāditya did not build any structure of this kind.

Stūpa of Chaṅkuṇa.

This stūpa must have been an important landmark in the valley of Kashmir. The stūpa itself has been completely razed by the hands of the destroyer, and nothing remains of it but a few fragments which will be noticed presently. The basement (Pl. XXXV, *a*), however, is in an excellent state of preservation. It consists as usual in Kashmir, of a double platform, thus providing two passages, one above the other for the pilgrim to go round the shrine. The upper platform is 12′ high, the lower 8′ 9″. These platforms are of the massive type and are built in the usual design followed in other structures of this period. It is interesting to note that the torus member which crowns the upper plinth is adorned with plain spiral bands such as we notice frequently in Greek art. The basement is square in plan, measuring 127′ 6″ × 127′ 6″ with a single projection on each face.

The stairways, which face towards the cardinal points, are placed in the middle of these projections. The steps of these stairs are mostly ruined, but the flank walls are fairly well preserved. The front (Pl. XXXV, *b*) of each of these flank walls is occupied by a square panel containing a figure of an Atlant seated cross-legged and ornamented with garlands and jewellery. The outer faces of these flank walls are embellished with fabulous elephants with long foliated tails, and holding rosaries or flower garlands in the trunk.[4] The upper stairs

---

[1] *Anc. Geography*, p. 101.

[2] Kalhaṇa, *Rājat.* trans. Stein, Vol. II, p. 300.

[3] *Ibid.* Bk. IV, v. 211.

[4] For a fragment of a similar sculpture dating from the early centuries of the Christian era, *vide* *Annual Report Archæological Survey of India*, Part II, 1906-7, Pl. XIX, 2.

are much more ruined, as even the flank walls have not survived. It is, however, obvious that the flank walls of the upper stairs were also adorned on the front with standing Atlants. One of these is illustrated in Pl. XLVII, *a*. The drum of the stūpa, as has been hinted above, was ornamented with niches containing standing and seated figures of Buddhas and Bōdhisattvas. The only complete standing Buddha that was found resembles in all respects those of the late Gupta and mediæval sculptures of Sārnāth. We mark the jewelled crown on the head of the Buddha which is uncanonical. I have re-constructed one of the niches that contained seated Buddhas. The structure was surrounded by a roughly built enclosure wall which is 400′ from north to south and 300′ from east to west. There are no other structures of any kind in the compound.

Rājavihāra.

This structure has now been completely excavated, Pl. XXXVI. Like the Buddhist monasteries of India proper, it is a quadrangle (*chatuḥśāla*) with an open courtyard in the middle surrounded by ranges of cells on all sides. The cells were as usual preceded by verandahs supported by columns. None, however, of the latter have survived, and of the cells, which are 26 in number, only the foundations remain. The basement, 10′ in height, is in good preservation. The monastery faces towards the east, the central cell on this side, before which the stair is placed, being somewhat larger than the others. The inner courtyard was paved with stone slabs, a few fragments of which have come down. Rain water was carried away by two stone built drains which pass out through cells 18 and 21. A reservoir cut out of a single block of stone is bedded in the courtyard. It was probably kept filled up with water, which was brought in by a covered channel entering the monastery through cell 17. In the verandah in front of cell 25 I found a small earthen vessel containing 44 silver coins of Durlabhadēva, grandfather of Lalitāditya-Muktāpīḍa, Jayāpīḍa-Vinayāditya, grandson of Lalitāditya and Vigrahatuṅga.[1] The absence, from this hoard, of any coins of Lalitāditya who built this monastery need not surprise us; for none have yet been discovered anywhere and apparently he never struck any coins of his own.

Chaitya C.

This chaitya (Pl. XXXVII), which I believe to be the one erected by Lalitāditya, is a square chamber measuring 27′ × 27′, surrounded by a circumambulatory passage (*pradakshiṇā*) and supported on a set of four stone columns, only the bases (Pl. XXXVII) of which have survived. The roof was most probably of the usual pyramidal type similar to that of the Brahmanical temples of Kashmir. The outer facing of the walls has all been destroyed and their thickness cannot be ascertained. The entrance, which faces towards the east, was covered with a large trefoiled arch enclosed in an imposing pediment. The corners of the structure were emphasised with pilasters having moulded bases and capitals. The cornice consisted of a string course of *kīrtimukhas* alternating with trefoil arches. The inner chamber contains a single block of stone 14′ × 12′ 6″ × 5′ 2″, upon which rested the sacred image. It is possible that the great

[1] Cunningham and Smith were unable to read the second part of the name, which is undoubtedly *tuṅga*.

Buddha image of copper which Lalitāditya erected and which escaped destruction at the hands of Harsha was worshipped in this very chapel.

The basement upon which the *chaitya* rests, consists of two platforms with the same mouldings as in stūpa A. The flank walls of the stair were adorned with seated Atlants of the usual type. No other sculptures or inscriptions were found in this monument except a small epigraph in early Śāradā, which I read as *Chaṅaṇa*. On several stones of stūpa A are carved the syllables *Chaṁku*. A favourite minister of Lalitāditya, whom he brought from Tuḥkhāra, *i.e.*, probably Bukhara, was called Chaṅkuṇa. I assume that Chaṅaṇa and Chaṁku refer to the same minister, who may perhaps have superintended the erection of these Buddhist edifices for his master.

Purāṇādhishṭhāna or the ancient capital of Kashmir which stood near the present village of Pāndrēṭhan nearly three miles above Śrīnagar, is well known to visitors to the valley from the well-preserved Brahmanical temple on this site. All that remains of the ancient city is the level terraces which might have been fields in ancient times, lines of rubble walling, and mounds of stone rubble. The principal object of my search on this site was the Jayēndravihāra in which Hiuen Tsang lived, and any of the earlier stūpas that might have escaped destruction. None of these early structures seem to have survived, but my excavations revealed the remains of two Buddhist stūpas of the early mediæval period and an open courtyard surrounded by a rubble built wall which may have belonged to a monastery of about the same date (Pl. XXXVIII). These structures are situated close together. Purāṇādhishṭhāna.

Stūpa A was found in a mound of débris which rose about 20′ high. The whole facing has been stripped off, but the few stones which have been found in position enable us to restore the plan of the structure with certainty. They show that the structure was built in the usual style on the top of a basement, 72′ square, with four recesses in each corner. The drum of the stūpa was ornamented with sculptural carvings, a few of which are still well preserved. One of these representing the Bōdhisattva Padmapāṇi (ht. 5′ 4½″) is illustrated in Pl. XLVII, *b* while a large-sized standing Buddha (ht. 6′ 7″) and a fragment of the Lumbinī scene are also worthy of mention.

The other stūpa (C) has been so effectually destroyed, that parts of the stairs on the west and north only have survived. The hemispheric stone objects found in the interior of these two structures have already been noticed above.[1] Judging by the style of the sculptures unearthed in these structures and the few architectural members that have survived, the buildings may be assigned to about the 8th century A.D.

The only other Buddhist structure of Kashmir which survived to a comparatively recent date was a Buddhist stūpa at Ushkur (Hushkapura). This was presumably the same as the Stūpa of Lalitāditya. According to Sir Walter Lawrence, it was razed to the ground by Mr. Garrick who was deputed by Gen. Cunningham to explore it. It is possible, however, that some parts of the structure may lie

---

[1] See page 52 above.

buried in the ground. The site has, therefore, been acquired at my instance and it is hoped that its excavation will shortly be carried out.[1]

Brahmanical Temples.

Mārtāṇḍa.

The great temple of Mārtāṇḍa consists of a central shrine preceded by an *antarāla* and *ardhamaṇḍapa*, with a small chapel on either side of the ante-chamber (Pl. XXXV, *c*). The temple stands in the middle of an open courtyard, which is surrounded by a peristyle of the usual style. Gen. Cunningham was of opinion that the central shrine with its adjuncts was built sometime between the years 370 and 500 A.D., while he attributed the construction of the peristyle to king Lalitāditya. Sir John Marshall has discussed[2] this question in detail with special reference to the passages referring to it in the Rājataraṅgiṇī, and rightly concludes that the whole edifice, the temple with its wings and the colonnade must have been erected in the 8th century A.D., and probably by Lalitāditya himself. The courtyard of the temple is still covered with débris and its excavation may yield evidence in the way of inscriptions, etc., which will determine the date exactly.

The cella of the temple is rectangular, measuring, 18′ 5″×13′ 10″ internally. The walls are plain except for a small portion of the moulded cornice at the height of 17′ 6″ above the level of the floor. The ceiling was probably constructed on the principle of intersecting squares, though we can not be quite sure about it. The image and the paving of the sanctum must have been removed when the temple was destroyed by Sikandar. The entrance to the sanctum is a rectangular one covered with a huge horizontal lintel.

The ante-chamber is 18′ 10″ square internally and has entrances in the north and south walls also. Among the images carved on the walls of the *antarāla* and the ante-chamber, we notice, on the left wall of the former, a well-executed image of the river-goddess Gaṅgā, standing upon her vehicle the crocodile, which is looking up towards her. A female attendant on her right holds an umbrella over her head, and we observe a *chauri*-bearer to her left. She holds her usual emblems, a water-pot in her left hand and the stalk of a lotus flower in her right. On the opposite wall of the *antarāla* is the river-goddess Yamunā with her vehicle, the tortoise. Above the niche on the north wall is a relief consisting of a pair of Gandharvas in flight, with an umbrella over them. The statues on the western walls of the ante-chamber are undoubtedly representations of Vishṇu, and what Mr. Fergusson mistook for hoods of snakes are in reality points of their coronets. Each one of them is three-faced, like the Vishṇu image found in the Avantisvāmi temple, the left face being that of a boar (Varāha) and the right one that of a lion (Nṛisiṁha). Both are eight-armed and their lower hands are placed on the heads of *chauri*-bearers, as in the other images of Vishṇu found in the valley. Furthermore, they both wear the garland (*vanamālā*) and we also notice the

[1] The monument has since been excavated. The operations revealed the basement of a large stūpa and a collection of terracotta figures of the late Kushān period.

[2] *Note*, p 30.

bust of the earth-goddess (Pṛithivī) between the feet of the statue on the north wall. Most of the hands of the images are unfortunately broken and weather-worn, and the emblems they held can no longer be identified. Nor can the fourteen seated male figures, which occur on the walls of the ante-chamber below the cornice, be identified with certainty. Twelve of them occur on the north and south walls, *i.e.*, six on each, and two on the east wall. Of the two panels on the east wall, the right hand one seems to represent Aruṇa, the charioteer of Sūrya, holding the reins of his seven horses. The pilasters of the great trefoil arch of the ante-chamber are adorned with niches containing images which can not yet be identified.

The chapels to the north and south of the ante-chamber contain, each, two niches 5′ 9″ by 4′ internally, which face to the east and the west respectively, possibly in allusion to the rising and setting of the sun.

As to the form of the roof of the shrine and its adjuncts, the most plausible view in the present state of our knowledge is that advanced by Gen. Cunningham, who believed that all these roofs were of the usual pyramidal type and built of stone, like those of Pāndrēṭhan and Pāyar. Mr. Fergusson's doubts as to the juxtaposition of oblong and square pyramids on adjoining chambers need not deter us; for the same design is frequently met with in wood in the dwelling houses of the present day. It is possible that a careful examination of the top of the walls, which has not yet been made, will reveal further evidence in support of the above view.

The peristyle, which was by far the most imposing structure of its kind in the Kashmir State, is largely in ruins. The basement on which the colonnade rests as well as the stairs of the gateway and of the central shrine is buried under the ground. It is obvious, however, that, like the peristyle of the Avantisvāmi temple at Avantipura, that of the Mārtāṇḍa temple consisted of rows of cells preceded by porticoes supported on fluted columns and covered with horizontal architraves. Sir John Marshall[1] has suggested that the west outer façade of the peristyle was adorned with a series of columns, like those on the inside. This is the case with the two temples of Avantipura which have been excavated since Sir John Marshall's note was written; and the gateway of the Mārtāṇḍa temple was presumably similar to that of the Avantisvāmi temple, inasmuch as it seems to have had a portico supported on advanced columns on each face. It is difficult, however, at present to be certain on this point, as it is not known whether the bases of the columns concerned are in their original position.

The Brahmanical temples built at Parihāsapura by Lalitāditya were called Parihāsakēśava, Muktākēśava, Mahāvarāha and Gōvardhanadhara. Besides these, Lalitāditya's minister Mitraśarman put up a Śiva-liṅga; and other temples and images were also erected. Of these the temple of Gōvardhanadhara has been identified with tolerable certainty as a ruined structure (F in Sir Aurel Stein's plan)[2] situated on the south-east corner of the plateau on which the Parihāsapura.

[1] *Note*, p. 29.

[2] Kalhaṇa, *Rājat.* trans. by Stein, Vol. II, plate facing p. 430.

city of Parihāsapura stood. The ruin is known to the villagers under the name of Gurdan, which Sir Aurel Stein believes to be a corruption of Gōvardhanadhara. The central shrine which contained the sacred image has perished, and of the surrounding peristyle only the foundations remain. Among the heap of stones which mark the position of the sanctum is a fragment of a stone lintel (w. 3′ 3″, ht. 2′ 7″) carved with a row of geese and lotus medallions. The only other sculptured stone visible at this site is a capital. To judge from the remains of the enclosure wall the temple must have been one of respectable dimensions. Kalhaṇa mentions the erection of a Garuḍa standard, 54 cubits high, in connection with this temple.[1] This column no longer remains. Vigne's idea, that the capital of this column had been carried away to Purāṇādhishṭhāna and was identical with the fragmentary Śiva-liṅga lying on the spur near the village of Pāndrēṭhan, has already been shown by Gen. Cunningham to be incorrect.[2] It is interesting to note, however, that, according to the Persian manuscript chronicles of Nārāyaṇa Kaul and Muḥammad 'Aẓīm, fragments of this same pillar were still visible up to the early part of the 18th century.[3] If this statement is correct, the column may have been converted into road metal for the Jhelum Valley road.

None of the other structures that have survived on the site of Parihāsapura can be identified. Two of them would seem to have been the largest of all the temples of Kashmir. The temple marked D in Sir Aurel Stein's plan is of the usual plan and consists of a central edifice surrounded by an open courtyard and colonnade. The outer dimensions of the peristyle are about 258′×209′. The average inner dimensions of the cells are 7′ 8″×7′ 4″. Some fragments of fluted columns have survived.

Temple E measures 295′×247′. The sanctum and the colonnades are all heaps of stones. The corners of the courtyard were presumably occupied by smaller shrines. The one in the south-east corner contains a Śiva-liṅga, 4′ 5″ high and 3′ in diameter. It is possible that this image belonged to the central shrine. I am inclined to think that this temple is the same as that of Śiva-Mitrēśvara built by Lalitāditya's minister Mitraśarman.[4]

Vāngath.

The village of Vāngath is situated at a distance of 27 miles from Srīnagar. Four miles above this village are two groups of temples with separate enclosure walls, situated at a distance of 200 yards from each other. Lt. Cole[5] describes these groups under the names of Rajdainbal and Nagbal, which are not known to the inhabitants of the neighbourhood. Sir Aurel Stein identifies the principal temple of the eastern group with the temple of Śiva Bhūtēśa, and the largest temple of the western group with that of Śiva Jyēshṭhēśa[6] erected by Lalitāditya. The shrine of Bhūtēśa must have been a place of pilgrimage from

---

[1] *Rājat.* trans. by Stein, Bk. IV, vv. 198-99.
[2] *J. A. S. B.*, 1848, p. 324.
[3] Kalhaṇa, *Rājat.*, trans. Stein, Vol. II, p. 303.
[4] *Ibid.* Bk. IV, v. 200.
[5] *Illustrations of ancient buildings in Kashmir*, p. 11 sq.
[6] Kalhaṇa, Bk. I, v. 107 and IV, v. 190 n.

a very early time; for, according to Kalhaṇa's *Rājataraṅgiṇī*,[1] Aśōka obtained a son from this deity, and Jalauka,[2] son of Aśōka, made a vow that he would ever worship Jyēshṭhēśa. It was probably on account of these statements that Lt. Cole assigned these buildings to the commencement of the Christian era.[3] These temples were still held in reverence in the 12th century A. D., as Kalhaṇa refers to several visits of his father to them. The temples are described in detail by Mr. Cowie.[4]

Group I.

The enclosure wall is 130′ north to south by 137′ east to west, and is provided with a gate in the north wall. The principal temple (Pl. XXXIX, *a*) stands on a terrace 36′ 6″ square and 3′ 3″ high. Internally, the temple is a square of 17′ on each side and has doorways on E.-N.-E. and W.-S.-W., and closed niches equal in size to the entrances on the other two sides. These niches contain pedestals of images. The ceiling is of the dome-shaped type composed of blocks of *kanaiṭ* stone laid in horizontal courses. The roof, of which the covering has fallen off, was no doubt pyramidal. The exterior as well as the interior is quite plain. There is nothing in the style which militates against Sir Aurel Stein's identification of this temple with that of Jyēshṭhēśa built by Lalitāditya. It must be noticed, however, that the block of stone, 5′ 6″ square, which Mr. Cowie[5] believed to be the pedestal of the image of Jyēshṭhēśa, is in reality the ceiling stone of one of the smaller temples in this group.

The other five temples in this group are built on the same general plan as the principal temple, but they have only one doorway and face in different directions. Of the two temples marked H and K in Bishop Cowie's sketch, one faces towards the east and the other towards the south. Bishop Cowie's sketch shows the doorways in wrong directions. It is noteworthy that the ceilings of all the smaller temples, unlike that of the principal temple, were constructed of intersecting squares.

In addition to the six temples just described, there were in this enclosure at least two others, the foundations of which can still be traced. The gateway in the north wall of the enclosure was built on the usual plan, with pediments supported on independent columns on the front and in the rear. Nothing is known about the date of these smaller temples, though some of them are certainly later in date than the principal temple.

The two groups were connected by a roadway, 35′ broad. Midway between the two groups of temples on the right hand of the roadway is a platform 103′ 6″ by 67′ 6″, which supported some sort of a pillared hall. Bases of the columns are in position.

---

[1] *Ibid*, Bk. I, v. 107.

[2] *Ibid*, v. 113.

[3] *Illustrations of ancient buildings in Kashmir*, p. 12.

[4] *J. A. S. B.*, 1866, pp. 101 sqq.

[5] *Ibid*, p. 104.

Group II.

This group includes more than a dozen temples, very badly ruined. The enclosing wall is built of massive stones and measures 160′ by 148′. The gate of the enclosure occurs in the west wall and consists, as usual, of two chambers. The bases of the columns which supported pediments on each façade are extant. All these temples are described very accurately in Bishop Cowie's notes and only a few salient facts need be mentioned here. The principal temple (Pl. XXXV, *d*) has the same dimensions and is built on the same style as the largest temple of group I. Sir Aurel Stein recognizes in this shrine the temple of Bhūtēśa. This temple, or rather, its site, has enjoyed sanctity from very ancient times. A temple of Bhūtēśa was built here by Jalauka.[1] The present structure is undoubtedly mediæval in character. In the south-west corner of the enclosure we notice a pedestal broken into two halves, measuring together 2′ 10½″ square. It has an octagonal hole in the centre and must have belonged to a Śiva-liṅga. Among the débris of the surrounding wall in the south-west corner is lying a capital of a pilaster which is carved with a pair of geese in good style.

The spring to the north of group II has been identified by Sir Aurel Stein as the tank into which the minister of Avantivarman threw the bleeding body of Dhanva, who had confiscated the lands endowed upon the temple of Bhūtēśa.[2]

Jayapura-Andarkōṭh.

This is the name of a modern village which occupies a part of an ancient site 5 miles below Shādipūr (Shahābu-d-dīnpūr) on the left bank of the river Vitastā. Prof. Bühler identified it as the city of Jayapura founded by Jayāpīḍa-Vinayāditya towards the end of the 8th century A. D. The principal religious buildings erected at this place by the king were a large *vihāra* with a Buddha image and a temple of Kēśava. No remains of the *vihāra* appear to have survived. There are, however, remains of several Brahmanical temples, in one of which, standing on the western corner of the site, Dr. Bühler recognised the temple of Kēśava.[3] Among the remains of the temple, Dr. Bühler noticed a sculptured block. It was afterwards seen by Dr. Konow, who was unable to photograph it. I have had no time yet for a proper exploration of this temple, beyond a little excavation at this point which showed that the block belonged, not to a corner of the temple as supposed by Dr. Bühler, but to the left flank wall of the principal stair which led up to the basement on which the temple stood. The block is sculptured on two sides, the subject of each scene being a four-armed image of Vishṇu seated in easy attitude between the goddesses Lakshmī and Bhūmi. The relief on the front is illustrated in Pl. XLIII, *a*. It will be noticed that the panel containing this relief is rectangular. Dr. Konow thought that the figure of Vishṇu was reclining on the serpent Śēsha, but this is not the case. The description[4] of

[1] *Rājat.* trans. Stein, Bk. I, v. 148.

[2] *Ibid*, Bk. V, vv. 55-59n.

[3] *Report of a tour in search of Sanskrit manuscripts in Kashmir, etc.*, 1877, pp. 13-15.

[4] *Rājat.* Bk. IV, v. 508.

the image recorded by Kalhaṇa refers to the statue which was worshipped inside the central shrine and which must have been a representation of the Śēsha-śāyi Vishṇu. The images on the stair, however, should not be confounded with the statue of the central shrine. This temple is just a hundred years older than the Avantisvāmi temple and may well have served as a model for the latter.

This is the name of the temple situated about two miles above Rampur, quite close to the Jhelum Valley Road. Gen. Cunningham spells the name as Bhaniyār or Bhavānīyār, which he believes to be due to its dedication to the goddess Bhavānī. We shall see presently that in reality the temple must have been dedicated to Vishṇu. The monument is by far the best preserved temple of Kashmir. This is due to its being constructed, unlike other Kashmiri temples, of a kind of granite stone. It is also obvious that it was not injured by Sikandar. Gen. Cunningham did not inspect this temple. It has, however, been described in great detail by Bishop Cowie, with detailed dimensions of different parts, and it is not necessary to repeat these details here. The accompanying drawings (Pls. XL and XLI) will supply all such information. Here I offer only a few general remarks, which will be found to supplement the information contained in Bishop Cowie's notes. **Buniār.**

Internally, the central shrine (Pl. XXXIX *b*) is cubical, each dimension being 14′. The walls are quite plain up to the cornice. The original roof and ceiling have both disappeared, except a few stones of the lowest courses of the pyramid on the outside, which show that the roof must have been of stone of the usual double-divisioned pyramidal type. The old ceiling existed in the time of Bishop Cowie, who tells us that it was a hemispherical dome of which the centre was decorated with an expanded lotus flower.[1] The ceiling either tumbled down or was taken down and replaced by the present wood and brick superstructure after his time. The pedestal of the image is a rectangular block of stone, 9′ by 4′ by 2′ 9″ in height, adorned on three sides with the same mouldings as the basement of the temple. It is obvious that it has always rested against the back wall of the temple, as is everywhere the case with pedestals of Vishṇu images. Śiva *liṅgas* are necessarily placed in the centre of the shrine to enable the pilgrim to go round it, as, for instance, in the Pāyar temple.

The courtyard, which was covered with earth and other débris, has been excavated down to the floor, which is paved with flag stones and in good preservation. Bishop Cowie's statement[2] that the quadrangle had two large wells in the W.-S.-W. and E.-N.-E. corners, which he believed to have been intended for supplying water for flooding the enclosure, is based on a false assumption; and he is also in error in suggesting that the square platform, remains of which have been found between the stairs to the central shrine and the gateway, held a prop to a raised pathway. The platform in reality must have supported a statue of the vehicle of the deity, *i.e.*, Garuḍa.

---

[1] *J. A. S. B.*, Vol. XXXV, part I, 1866, p. 92.
[2] *Op. cit.*, p. 95.

The peristyle (Pl. XLII, *b*) is similar in all respects to that of Mārtāṇḍa, with this difference, that the columns have everywhere only twelve flutes. It is also to be noted that all capitals are of the usual Hindu type, as has been stated above in the introductory remarks. The peristyle contains 56 cells including the gateway. The corner cells in the front line open outwards towards the road: the corners of the back row are built up solid and contain no cells.

The gateway (Pl. XXXIX, *c*) has lost the original roof. The present roof is a modern one of brick and wood which will soon be removed. The side walls of each of the two chambers into which the gateway is divided, have each a rectangular niche of the same design as the temple itself. Bishop Cowie states that the flank walls of the stair to the gateway were adorned on the front with standing figures, which the pandits told him represented the servants of Śiva. The sculptures are now invisible and can not be exposed without a diversion of the road which runs quite close to the front.

The date of the temple is not known. Lt. Cole makes it 500 to 600 A. D. My own opinion is that it was built about the eighth century A. D.

Temple between Uri and Nowshera.

Gen. Cunningham, relying on Baron Hügel who calls this temple Brangutri, expresses the opinion that this name is a corruption of *Varnakoṭri*, meaning golden Durgā. The name given to the temple by Hügel is unknown to the people, and the temple was undoubtedly dedicated to Vishṇu, as fragments of a life-sized statue of this deity were found in the courtyard.

The temple is built on the same plan as the one described above, the only difference being that the peristyle of this temple has no colonnade attached to it, the only columns used in the temple being those in the front and the rear of the gateway, which are 16-sided. One of these, which is intact, is 17′ high including the base and the capital, which are 3′ 2″ and 2′ 2″ respectively.

There is nothing to be specially noted about the central shrine, except that the ceiling, which is now missing, must have been of the same dome-shaped type as that of Buniār. The throne of the image has escaped destruction at the hands of a road-contractor, though it was taken out and left in the entrance. It has now been put back in its original position against the back wall.

The gateway follows the usual plan. The jambs of the entrance in the transverse wall were ornamented with vertical rows of panels, all the figures in which, except the lowest ones representing the river-goddesses, are now defaced. When Bishop Cowie wrote about this temple, the courtyard and the peristyle were so completely buried that he doubted if any ever existed. These have now been excavated by me, and are being conserved on suitable lines.

Of temples which can be definitely attributed to the 9th century A. D. the only examples are those of Pāmpạr (anc. Padmapura), Kāk:pōr (anc. Utpalapura), Vāntipōr (anc. Avantipura) and Paṭan (anc. Śaṅkarapurapattana). The temples at Avantipura I have completely excavated and have already contributed a special article on them to last year's report. A considerable amount of excavation and conservation has also been effected among the temples of Paṭan.

Padmapura-Pāmpar.

Pāmpar is the name of the ancient city of Padmapura which was founded by Padma, a maternal uncle of Chippaṭa-Jayāpīḍa, in the first half of the 9th century A. D., who also built here a temple of Vishṇu called Padmasvāmi. Gen. Cunningham identifies this temple with a small ruined structure (Pl. XLII, *a*) situated to the east of the tomb of Mīr Muḥammad Hamadānī. The ruin is standing to a height of about 8′ above the ground, but the interior is filled with débris. The entrance was in the east wall. The other sides had niches, 4′ in width and 2′ 6″ in depth. The walls on the outside are defaced and cracked. The outer dimensions of the chamber are about 25′ along each side and not 22′, as stated by Gen. Cunningham. From the two fluted columns which support the porch in front of the entrance of the tomb referred to, Gen. Cunningham surmised that the temple must have had a colonnaded peristyle with larger cells in the middle of the long sides. There are no vestiges of any such colonnades on the surface, though it is possible, of course, that other columns may have been carried away by the people.

The remains at Kāk.ᵃpōr (anc. Utpalapura) consist of two insignificant shrines which are mostly buried under the ground.

Avantipura.

The city of Avantipura was founded by king Avantivarman (855-883 A.D.). Among the ancient remains of this city that have come down to us are two temples which are identified by Gen. Cunningham as those of Avantisvāmi and Avantīśvara built by Avantivarman. Gen. Cunningham considered both of them to be Śaiva temples, because he did not know that in Kashmir, as in other parts of India, the terminations *svāmi* and *īśvara* are essentially different and are applied exclusively to the temples of Vishṇu and Śiva respectively. The excavations that have been carried out at these temples have shown conclusively that the smaller and more ornate of the two structures nearer the village of Avantipura is that of Vishṇu-Avantisvāmi and the other of Śiva-Avantīśvara.[1]

The Avantisvāmi temple has, after the recent excavations, become an object of special interest. This is due to the fact that the peristyle, the courtyard and the basement of the central shrine, which were hitherto almost completely buried under the ground, have now been reclaimed in an excellent state of preservation. This fact will be evident from the photographs which accompany the special article referred to above, and it serves to vindicate Gen. Cunningham's idea that the lower parts of the temple had already become buried before its destruction in the 15th century A.D.

The central shrine, which measures about 33′ square externally, has almost entirely disappeared, the only remaining fragments being some portions of the lowest course. The entrance was in the west wall; the other sides contained niches of the same size as the entrance and preceded, like it, by the usual porticoes. The image of Vishṇu, which was worshipped in the sanctum, has not been recovered. There is, however, no doubt as to its general form and character, since it must have been of the same type as the many images of

[1] For detailed information about these temples, a reference may be made to a special article on the subject in last year's Report.

smaller size that were found in the excavations and must originally have been worshipped in the cells of the peristyle. Pedestals of some of these are still *in situ* in those cells. One of these smaller images of Vishṇu is exemplified in the article referred to.

The stair to the central shrine must have been an important feature of the temple. The sculptures carved on the front and inner sides of the flank walls are in perfect condition. Those on the front represent Vishṇu seated between the goddesses Śrī and Bhūmi, with pairs of parrots in front of the throne. It is interesting to note that, whereas the images of Vishṇu in these scenes have four or six arms, the goddesses have, in accordance with prescribed rules, only two arms each. As regards the parrots, they are frequently noticed in the hands of Durgā and other goddesses in Southern India.[1] The courtyard, which is paved throughout with stone slabs, measures 174′ east to west by 148′ 8″ north to south. In front of the stair to the central shrine is a moulded base which may have supported a Garuḍa column. The subsidiary shrines in the corners of the courtyard show that the temple was of the *pañchāyatana* or *pañcharatna* class. The shrine in the north-east corner must have been dedicated to the river-goddess Ganges as the pedestal which supported the image has a crocodile engraved on its spout.

The peristyle comprises 69 cells, whose inner dimensions average 3′ 8″ by 4′ 10″. With the exception of the square ones in the corners, the columns which support the portico in front of it are 16-sided.

The gateway is, as usual, divided into two chambers of equal size. Among the sculptures with which the gateway is adorned, we notice figures of the river-goddesses on the base of the jambs of the entrance in the middle wall and larger images of the same deities on the side walls, with friezes of Garuḍas below them. A peculiarity of this gateway, which is observable in only one other example, namely, that of Mārtāṇḍa, is the projecting porticoes supported on advanced columns on each side of it.

The Avantīśvara temple, which is situated half a mile below the town of Avantipura, has also been excavated, though the work is not yet complete. The sanctum is of the *maṇḍapa* type, and had an entrance and a staircase leading to it on each side. The basement on which the sanctum stands is 57′ 4″ square and about 10′ high. To each of its corners was attached a platform about 16′ square, which must originally have supported a small subsidiary shrine. As the hollow spaces between these shrines and the stairs had been built up at a later date, Gen. Cunningham thought that the temple must have been 82½′ along each side and 165′ high and thus the loftiest structure not only in Kashmir but in India.[2] The peristyle and the gateway do not call for any special remarks except that Gen. Cunningham's plan shows columns in front of the cells which never existed.

The smaller antiquities found in the temples of Avantipura included large numbers of coins, both Hindu and Muhammadan, and other objects, but no-

[1] *Cf.* T. A. Gopinatha Rao, *Elements of Hindu Iconography*, Vol. I, part II, p. 11.

[2] *J. A. S. B.*, 1848, p. 280.

inscriptions except a small but interesting record cut on a large-sized jar, which is dated in the year 1583 and contains the name of Avantivarman. This is the only epigraphical evidence of Avantivarman's connection with the town and the temples.

Śaṅkarapura-pattana. Patan.

The modern town of Paṭan marks the site of the ancient city of Śaṅkarapurapattana founded by king Śaṅkaravarman (A.D. 883-902). Kalhaṇa records the erection at this place of two temples, one by the king himself and named Śaṅkaragaurīśvara, and the other by his queen and called Sugandhēśa after her. Śaṅkaravarman's minister Ratnavardhana built a third temple named Ratnavardhanēśa. Of these, Gen. Cunningham recognized the king's temple in the larger temple near the modern town and the temple of Sugandhēśa in the smaller structure situated half a mile higher up towards Śrīnagar. The third temple has perished, but it is possible that its material has survived in the walls around the *baolis* recently excavated near the Dak Bungalow which supported a later shrine to be noticed later on. Photographs taken by Lt. Cole show the first two temples in a much better condition. They were damaged considerably by an earth-quake thirty years ago.

Sugandhēśa Temple.

Of this temple only the sanctum has hitherto been visible above the ground. Gen. Cunningham suspected the existence of the peristyle around it, and this suspicion has been proved correct by my excavations. The sanctum (Pl. XLIII, *b*) which is of the closed or *vimāna* type, measures 12′ 7″ along each side internally. The entrance, which faces towards the east, was covered with a horizontal lintel, and in front of it is a smaller chamber 9′ 6″ by 7′ internally. As at Mārtāṇḍa, the front of this chamber must have been surmounted merely by a trefoil arch. The niches in the other three walls of the sanctum, which measure 6′ by 4′ 2″ internally, have had trefoil-headed entrances surmounted with pediments of the usual type. Their entrances were originally provided with wooden doors and contained images of Śaiva deities. The basement of the central shrine which has been partly excavated consists, as at Avantipura, of two platforms. The stair which led up to the entrance of the sanctum is well preserved. It will be seen, however, that the carvings on the stair were never finished. The construction of the temple must have been stopped before its completion.

The gateway to the peristyle has the usual plan, each of the chambers into which it is divided being 13′ 2″ by 7′ 8″ internally. The cells of the peristyle (Pl. XLIII, *c*) are 4′ by 2′ 9″. The pillars which supported the portico in front of these cells were 16-sided.

Of the statue which was worshipped in this temple a few small pieces were found. They show that it must have been one of Śiva, as the fragments include pieces of a trident. But, while it is evident that the temple was dedicated to Śiva, it is impossible as yet to ascertain which of the two temples erected by the king and the queen this one is. For the present, therefore, we may retain the identifications proposed by Gen. Cunningham.

Śaṅkara-gaurīśvara temple.

The temple of Śaṅkara-gaurīśvara is similar in plan to the one described. The sanctum (Pl. XLIII, *d*) was filled up with blocks of stone from the superstructure which hid the outer walls also to a considerable height. All this débris has now been cleared away, exposing the floor, which is paved in stone and in excellent preservation. The cella is 17′ square. The central stone of the floor, which measures 12′ 6″ by 10′, has nine circular holes arranged in three rows, the central one, which is the biggest, being 3½″ in diameter and the same in depth. These holes may have held Śiva *liṅgas*, though none of them have been found, and it is also possible that these holes were only meant for the tenons of a large throne for the image. The south inner wall of the portico has a niche with a double-divisioned roof and containing a four-armed figure of Mahādēva piercing the demon Tripura with his trident. The chambers in the south, west and north walls of the temple measure 8′ 5″ by 5′ 9″ internally and are paved with stone slabs. The pilasters which flank these porches are adorned with elegant patterns.

The Śaṅkarāchārya temple on the Takht Hill.

The Śaṅkarāchārya temple (Pl. XLIV, and Pl. XLV, *a*) consists of a single chamber built on an octagonal basement which is approached by a broad flight of steps. The plan of the sanctum is a square with a double projection on each face, the interior being circular 13′ 2″ in diameter. The entrance faces east. The maximum thickness of the walls in the middle of each face is 8′ 2″. The cella is covered with a modern ceiling composed of flat stone slabs and wooden boards, which rest on two lintels of the same material, themselves supported on four columns in the centre of the room. The south-west column bears two Persian inscriptions, one of which states that the column on which it is engraved was carved by a mason named Bahishtī in the year 54, *i.e.*, 1054 A. H. corresponding to 1644 A. D. This date falls in the reign of Shāh Jahān. It is obvious, therefore, that this ceiling with its columns was erected in the time of that king. Mr. Fergusson[1] wrongly considered this ceiling and its columns to be a part of the original temple, and assigned the whole structure to the 17th century A. D. It is interesting to find that the original Hindu ceiling is still extant and is only hidden from view by the ceiling referred to. The ancient ceiling is of the same dome-shaped type as that of the temple of Jyēshṭhēśa erected by Lalitāditya, which Sir Aurel Stein identifies with one of the temples near Vāngath, and, like it, constructed of horizontal courses of *kanaiṭ* stone. This circumstance alone should suffice to dispose of Mr. Fergusson's theory. It is also to be noted that Sir Aurel Stein's and Mr. Fergusson's suggestion that the circular form of the cella was due to repairs carried out in Muhammadan times is untenable. This error seems to have been due to the fact that the inner wall is covered with a thick coating of lime plaster which might have been applied in the Mughal period. But, behind this plaster, the wall is composed entirely of stones of the Hindu period. It is also to be noticed that the same form of cella also occurs in another pre-Muhammadan temple, *i.e.*, the bigger temple at Ladu.

The Śiva *liṅga*, which is now worshipped in the temple, is a modern one and was erected some years ago. The original image which existed in the time of Lt. Cole was a *liṅga* encircled by a snake.[2]

---

[1] *History of Indian and Eastern Architecture*, 1910, Vol. I, p. 254.

[2] *Illustrations of ancient buildings in Kashmir*, Pl. 1-68, D.

The parapet which surrounds the basement of the temple is also octagonal, 23′ 6″ along each side. This wall is adorned on the inside with round-headed recesses. Gen. Cunningham considered these arches to be the origin of the mediæval trefoil, whereas Mr. Fergusson held that they were necessarily Muhammadan, as they were pointed. Sir John Marshall has shown that neither these arches nor those in the wall around the tomb of Zainu-l-'ābidīn are as distinctly pointed as the Musalmān arches, and that they must be pre-Muhammadan. It is interesting to note that one of the temples in Group II near Vāngath and the bigger temple at Ladu have the same kind of arch in their entrances.

In examining[1] the several theories that have been advanced as to the age and founder of this temple Sir John Marshall concludes that, while there is no evidence to show which particular prince erected it, it is clear from its style that it appertains approximately to the same age as the other temples of Kashmir. It is interesting to find further internal evidence in favour of this conclusion. It is also inferable that the so-called pointed arch of the enclosure walls of this temple and of the tomb of Zainu-l-'ābidīn is, as hinted above, not the prototype from which the trefoil is evolved, but rather a decadent form of it with the side curves greatly diminished or altogether eliminated.

Tomb of Zainu-l-'ābidīn.

This building is situated in a large enclosure on the right bank of the river below the 4th bridge of the city of Śrīnagar. The grave in which the remains of Zainu-l-'ābidīn lie buried is an insignificant one, hardly recognizable from the other graves around it. But the enclosure wall surrounding it is one of considerable interest, as it undoubtedly belonged to an ancient Hindu temple, though no vestiges of the temple itself now survive. The peculiarities of the enclosure wall are illustrated in the accompanying photograph (Pl. XLV, *b*). It consists of a low parapet wall pierced with a series of recesses and surmounted with a triangular coping. These arches are all nearly semi-circular in section and very slightly pointed at the top, with the exception of a single arch at the west end of the south side, which is trefoiled. The basement on which this wall rests is moulded like the basement of the Sugandhēśa temple at Paṭan, with a torus moulding at the base and a *cyma recta* at the top. The gateway that now remains in the south side is of the usual Hindu type, divided into two equal chambers by a cross wall which contains the entrance, the side walls of the chambers being adorned with unfinished Hindu niches crowned with the usual pyramidal roof. The flank walls of the stair which led up to the floor of the gateway are extant. They were adorned on the front with panels containing sculptured scenes. The one on the left wall presumably represents a standing figure of Vishṇu. This fact is noteworthy, since we may infer that the enclosure wall must have belonged to a Vaishṇava temple, which has now entirely disappeared.

The ancient name of the temple will, perhaps, never be known. There seems, however, no doubt that it was a temple of a Vaishṇava deity and that it was erected about the 9th or 10th century A.D. It is, therefore, not a little surprising that two such high authorities as Gen. Cunningham and Mr. Fergusson

[1] *Note*, p. 12 *seq*.

should have been so much misled about the age of this building, that the one assigned it to the early centuries of the Christian era, the other to the Muhammadan period. Mr. Fergusson stated emphatically that the enclosure wall including the gateway was erected by the prince, whose name it bears, to surround his tomb. It is a pity that Mr. Fergusson had no opportunity of seeing it personally. Nor does he appear to have examined carefully the photograph[1] of the structure in Lt. Cole's book, for if he had done so, he could not have failed to observe in it an entrance in the real Muhammadan style added to the same enclosure wall by Sulṭān Ḥabīb of Kashmir in A. H. 981 (A.D. 1573).[2] The contrast afforded by this entrance, the inscribed lintel of which is still extant, to the other gateway which is in the Hindu style, must have rendered impossible the conclusion at which Mr. Fergusson arrived.

Śiva temple at Purāṇādhiṣṭhāna.

This temple (Pl. XLV, *c*) is very familiar to visitors to Kashmir owing to its excellent preservation and its proximity to the capital of the valley. It consists of a single chamber measuring 11′ 6″ along each side internally and 17′ 6″ square along the outside. It is a temple of the *maṇḍapa* type with a doorway on each side, that on the north side being the principal entrance. The trefoiled niche above it contains a seated figure, which I believe to be a representation of Lakulīśa, showing that, like the temple of Pāyar, this temple was also dedicated to Śiva. The opening in the back wall seems to have been made at a later date. The roof of the temple was of the usual pyramidal type, divided into two sections by an ornamental band. The ceiling is composed of intersecting squares and exquisitely adorned with sculptures consisting of a large expanded lotus on the central slab, and Gandharvas in the angles of the several courses. I am sorry I have not yet been able to take a good photograph of the ceiling. The sketch[3] published by Mr. Cowie, who describes Gen. Cunningham's drawing[4] as incomplete, is not a great improvement upon that of the latter. Both are wrong in representing the angels as naked because they are clearly clad in a *dhōti* and a scarf. Each of the figures in the angles of the middle square has a lotus stalk in the left hand. Gen. Cunningham's sketch shows this stalk in the right or in the left hand while Mr. Cowie mistakes it for drapery.

Above the ceiling, the roof is hollow, and was ventilated with trefoiled windows one on each side of the upper division of the roof. It is interesting to note the similarity of the outer form of these windows to that in the slab from Muhammad Nāri,[5] and in the monuments of Taxila.

The basement upon which the temple stands is hidden under mud and water. But that it exists in good condition, is certain. An interesting feature of the walls of the temple is a string course of elephants' heads which runs round their bases. The interior of the temple is paved with stone slabs. The central portion, about seven feet square, held the pedestal of the cult image which

---

[1] *Illustrations of ancient buildings in Kashmir*, Pl. 5-68.
[2] *J. A. S. B.*, 1864, p. 282 seq.
[3] *J. A. S. B.*, Vol. XXXV, pt. I, 1866, Pl. XVIII.
[4] *J. A. S. B.*, 1848, Pl. XXI.
[5] Smith, *Fine Art*, Pl. XXIV.

must have been a Śiva *liṅga*. Gen. Cunningham's idea[1] that the northern door was kept closed as the image was placed on that side has nothing to support it.

Gen. Cunningham identified this temple with the temple of Mēruvardhanasvāmi built by the minister of Pārtha (906-921 A.D.), and this identification has so far been accepted as correct. The remarks I have made above clearly show that Gen. Cunningham's view can no longer be upheld: (*a*) because the inner arrangement of the floor of the temple can only admit of a Śiva image; (*b*) the figure of Lakulīśa over the north doorway has no place in a Vaishṇava fane; (*c*) the only other temple in Kashmir (namely, that of Pāyar) which has a figure of this deity, is dedicated to Śiva.

It may, therefore, be assumed that the temple of Vishṇu founded by the minister referred to has perished. On the other hand, nothing is known as yet about the founder of the temple which now exists in such good condition at Pāndrēṭhan. The only Śiva temple of any importance whose erection at Purāṇādhishṭhāna is recorded by Kalhaṇa was that of Śiva-Rilhaṇēśvara founded by a minister of Jayasiṁha (1128-49 A.D.). Our temple, however, is certainly quite two hundred years older than the temple of Rilhaṇa.

The water that surrounds the temple during some seasons of the year is due to a spring which has burst out inside the temple, and many smaller ones in the area around it. It is obvious that the site must have been free from springs when it was selected for the erection of this temple, as according to the prescribed rules quoted by Rām Rāz, moist ground must not be selected for a building.[2] It cannot yet be ascertained if there was a paved courtyard and a peristyle around the temple until the area around it is properly excavated.

Other Brahmanical antiquities have survived at Purāṇādhishṭhāna. These are a capital[3] of a pilaster and fragments of several large-sized Śiva *liṅgas*, a few of which, Gen. Cunningham[4] thought, could be joined together and supply the well-known Pravarēśvara symbol set up by Śrēshṭhasēna, whose reign he places between A.D. 400 and 415. I have examined these fragments carefully and can find no reason for supposing that they were connected with each other. Gen. Cunningham's idea[5] therefore must be regarded as merely fanciful.

This temple, which is by far the most perfect specimen (Pl. XXXIX, *d*) of the Kashmiri Hindu style, is situated at a distance of about six miles south-east of Avantipura. Gen. Cunningham, following Mr. Vigne, spells the name of the village as Pāyech or Pāyachchhagrāma "the village on the clear stream." The only name known to the villagers is Pāyar, which they derive from Pārvatīpura, but I am unable to verify the correctness of the latter derivation. **Śiva temple at Pāyar.**

Gen. Cunningham, relying on an unknown tradition which attributed the temple to a certain Rājā Nal or Nar, identified it with the temple of

[1] *J. A. S. B.*, 1848, p. 287.

[2] *Hindu Architecture*, pp. 16-17

[3] Cole, *Illustrations of ancient buildings in Kashmir*, Pl. 11-63

[4] *J. A. S. B.*, 1848, pp. 322 seq.

[5] *Ibid*, Pl. VII.

Narendrasvāmi founded by Narēndrāditya, whose reign he places between the years 483 and 490 A.D., adding that the Pāyar temple is one of Śiva and that *svāmi* is a name of Śiva. Now, we know that this is not the case, the termination *svāmi* being applied exclusively to the names of Vishṇu temples. But a stronger evidence against the identification proposed by him is afforded by the style of construction of the temple, which is very simlar to that of the temple at Purāṇādhishṭhāna.

The temple consists of a single square chamber, 8′ along each side internally, with a roof of the usual Kashmiri type and a doorway on each side (Pl. XLVI). The superstructure above the basement, except the base, is constructed of ten stones and not six, as stated by Gen. Cunningham. The temple has always been one of Śiva and the old *liṅga* is intact. As observed by Gen. Cunningham, the figures of bulls on the capitals of the pilasters, which flank the doorways, are intended to emphasize the Śaiva character of the temple. Another Śaiva symbol, as I have stated above, is the figure of Lakulīśa over the principal entrance.

Bumᵊzu temples.

Bumᵊzu is the name of a small hamlet about a mile north of the sacred springs of Mārtāṇḍa (vulgo Bavan). The name Bumᵊzu figures in the Māhātmyas under the form of Bhīmādvīpa, that is, the island of Bhīmā, one of the *śaktis* of Mārtāṇḍa.

This village contains three ancient temples, which probably all date from the 10th century A.D. The most important among them is the temple now converted into a Muhammadan tomb and known as the Ziārat of Bābā Bāmᵊdīn Ṣāḥib. Sir Aurel Stein[1] recognises in this name a corruption of the Sanskrit name Bhīma Śāhi and concludes that the structure is identical with the shrine of Bhīmakēśava, which was erected by Bhīma Śāhi, maternal grandfather of Diddā, queen of Kshēmagupta (A.D. 950-958). The temple (Pl. XLV, *d*) has been fully described by Mr. Cowie.[2] It is now covered completely, both inside and out, with a coating of mud plaster two inches thick, which prevents an examination of the structure. The ceiling is quite intact and composed of intersecting squares. The roof, which must have been pyramidal and divided into two sections, has entirely disappeared. The temple faces towards the north.

At a distance of 30′ to the west of the temple just described is a smaller shrine[3] which has no special interest.

The little temple (Pl. XLVII, *d*) in the cave near this village was assigned by Gen. Cunningham to the commencement of the Christian era. Sir Aurel Stein[4] and Sir John Marshall[5] have already shown that it has no claims whatever to that great antiquity, and that it must be a good deal later even than the time of Bhīma Śāhi. A comparison of this temple with any of the other authenticated examples of the style leaves no doubt as to this structure being

---

[1] Kalhaṇa, *Rājataraṅgiṇi*, trans. Stein, bk. VI, 177-78.
[2] *J. A. S. B.*, Vol. XXXV, pt. I, pp. 100 sq.
[3] *Ibid*, p. 101.
[4] *Rājat.*, bk. VI, vv. 177-78.
[5] *Note*, pp. 24-25.

one of the latest specimens of the Kashmir Hindu architecture. The temple is certainly later than those of Pāyar, Kōṭhēr and Māmal, and the earliest date we can assign to it is the 13th century A.D.

The shrine is situated at the rear of the cave and faces towards the west. It is 9′ 5″ square externally and rests on a basement 4′ 6″ in height. There is nothing else to be recorded about this structure, except that the outer gate must have been built about the same time as the shrine itself.

Kapaṭēś'vara. Kōṭhēr. This village is known after a spring of Pāpasūdana-Kapaṭēśvara-Śiva which was surrounded with a round tank by Bhōja,[1] king of Mālava in the time of Ananta (1028-1063 A.D.). The stone wall built by Bhōja is still in good condition. By the side of this spring there are two little shrines, not noticed by Gen. Cunningham or Mr. Cowie, which, as Sir Aurel Stein states, must have been built at the expense of the same ruler. The bigger one of these two shrines, which faces towards the south-west, has lost its roof. It must have been destroyed with fire. It is 8′ 4″ square internally, the doorway being 3′ 8″ wide by 6′ high. The niches on the remaining three sides, which in earlier examples are equal in dimensions to the entrance, are, in this case, much smaller than the entrance.

The smaller shrine faces to the west and is 6′ 4″ square internally. The ceiling is composed of intersecting squares. The lower part of the temple is buried under earth.

A large area around the spring and these temples was in ancient times enclosed in a surrounding wall 12′ in width. On the north side, where this wall is complete, it is 246 feet in length. The enclosed area might with advantage be excavated to the original level.

Māmalaka. Māmal. This is the name of a village near Pahlgām now known as Māmal, which Sir Aurel Stein[2] identifies with the ancient Māmalaka. In the small shrine of Śiva situated near this village, that scholar recognises the temple of Mammēśvara which Jayasiṁha (A.D. 1128-49) adorned with a golden *āmalaka*. The late style of architecture exhibited by the shrine leads me to think that its original erection can not have been much earlier than the 12th century.

The temple faces E.-N.-E., and is standing up to the cornice. It is 8′ square internally and is preceded by a portico supported on two fluted columns. In front of the temple is a spring of water surrounded by a stone wall.

All the temples that I have described in the preceding paragraphs were erected during the Hindu period of Kashmir history. In 1339 A.D., the country passed into the hands of Musalmān rulers, when Queen Kōṭā, the widow of the last Hindu ruler, was murdered by Shāh Mīr. No Hindu religious buildings of any consequence were erected in Kashmir in the Muhammadan period. The only Hindu remains of this period are insignificant shrines constructed of one, two or three blocks of stone, which alone could be undertaken by private individuals of small means. Such shrines are frequently met with in the valley of

[1] Kalhaṇa, *Rājat.* trans. by Stein, bk. VII, vv. 190-93.

[2] *Rājat.* bk. VIII, v. 3360.

Kashmir. Mr. Cowie has described the one at Kohil[1] near Pāyar. One other shrine of some interest (Pl. XLVII, *e*) I brought to light in the spring near the Dak Bungalow at Paṭan. It was constructed of three stones; the uppermost, which formed the upper section of the roof, could not be recovered. The shrine is 2′ 8″ square externally and exhibits all the principal features of the earlier temples. All the four openings were originally closed with wooden doors. On the floor of the shrine we notice a pair of feet (*pādukā*) and holes for miniature *liṅgas*. Another class of antiquities of this late period which are very common everywhere in Kashmir, are a kind of memorial slabs which might have been *satī* stones. A typical example is illustrated in (Pl. XLVII, *c*). The face of the slab is divided into two compartments, the upper one containing a standing figure of Bhairava with his usual emblems, and the lower a female figure seated between a bird and a dog, the vehicle of the deity referred to. In some examples the female is represented as seated by the side of her deceased husband.

DAYA RAM SAHNI.

[1] *J. A. S. B.*, Vol. XXXV, Pt. I, 1866, p. 110.

a. PARIHASAPURA: STUPA OF CHANKUNA FROM S.-W.

b. PARIHASAPURA: STUPA OF CHANKUNA: RIGHT FLANK WALL OF EAST STAIR.

c. MARTANDA TEMPLE, FROM S.-W. CORNER OF COURTYARD.

d. VANGATH: TEMPLE OF BHUTESA.

Photo-engraved & printed at the Offices of the Survey of India, Calcutta, 1917.

MONUMENTS OF KASHMIR. PLATE XXXVI.

PARIHASAPURA: PLAN AND SECTION OF THE RAJAVIHARA.

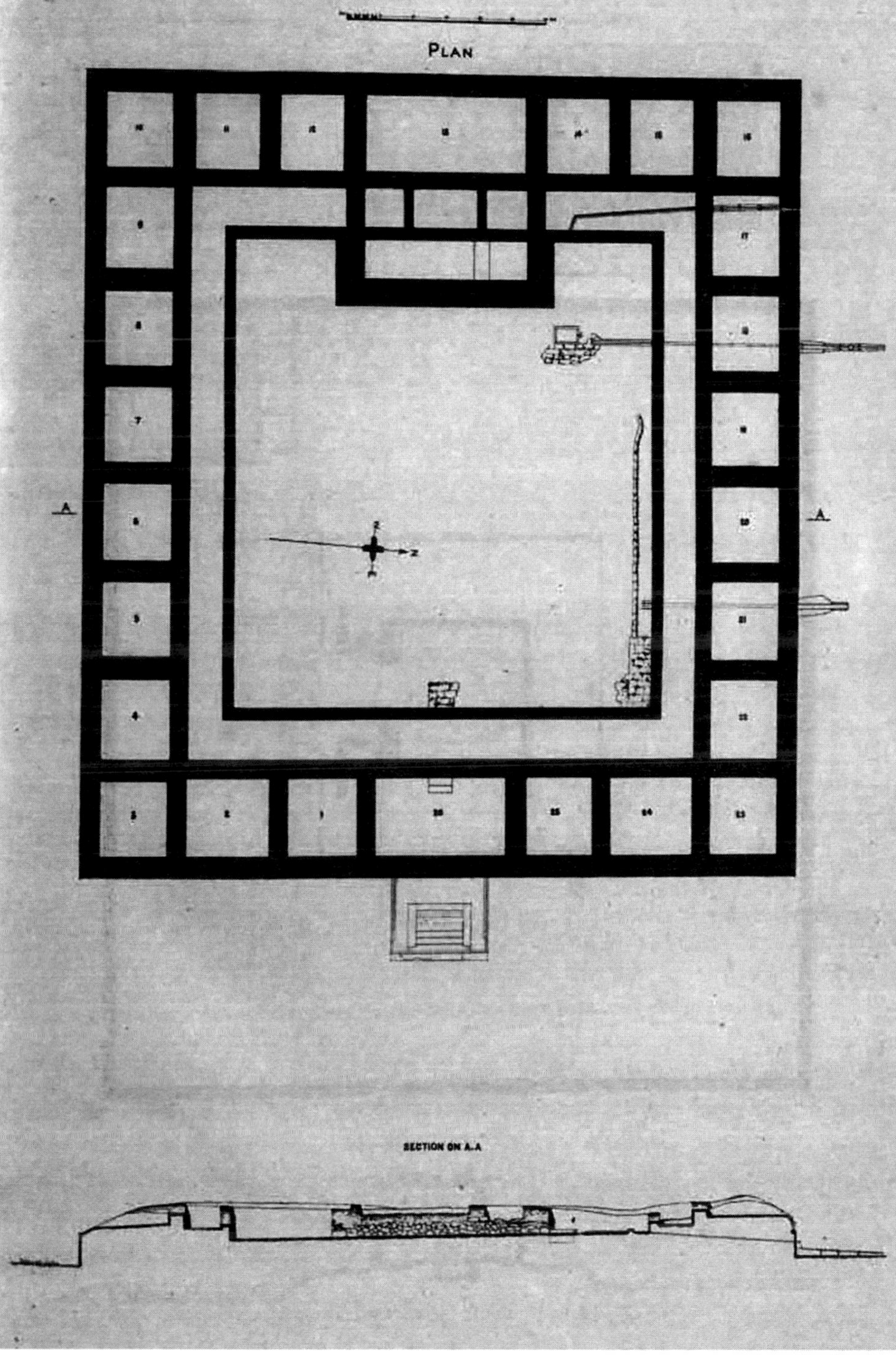

BUDDHIST CHAITYA (C).

— BASE OF COLUMN —

ELEVATION

SCALE

— FROM CORNICE OF SHRINE —

SCALE

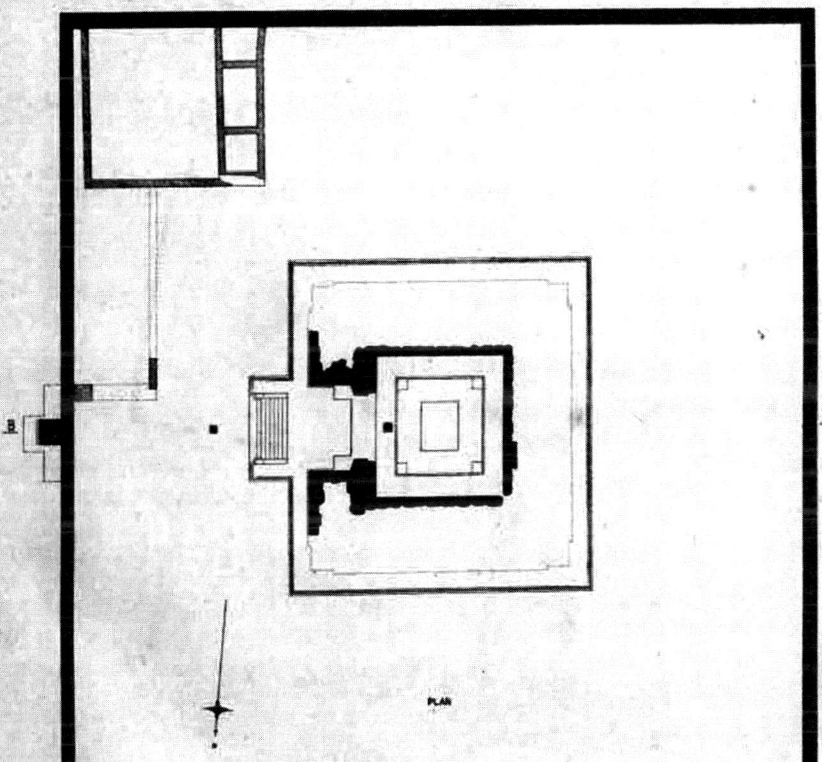

— SECTION ON B.B —

SCALE

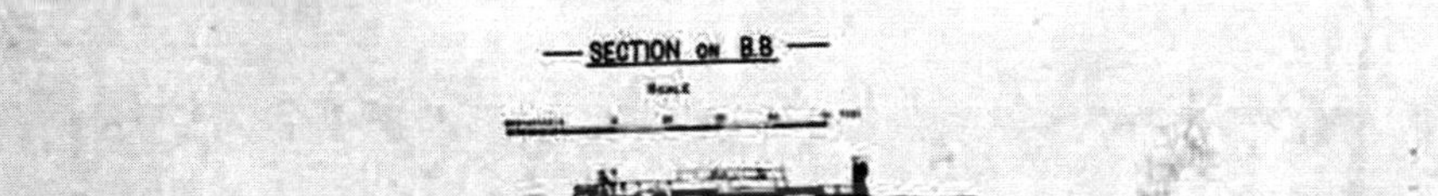

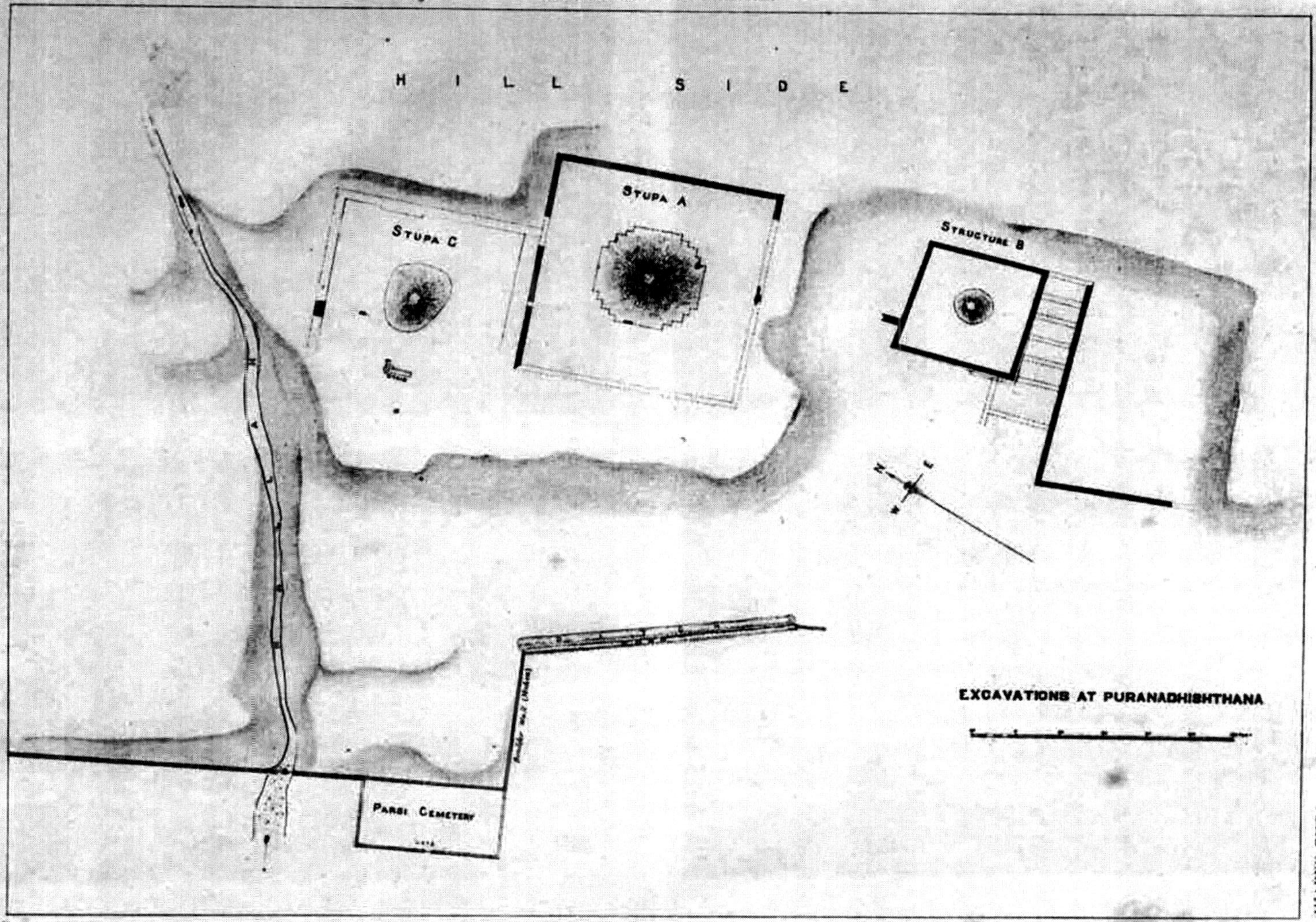
HILL SIDE
STUPA A
STUPA C
STRUCTURE B
N
E
W
PARSI CEMETERY
EXCAVATIONS AT PURANADHISHTHANA

MONUMENTS OF KASHMIR.

a. VANGATH: TEMPLE OF JYESTHESA FROM W.

b. BUNIAR: CENTRAL SHRINE IN VISHNU TEMPLE.

c. BUNIAR: GATEWAY OF VISHNU TEMPLE.

d. PAYAR: SIVA TEMPLE FROM EAST.

PLAN OF TEMPLE OF VISHNU AT BUNIAR.

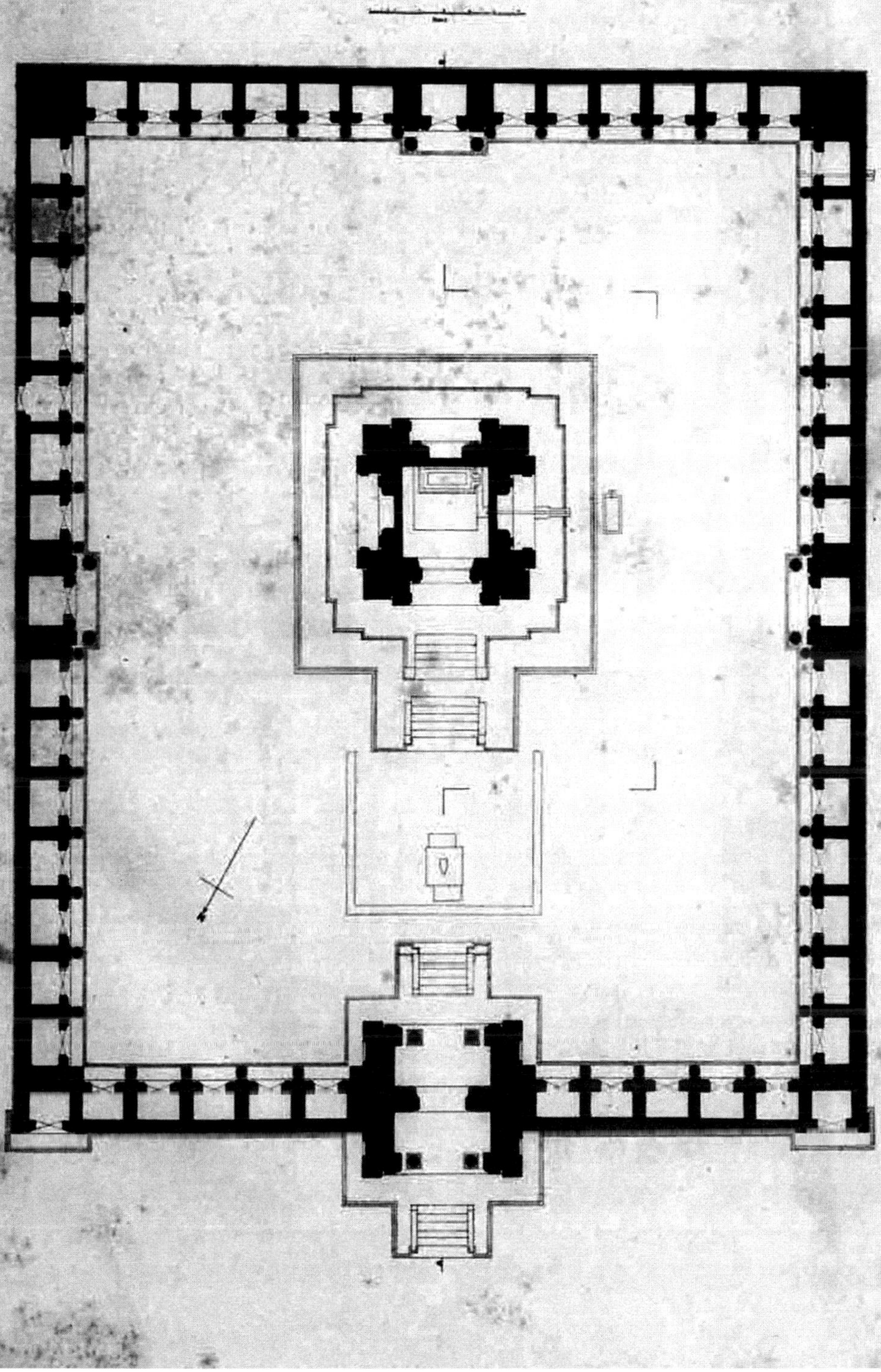

MONUMENTS OF KASHMIR.

FRONT ELEVATION AND SECTION OF TEMPLE OF VISHNU AT BUNIAR.

FRONT ELEVATION

SECTION ON A.B

MONUMENTS OF KASHMIR.

a. PAMPOR: PADMASVAMI TEMPLE.

b. BUNIAR: PERISTYLE IN VISHNU TEMPLE.

a. JAYAPURA: TEMPLE OF KESAVA: RELIEF FROM STAIRWAY.

b. PATTAN: TEMPLE OF SUGANDHESA.

c. PATTAN: TEMPLE OF SUGANDHESA: CORNER OF PERISTYLE.

d. PATTAN: TEMPLE OF SANKARA-GAURESVARA FROM WEST.

Photo-engraved & printed at the Offices of the Survey of India, Calcutta 1917.

MONUMENTS OF KASHMIR.

Plan, section and elevation of Siva Temple on Takht Hill.

a. SRINAGAR: SIVA TEMPLE ON TAKHT-I-SULEIMAN.

b. SRINAGAR: ENCLOSURE WALL AT TOMB OF ZAINU-L-ABIDIN.

c. PURANADHISHTHANA: SIVA TEMPLE FROM S.E.

d. BUMAZU: ANCIENT TEMPLE CONVERTED INTO TOMB OF BAMADIN SAHIB.

Photo-engraved & printed at the Offices of the Survey of India, Calcutta, [illegible]

MONUMENTS OF KASHMIR.

SECTION, PLAN AND ELEVATION OF SIVA TEMPLE AT PAYER.

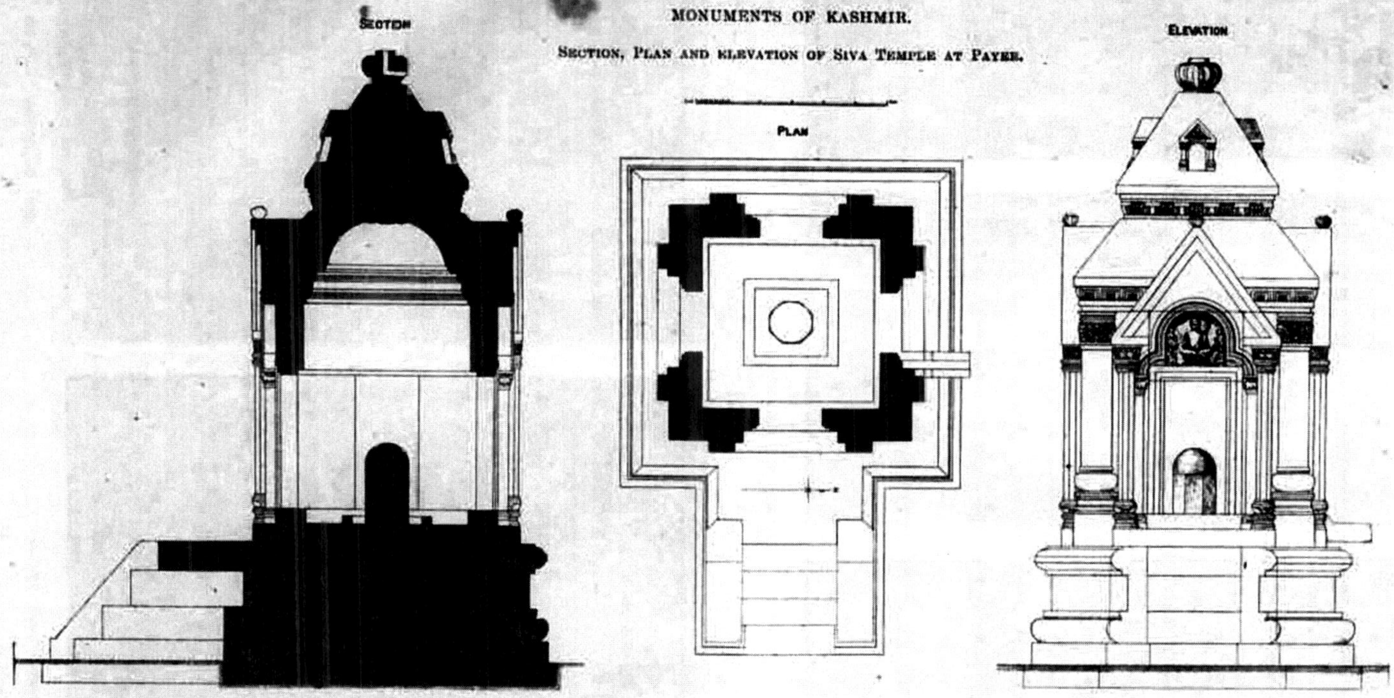

PLATE XLVI.

MONUMENTS OF KASHMIR.

a. PARIHASAPURA: STUPA OF CHANKUNA: SCULPTURE FROM UPPER STAIR.

b. PURANADHISHTHANA: STUPA H: IMAGE OF PADMAPANI.

c. PARIHASAPURA: MEMORIAL SLAB.

d. BUMAZU: TEMPLE IN CAVE.

e. PATTAN: SMALL SHRINE.

Photo.-engraved & printed at the Offices of the Survey of India, Calcutta, 1917.

THE ARĪ OF BURMA AND TĀNTRIC BUDDHISM.

THE religious history of Burma from the opening centuries of the Christian era up to the XIth century is still practically a blank; for among the great countries of Indo-China, Burma is the one about which we know least, so far as knowledge based on solid documents goes. For instance, the same period in Cambodia and Champa is much better known, owing to the evidence furnished by very early inscriptions. The fact is that apart from a few Pyu inscriptions on funeral urns,[1] which have no reference whatever to religion, the Pali extract on the Hmawza stone deciphered by M. L. Finot, the Maunggan inscription[2] and a few votive tablets from Eastern and Northern India inscribed with a line or two in Sanskrit in characters of the XIth century, and which were imported to Pagan, no records whatsoever, lithic or otherwise, have as yet been found antedating the middle of the XIth century. The very little we know has been obtained from foreign, principally Tibetan and Chinese, sources;[3] and even these tell us no more than what the pagodas and temples at Tagoung, Prome and Thaton and a few at Pagan bear witness to, namely: that Buddhism was then established in the land. As to the time at which its introduction into Burma took place, we are still in the dark. As regards this point, however, the religious history of Burma is integrally bound up with the general history of the expansion of Buddhism towards the East and South-East, and it is only by a close study of that expansion that we shall arrive at more conclusive results. From the researches of eminent scholars in French Indo-China and the Dutch Indies, it seems clear that the active and far-reaching expansion of Buddhism in Burma does not much antedate the fifth century A.D. That Buddhism within closely restricted limits and practically confined to the few Indian settlements of the deltaic provinces, was already existent

[1] See *Reports of the Superintendent, Archæological Survey, Burma*; C. O. Blagden, *The Pyu Inscriptions*, Epigraphia Indica, Vol. XII, p. 127.

[2] L. Finot, *Un nouveau document sur le Bouddhisme birman*, Journal Asiatique, 1912, p. 121; Epigraphia Indica, Vol. V, p. 101.

[3] Tāranātha, *Geschichte des Buddhismus in Indien*, Schiefner's translation, p. 262 *ff.* and other footnotes below; S. S. Chandra Das, *Indian Pandits in the land of Snow*, pp. 23, 50; *A Record of the Buddhist Religion*, by I-tsing, translated by Takakusu, pp. 9-10, Parker's *Burma*, p. 12.

in Burma at that time, there can be no reasonable doubt; but whether, following the rather late chronicles of Ceylon[1] on which the still very much later native chronicles are solely based, Buddhism was introduced in the Eastern maritime provinces of Burma by the mission of Soṇa and Uttara from the council of Pāṭaliputra, is still a moot point. This mission of Soṇa-uttara, absolutely unknown to the oldest Pāli documents as well as to Aśoka's edicts, has been completely rejected by some scholars,[2] while others are inclined to accept it.[3] But perhaps the two opinions may be to a certain extent reconciled, if it be conceded that this mission, independently of the Pāṭaliputra council and long after it, did in fact evangelize the coasts of Burma, and was inaccurately recorded in the Dīpavaṁsa (from which the Mahāvaṁsa merely copies) among the missions of Aśoka. That such an historical error might well have been committed, is shown by many other such errors which occurs in the Singhalese chronicles. Moreover, the fact that this mission to Suvaṇṇabhūmi, whatever its exact date, was recorded in the oldest chronicle of Ceylon, whose authors had no particular interest in so recording it, cannot be rejected *in toto* without convincing and conclusive proofs to the contrary.

Of the expansion and vicissitudes of Buddhism after its introduction, we know practically nothing. The Tibetan historian of Buddhism, Tāranātha, a diligent compilor and industrious recorder of current legendary and historical tradition, mentions Pagan[4] several times. Unfortunately, his knowledge of and information about Indo-Chinese countries seem to be very vague and hazy. However, his references are useful, though the dates implied (he practically never gives any direct ones) are often open to suspicion. He tells us that many temples were built at Pagan, and places its architectural activity in the time of Nāgārjuna; that a tooth of Buddha was taken from Assam to Pagan, during the time of a king Sīla;[5] that in the time of the Senas (XIth-XIIth centuries), under the pressure of Muhammadan invasion, many learned doctors and disciples fled from Magadha to Pagan, Cambodia and other lands (P. 255); that very early, Buddhism, especially Mahāyāna Buddhism, spread over the Koki land, in which he includes, among other places Pagan, Arakan and Haṁsavatī (Pegu). This mention of Mahāyānism as being extant at Pagan is particularly interesting, because it is corroborated by votive tablets found at Pagan, as well as frescoes, some stone carvings, and bronze statuettes (among which are figures of Avalokiteśvara and one of Tārā), the Mahāyānist character of which is unmistakable. It is corroborated also, though only indirectly, by the Burmese chronicles.

This rapid aperçu,[6] divested of all speculation, however plausible, and based

---

[1] Dīpavaṁśa, VIII, 12; Mahāvaṁśa, XII, 6, 44.

[2] Kern, *Histoire du Buddhisme dans l' Inde*, 11, p. 289; V. Smith, *Asoka's alleged mission to Pegu*, Indian Antiquary, 1906, p. 180 *ff*.

[3] L. Finot, *opus-cit.*

[4] Which he writes indifferently *Pukam*, *Pukham* and *Pukhang*.

[5] ? Śīlāditya=Harsha Vardhana, VIIth century A.D.

[6] For a more developed sketch, see Taw Sein Ko's *Burmese Sketches*, p. 179.

only on such meagre written documents as are now available,[1] brings us up to the XIth century, and to the subject of our enquiry—the Arī. Up to this time and for the same reason, namely, the total absence in Burma of any written documents, the political history of the country is but little known, though somewhat better, it is true, than the religious one; and we owe this knowledge again, apart from the native traditions, to Chinese, Arab and Indian sources.[2] This has been called the pre-historic period of Burma, in contradistinction to that which follows, in which we are treading on firm historical ground, and in respect of which we possess a variety of monuments, sculptures, paintings and inscriptions, which enable us to check the statements made in the Burmese histories.

The career of Pagan as a great political power opens suddenly in 1057 A.D., in the reign of king Anorata (1044-1077), by the destruction of some Indian settlements on the seashore and the sack of Thaton, the capital of the Talaing country or Lower Burma. The histories of the two countries, Burmese and Talaing,[3] agree in the essential points, and tell us that Anorata, after the sack of the city, carried away to the Burmese capital many sets of the Pali scriptures and their commentaries, as well as a large number of the most learned monks. This was the beginning of the establishment, at Pagan, of the Hīnayānism of Ceylon, which had been imported into Thaton at some undetermined date prior to this event. The Burmese chronicles go on to say that, before this time, Buddhism did not exist at Pagan.[4] This is merely a sectarian endeavour to make the nation forget that there had once existed at Pagan a Buddhist sect, outside the pale of Singhalese Hīnayānism, and very strongly tainted with grossly immoral practices which were repulsive to the purer faith they now professed. They ignored a whole phase of distasteful religious development by shortly stating that the religion of the Arī with an admixture of nāga worship held supreme sway in the land.[5] Burmese histories,[6] no doubt purposely, tell us practically nothing about these Arī; and the only two manuscripts which purport to treat exclusively of them, are merely a collection of the short notices found in the chronicles, interspersed with the compilers' own reflections, and throw no further light on this sect. This dearth of information is reflected in the several opinions of Orientalists who have touched on the subject. Phayre says "they lived in monasteries like Buddhist monks and their practices resembled those attributed to the votaries of the sect of Vāmāchāris

[1] The works mentioned in the previous notes are those that give the most exact informations.

[2] Parker's *Burma*; Pelliot, "*Deux itinéraires de Chine en Inde*" in B. E. F.E.-O. 1904, 131, a very interesting and important work; Ferrand, "*Relations de voyages et textes géographiques relatifs à l'Extrême-Orient*," under "Pégou" in index: V. Smith, "*Early History of India*," 3rd edit., p. 466.

[3] *Mhan-nan Mahārājawan to kri*, the standard history of Burma, and several others in manuscript. The Talaing history *Dhammachetī* p. 19, places this event in 1000 A.D., the Burmese in 1057.

[4] See *Pictorial representations of Jātakas in Burma*, in Archæological Survey of India, 1912-13, p. 87.

[5] The Talaing chronicle, *opus. cit.* simply states that the monks then at Pagan were *alajji*, shameless, and that Anorata followed their teaching.

[6] It must be remembered these were compiled from old records at a time when religious unity had been attained and the subject of the Ari was unpleasant.

in Bengal;"[1] he does not seem to think that they were Buddhist in any sense of the term. M. Louis Finot[2] thinks that Vishṇu was the *devatā* of the Arī, and that their cultus was a purely indigenous and savage one, though dignified by some Indian forms; he too does not see in them Buddhist monks, even of a lax and degraded sect; he doubts also whether they were in the least affected by Saivism. Others have thought they must have been a Mahāyānist sect, fallen away from the primitive teaching at the time of its introduction at Pagan, and strongly influenced by the Nāga worship, Tāntrism and Śaivism.[3] Up to the present year, no archæological find of any kind had been made which might help in deciding whether or no these Arī were Buddhists and what was the character of their cultus. But a discovery has now fortunately been made which gives us some insight into this much discussed question.

Min-nan-thu, a small locality not quite five miles to the north-east of Pagan, is full of interest. It is covered with rather extensive ruins, among which are those of a number of brick monasteries and temples, with various interesting architectural features. The principal interest of this locality, however, is to be found in the stone and plaster carvings and in the frescoes which adorn not a few of the temples and monasteries, and many of which are distinctly Mahāyānist and Tāntric in character. Min-nan-thu was no doubt one of the strongholds of some sect of Northern Buddhism, and this is borne out by the fact that it is only about one mile distant from Thamati, which latter was, according to all traditions and histories, the place in which the so-called Arī religion arose and endured for many centuries. Among the Min-nan-thu ruins is that of a temple now known as Paya-thon-zu, the date of which is not known, for no mention of it is found either in the inscriptions or in the chronicles. Its name, which signifies "The Three-Temples," has been given it because it consists of three distinct small square buildings with vaulted corridors and porticoes, joined together by two vaulted narrow passages leading from the one into the other (Pl. XLVIII*a*). This is a unique feature in Burma. The interior walls of the corridors and the roofs are covered with frescoes which are amongst the best executed and preserved in Pagan. Moreover, the subjects of these paintings are quite peculiar and unlike any others as yet found. Shortly, they represent that phase of religion, so much abhorred later, when the Theravāda school of Ceylon had been firmly established at Pagan, the priests of which were the Arī. All the accompanying plates are photographs of frescoes in this temple. A few hundred yards away, there is another temple, the Nandamaññā, close by a brick monastery, and also decorated with similar paintings; but whereas the Min-nan-thu frescoes, though suggestive, have nothing in them particularly offensive; some in the Nandamaññā are of a character so vulgarly erotic and revolting, that they can neither be reproduced nor described. The character of all these paintings tallies exactly with oral tradition and with what

---

[1] Phayre's *History of Burma*, p. 33.

[2] *Opus. cit.*, 125, 126.

[3] E. Huber, *B. E. F. E-O*, 1909, p. 584; Taw Sein Ko *opus. cit.*; Chas. Duroiselle, *Journal of the Burma Research Society*, 1911, Vol. I, Part 1, p. 126.

the histories vouchsafe to tell us about the Arī practices; as a matter of fact, those practices have not, at least in some parts of Burma, quite disappeared, as we shall see later on. An inscription in Burmese was found near the Nandamaññā temple, which had been originally erected within the precincts of the monastery near by. It is dated 610 Burmese Era=1248 A.D.[1]; though it is the original stone, it is the record of an event which took place some time previously, but the exact date of which is not recorded in it. The original document, referred to in the inscription, must have been composed long before, as it is clear from internal evidence. It is there said that Narapatisithu, otherwise known as Alaungsithu, who ascended the throne in 1112, urged one of his ministers to build this temple and the monastery close by; and that he, the king, sent Shin Arahan, the Talaing apostle of Pagan, to Tenasserim. Now, Shin Arahan began his work of evangelization in 1057; supposing him to have then been, at the lowest estimate, twenty years of age, he would, at the date of accession of Alaungsīthu (1112), have been already seventy-five. So his mission to Tenasserim, an arduous journey at that time, cannot have been long after that. Hence the foundation of the Nandamaññā can be placed somewhere between 1112 and 1130 at the latest, allowing the venerable monk a span of life of about ninety-five years.[2] Considering that the paintings of Nandamaññā and of Paya-thon-zu are identical in technique and character, we shall not be far out of our reckoning in attributing about the same date to the latter as to the former. The most interesting part of the inscription is the passage in which it is prescribed that, out of the revenues of the lands dedicated to the temple, the inmates of the monastery shall be daily provided with rice, meat and fermented spirits twice a day, morning and evening. This detail is important, in that it clearly shows that the inmates were not Hīnayānists; for the rules of the latter strictly forbid food after twelve in the day, and they hold the use of spirits, except when prescribed in a case of sickness, in abhorrence. The actual word "Arī" does not occur in the inscription; but considering that the locality has always been described as the home of the Arī, the erotic character of the paintings in the two temples, and the mention of meat and spirits to be provided morning and evening, there cannot be the least doubt that this monastery as well as the numerous others scattered about, were the homes of that mysterious sect. The very omission of their name further shows that the Arī were then recognized as a long standing and matter-of-fact institution; furthermore, the building of monasteries and temples and the providing of more than the usual necessaries of monkish life for their use, is a proof that, far from having been exterminated by king Anorata in 1057, as we are told, they were held, on the contrary, in high esteem, not only among the people, but also at the court. Another point worthy of remark is that contrary to all we are told in the chronicles about the intense enmity between the Arī and the professors of the newly implanted Theravāda

[1] *Inscriptions of Pagan, Pinya and Ava*, p. 250.

[2] The *Hman-nan*, I, 333, places the death of Shin Arahan in the reign of Alaungsithu which tallies with our inscription, but gives no date.

faith from Thaton, the two communities seem to have lived on a footing of amity; for, as the inscription tells us, Shin Arahan, the staunch Theravādī, goes to Tenasserim in Lower Burma to bring back a Buddha-relic for enshrinement in the Nandamaññā, an avowedly Arī temple. The fact no doubt is that, at Pagan as well as in India and elsewhere, Mahāyānism and Hīnayānism, at that period and probably long after, lived peaceably side by side, as I-tsing and Tārānātha tell us was the case.[1]

As has been seen, the frescoes found at Min-nan-thu are of the early part of the XIIth century; but they certainly do not hold good for that period only, and they certainly represent a much older order of things; careful search will no doubt bring to light others of the same kind and older. The question whether the Arī were Buddhists or not, is settled by the character of the two temples mentioned above; they are Buddhist places of worship; in each case, the cella contains a figure of the Buddha seated in the *bhūmisparśa* attitude; on the walls and ceilings, numerous Buddhas in divers attitudes are painted promiscuously with the other figures and whole series of Buddhas, surrounded by saints, are depicted on the roofs (Pl. XLVIII-*b*). In the Nandamaññā, a standing Buddha, in the *varada-mudrā*, or gesture of charity, is actually accompanied by his Śakti, Tārā. Thus, not only do we know they were Buddhists, but the presence of Tārā indicates that they were Mahāyānists. A remarkable thing about this Śakti is that, whereas the Buddha has Indian features, she looks like a Burmese woman standing in a rather voluptuous attitude; her right arm, invisible, seems to be embracing the Buddha behind. Had all these figures been absent, the riddle of the Arī would still have been unsolved; for, as will be seen from the plates, there is nothing in the other figures to suggest they are Buddhist rather than Hindu.

But from what can be gathered from oral tradition and the documents, the Arī were something more than mere Buddhists; they appear to have been the priests of some kind of Nāga worship as well as the Shamans who presided over the ceremonies of the indigenous Nat-worship and the animal sacrifices and drinking-bouts connected therewith. About the existence, at an early period of Mahāyānism in Upper and Central Burma, there can be no doubt; this is attested by Tibetan sources.[2] The exact date of its introduction into these regions it is impossible to fix with any degree of certainty; but it may with some probability be placed, according to the general consensus of opinion, somewhere in the fourth or fifth century A.D. The route followed from northern and north-eastern India was by way of Assam and Manipur on one side and through Arakan on the other. This is confirmed by the Burmese chronicles, which mention several immigrations from Northern India at an early time, one of which was responsible for the foundation of the city of Tagoung, on the Irrawaddy, about one hundred miles above Mandalay, the site of which is still covered with extensive ruins. This Tagoung is now generally believed to be

---

[1] Takakusu, *opus. cit.*, pp. XXII, 14, 51; Tārānātha, p. 262.

[2] Tārānātha; *The Land of Snow.*

the Tugma of Ptolemy.[1] The same route was still followed in the XVIIth century by Persian and other traders.[2] The Mhan Nan[3] (*vide* foot note No. 3, p. 81) vaguely records the fact that for an undetermined period, up to the VIth century A.D., some form of Buddhism existed at Pagan[4] which, from that time, gradually deteriorated almost past recognition up to the beginning of the Xth century, the period at which the execrated Arī worship had become absolutely supreme in the land. We are told that, at the beginning of the VIth century,[5] king Thaiktain shifted his capital from Thiyipyissayā (Sīripachchayā) to a place called Thamatī, a few miles to the east, which he renamed Tampavatī. He is credited with having introduced the Nāga worship at Thamatī, and it is from this time that mention of the Arī in connection with this worship begins. Is this worship to be connected with Buddhism or was it simply a native cult? Probably it was a compound of both. That snake-worship is a very ancient cult found in many countries, is well known; in the Burmese legends, as well as in those of India, the snake is often a *genius loci;* the Nāgas had also a prominent place in Buddhism, both Southern and Northern, as is attested by the texts, the sculptures and the paintings. The Arī, who, besides professing some form of Buddhism, were also the priests of the local worship, would naturally connect the Buddhist Nāga with the local snake. Plate LI*a* shows us two Nāga kings in the act of adoring the Master, which will be recognized at once as a familiar Buddhist conception. Pl. LIII*a* shows a large snake behind a squatting monster with human body flanked by two dragons. This, as well as the winged serpents not uncommon among these frescoes, may be referred to the local worship as distinct from the Nāgas of Buddhism. Old popular legends about snakes and dragons are numerous in Burma, as they are, in fact, over all Indo-China. Traces of Vishṇu worship have been found at Thaton, Prome and Pagan in the form of sculptures and statuettes, also in the name of several cities.[6] Vishṇu moreover, was revered up to the annexation of Upper Burma (1885) at great regal ceremonies, such as the king's coronation, the piercing of the ears of princesses, etc.; but this was due to the presence of *puṇṇās* or brāhmans, who were always considered indispensable at Burmese courts for the proper performance of those ceremonies. On the other hand, there is no evidence

---

[1] Phayre's *History*, p. 1 ff; Stuart's *Burma through the Centuries*, ch. 1; Taw Sein Ko, *opus. cit.*

[2] Ferrand, *opus. cit*, Vol. II, 556-57, where an itinerary from India through Assam to Burma is described (1663).

[3] Vol. 1, 232.

[4] By "Pagan" in connection with the earlier period of Burmese history, must be understood, in most European authors and Tāranātha, Central Burma, and the principalities which were established at various places around the site of the modern Pagan. The latter, as a matter of fact, was founded only in 849 A.D., and became generally known by this name to neighbouring countries, Chinese and others, only in the XIth or XIIth century.

[5] The *Mhan-nan* (1,241) gives an exact date: 438, Śaka Era = 516 A.D.: considering that the chronicles, written more than a thousand years afterwards, base themselves, for the early centuries, solely on tradition, these exact dates must be accepted with some reservation. The centuries given are, however, probably near the truth, for several are found to tally with contemporary events in India.

[6] Old Prome was known as Bissano-Myo (=Vishṇupura); so also Taungdwin, founded in 857, and which was called also Rāmavati, after Rāma, the seventh incarnation of Vishṇu; but Bissano and Rāmavati were quasi-classical appellations, and the town was always and is still popularly known as Taungdwin.

whatsoever, in the monuments, the inscriptions or the literature, to warrant the assumption that the worship of Vishṇu ever struck root among the people or that it was popular in Burma. It was only the faith of Indian traders and settlers and of some of the Indian royal astrologers at the court. Probably, therefore, it was not associated with snake-worship in Burma. It is also very probable that in the matter of snake-worship Central Burma may also have been strongly influenced by Manipur, which, under the name of Nāgasyanta and Nāgapura, is, in some Sanskrit works, mentioned as the reputed centre of Nāga-worship.[1] The chronicles give us to understand that, during the four centuries which followed the introduction of snake-worship in Thamatī, the influence and power of the Arī gradually developed, until, at the dawn of the Xth century, the Arī held all the people and the court under their spiritual sway. It is said that at that time king Sorahan (931-964),[2] an ancient gardener and usurper,[3] set up a dragon in a garden, which was an object of worship to the people and before which were placed offerings of meat and spirituous drinks. The Arī, it is stated, were the priests of this worship. This clearly has nothing to do with Buddhism proper, nor did it disappear with the persecution of king Anorata a century later; witness the beautiful Naga-yon temple, whose foundation at the end of the 11th century, as its name indicates, is connected with a snake-story. In fact, it has left lasting vestiges which can easily be traced even now. "The European and the Burman of to-day, who opens his eyes, can easily see that the Nāga has not yet been stamped out, of the national art at least, for the Nāga is to be seen everywhere in Burma, artistically, but not very much transformed, in every carving of the pagodas, at the extremity of the common carts and in pictures and frames. The observant reader will easily detect the cobra (nāga) everywhere on the platform of the Shwedagon at Rangoon."[4] In this reign, also, and under the king's patronage, the Arī built five temples, only one of which, the Patothamya, is still extant. These temples are said to have been built on the model of those of Prome and Thaton. Several others followed, and this activity appears to herald that architectural fever of four score years later which covered the land with a multitude of pagodas.

It is only when we come to Anorata (1044-1077), that is, not quite a century

---

[1] Duroiselle, *opus. cit.*, p. 126: Taw Sein Ko, *opus. cit.* p. 181.

[2] *Mhan-nan*, 1, 250. The interesting events, relating to architecture and religion recorded as having taken place during this reign, are doubtless worthy of credence, for with the foundation of Pagan it may be said we stand on the threshold of the political importance of Upper Burma: moreover, from the VIIIth century and coinciding with the steady decline of Buddhism in India an intense religious intercourse between this latter country and Lower and Central Burma was established; numerous bhikshus passed through on their way to countries further to the east and south-east, and many established themselves at Prome, Thaton and Pagan, bringing with them their ideals and learning. Then, again, the events connected with Sorahan took place barely a century before the Burmese language became the medium of written records. And last, but far from least, as the record of some of these events goes directly against national vanity and above all against sectarian bigotry, this evidently impartial record has a strong claim to the credence of the historian.

[3] For an interesting parallel between this gardener, who became a king and a strikingly similar Cambodian story, see E. Huber, *B. E. F. E-O.* 1905, 176.

[4] Duroiselle, *opus. cit.*, p. 123.

after Sorahan, that we learn something more about the Arī, their dress, their mode of living, their doctrines and practices. As has already been said above, the documents tell us, unfortunately, but little about their practices, but now something further can be deduced from the frescoes of the Paya-thon-zu and Nanda-maññā temples, which speak for themselves and clearly indicate certain influences from India, which, it was known indeed, must have been felt at Pagan, but of which there was hitherto no actual and visible proof. Anorata was the instrument of a great religious reform in Pagan, for it is through him, with the help of Shin Arahan, a bhikshu from Lower Burma, whose likeness in stone is still to be seen in the Ananda temple, that Hīnayānism was introduced into his capital in 1057, after the destruction of Thaton, and thence rapidly spread all over Upper Burma. He is represented as much dissatisfied with the doctrines and ways of the Arī, and as longing for a purer faith. The Arī are said to have numbered sixty thousand with thirty abbots at their head. They wore a robe dyed with indigo, resembling that of the Lamas of Tibet and China,[1] and we are told of a *blue robe* order of Tāntric monks in Tibet who "preached immorality and obscene doctrine."[2] The similarity in colour is striking and cannot but be attributed to Tibetan influence through Northern India. They kept their hair four finger-breadths long; they lived in large monasteries, the ruins of some of which are still to be seen a few miles to the south-east of Pagan; were addicted to much drinking; and were not observant of monastic celibacy. The use of meat and spirituous drinks for themselves and in their ceremonies, and their incontinency, recalling the five *m's* (mākāras), the five requisites for Tāntra worship,[3] point to Tāntrism. In the VII—VIIIth century, Buddhism was already declining in India, and becoming tainted with Tāntric ideas; sects arose in Bengal and Nepal, like the Vajrayāna and the Sahajiyas, who practised gross immorality; and the influence of the *śakti* cult in its most revolting form was making itself felt everywhere. It is also about this time that a great religious intercourse between Bengal, where there were several celebrated Buddhist Tāntric monasteries, and Northern India with Burma was established. It is owing to these influences that Tāntrism, as practised by the Arī, became established at Pagan. The frescoes from the Paya-thon-zu reproduced here are, it will be remarked, quite Tāntric in character, and the personages are distinctly Indian, as is clear from their dress (*e.g.*, the two women in tight short bodices in Pl. LI, *b*), and the mode of doing the hair and the large ornaments in the distended ear-lobes. They mostly represent a man, probably a Bodhisattva, embracing two women in voluptuous attitudes, in some cases half naked, and sometimes with a suggestive gesture of the hand. As already hinted above, there are some frescoes of so vulgar and grossly immoral a nature as to preclude any description. The central figures in the groups on the right hand of plates XLIX *a* and L *a* are interesting, because they seem to be Burmese

---

[1] Taw Sein Ko, *opus. cit.*, 182.

[2] S. S Chandra Das, *opus. cit.*, 56.

[3] That is: (1) *madya*, intoxicants; (2) *māṁsa*, flesh; (3) *matsya*, fish; (4) *mudrā*, mystic positions of the hands and (5) *maithuna*, sexual intercourse.

like the Tārā already mentioned in connection with a fresco in the Nandamaññā, and this promiscuity of Indian and Burmese (?) figures shows that these *left-hand* (*vāmācārī*) practices, though in their remote origins Indian, had been thoroughly absorbed by the Burmese Arī. Pl. L, *b* represents a deity with eight arms. It is not possible to identify exactly who this personage is; that he is a Boddhisattva is shewn by his head-dress and the stylized lotus flowers he is holding in two hands; in two other hands, he is holding what looks like a piece of cloth, for it is certainly not the "pustaka" or book of Avalokiteśvara; two hands are brought back before the breast in a peculiar *mudrā;* the two lowest hands are empty. There is nothing to allow exact identification. In the Nandamaññā is another figure with ten arms, the hands of which are all empty. Pl. LII, *b* represents a non-descript monster, in the manner of those so dear to Lamaism; it has the head of an elephant, with one eye on each thigh and looks like a grotesque image of Gaṇeśa. From its back, on each side, springs a nāga, whose neck is embraced by a lion and, lower down, by a goblin. There is nothing particularly Buddhist, and little that is Hindu about this figure, unless, indeed, we see Gaṇeśa in the central figure. Possibly this fresco belongs to the peculiar indigenous pantheon of the Arī, as influenced by Hinduism. In Pl. LII, *a* the central figure is a *bilū* (ogress), similar representations to which are still to be seen among the carvings of some temples and monasteries; she is flanked by two elephants on which are disporting two goblins. Pl. LIII, *b*, a leogriph on a caparisoned elephant, is one of the best paintings in the Paya-thon-zu; it is beautifully preserved and forms a very fine motif for decoration.

That the Arī, at the same time Buddhists, Shamans and Śāktas, were addicted to the grossest immorality, is therefore confirmed, not only by tradition, but by their temples themselves. Besides the sexual aberrations derived from Tāntric influence, they had the right to a kind of *jus primae noctis*, which, if we read between the lines, was in the end the means of their undoing; for this privilege does not appear to have survived the persecution of the Arī initiated by Anorata in the XIth century. Probably it was this practice to which the king took particular objection, for even the highest in the land were not exempt from it. On the eve of a marriage, the young bride, whatever her rank, peasant or princess, had to be brought in the evening to an Arī monastery, where she was deflowered by the pious men, and sent back in the morning to her bridegroom. This custom is purely a native one; it was not, in fact, confined to Burma. With slight differences in preliminary ceremonial it was known of yore in Cambodia, Siam and the Laos. In Cambodia, the practice was called by the Chinese *chen-tán*. At a fixed period each year, the time of the *chen-tán* was officially announced, and the parents of girls who had to go through it had to give notice to the officials. The latter gave the girl a taper, on which was made a mark; "on the appointed day, at night, the taper is lit, and when it has burned down to the mark, the moment of the chen-tān is come......The parents choose a monk either Buddhist or Taoist, according as they live nearer the temple of one or the other sect." [1] In Siam, according to the Chinese document which records the custom, "The monks go to meet the bridegroom; arrived at the house of the bride, one of them deflowers her, and makes a red mark on the forehead of the young man; this is called *Li she*."[2] It appears that the bhikshus of the Laos, one of whose privileges was, according to custom, to perform a similar ceremony, were very lax in their morals.[3] A strange custom, which in Burma is popularly referred to as a remnant of Arī practices, is still extant among the Khamti Shans, on the Upper Irrawaddy, who are Buddhists. It is thus described by an eyewitness. The monks have to observe the lenten season very rigorously; the people themselves see to that, and provide them with all that is necessary. They are not allowed to leave their dwelling. At the end of the period, all the young girls in the locality are drawn up in a line, the upper part of their body bare; a monk passes along the line; this is called the "breast-offering." He designates the one who pleases him by touching her breasts; she follows him to his monastery and lives with him till the next lenten season comes round, at the end of which the ceremony is repeated. The young lady thus chosen is much honoured by the people and so is the offspring, if any. It may be remarked that, among the Burmese, the Shan monks in general are regarded with little favour; they are said to be very lax as to the observance of their vow of chastity, and this laxity is ascribed to lingering Arī influences. Such practices, in any form, seem to have been long extinct among the Burmese.

As priests, properly so called, of the indigenous Nat-worship, the Arī officiated at the extensive animal sacrifices which yearly took place at Pagan and at Mount Poppa, the sacred mountain. The king, his queens and the people, preceded by the Arī, repaired to the appointed temple or temples and there large numbers of white buffaloes, goats and fowls were sacrificed, and their heads cut off and hung in festoons between the pillars of the temples. A characteristic of these festivals was the vast amount of spirits imbibed by everyone from the king downward, the priests included. Such bloody sacrifices, but on a much smaller scale, seem to have lasted for a long time after king Anorata; for mention of them is made in several inscriptions, in which it is said that, at the dedication of a pagoda or temple, animals were killed and toddy offered.[4] In remote places they seem to have endured even up to the XIXth century. Sir Arthur Phayre says "I have seen, in a remote part of Burma an idol placed in a small hollow temple in the midst of a secluded jungle, to which buffaloes and other animals were sacrificed by the surrounding Buddhist population."[5] These bloody sacrifices may be considered as belonging to the aboriginal cult, which, as we have seen, existed along with, if it was not to

[1] Pelliot, *B. E. F. E-O*, 1902, 154.

[2] *Ibid.*

[3] *Ibid.* M. Finot, *opus. cit.*, 127, is inclined to think this custom was not a "droit de jambage" properly said, but a ritual ceremony independent of any Indian influence, and that it originated probably from a sexual taboo caused by the fear of blood. He is no doubt right.

[4] See, for instance, *Inscriptions of Pagan, Panya and Ava*, p. 293, an inscription found at Thamati, dated 1302.

[5] *History of Burma*, p. 21, note 2.

a great extent amalgamated in the Tāntric Buddhism of the Arī; for it must be borne in mind that in Burma as well as in other parts of Indo-China, notions purely Indian, belonging to whatever religion, did not displace the beliefs already extant in the countries which they penetrated. The adaptability of Hinduism and Buddhism in this respect are well known. In Burma, the long established native cults followed their own course side by side with the imported religion, both, as is patent in the case of the Arī, influencing each other to a greater or less degree.[1] Such was the case in Champa and elsewhere; "it is sufficient to point out the agrarian rites, of which traces still exist, among the Malais, the sacred interdictions (tabun), which appear, as this word indicates, to be borrowed from Polynesian religions; the sacrifices of buffaloes offered likewise by the Nepalese and the aboriginals of Indo-China."[2] The influence of Śaivism in connection with these bloody sacrifices may, therefore, be rejected. Moreover, only very feeble traces of Śaivism have, at least up to the present, been found in Burma; no *liṅga*, for instance, nor anything that could *irrefutably* be proved to be a *liṅga*, has yet been discovered—a fact which alone goes far to prove the comparatively small head-way made by this cult in this country. Śiva, as Maheśvara, is mentioned as one of the deities who presided at the foundation of Sarekkhetarā (old Prome); but it is now agreed on all hands that this city was founded by a small colony of Indians from southern India, who would, as a matter of course, bring with them their *ishṭā devatā*. One or two coins have been found with, possibly, a few traces of Śaivism; but the only certain trace of Śaivism in Pagan is a statue of Śiva about four feet high in the late mediæval style, which was originally found near a Vaishṇava temple erected between the XIth and XIIIth centuries,[3] and a few small figures of Gaṇeśa of the same period. As Vishṇu, so also Śiva was revered, through the influence of the Indian royal astrologers, at great court ceremonies,[4] but on no other occasions, and did not affect the people at large. In short Śaivism was not unknown in Burma, but never attained the status of a popular religion, even in a small degree; and there is nothing in tradition, oral or written, to authorize the assumption that these animal sacrifices were the outcome of Śaivite ideas.

The Arī preached the remission of sins through the recitation of certain texts. "Whoever commits murder, of father, mother, etc., is absolved by the recitation of this or that *sutta*,"[5] and so on through a long series of crimes and misdeeds; it is also hinted that payment to them in kind, according to a graded scale, did much to relieve the offenders from the consequences of their crimes in the next world. This highly pernicious doctrine could not but find some favour at an oriental court, where human life, especially when it stood in the way of ambition and power, was accounted so little. Nothing else is mentioned of their peculiar doctrines. The mention of *suttas* points to their

[1] Buddhism has not yet, for instance, displaced Nat-worship, which is rife throughout Burma, and not yet free from gross licentiousness, at least in many localities.

[2] Cabaton, "*Nouvelles recherches sur les Chams*," p. 49.

[3] *Vide*, *A. S. I.* Annual Reports, 1912-13, p. 137.

[4] *Cf.* p. 85 above.

[5] *Cf.* also *Sāsanavaṁsa*, Pāli Texts Society, p. 56.

having had some kind of sacred books; and, seeing that they were Mahāyānists, these books must have been in Sanskrit. Whatever they may have been, their names have unhappily not been preserved. Tradition, however, mentions one, still extant in Burmese garb under the title of Ādikappa (ādikalpa),[1] said to have been translated and compiled from Arī works. It is a collection of short chapters on quasi-Buddhist cosmogony, the description of some devatā and other beings, etc., which does not furnish an iota of new information about the sect. It is also said, but less affirmatively, that the Arī used the *Buddha Purāṇa*, a work now very rare and "interesting for the study of Nepalese Buddhism."[2] This Nepalese Purāṇa is no doubt the same as that reputed to have been in use among the Arī. It is to be regretted that the paucity of information as to the exact tenets of the Arī precludes at present the possibility of establishing by comparing them with the contents of the Buddha Purāṇa, a direct intercourse between Nepal and Burma: intercourse which is otherwise traceable in some elements of Burmese architecture.[3] There are widely read in Burma books known under the generic name of "Lokī-zā," about fifteen or twenty in number. Their principal interest lies in the fact that they contain a very large amount of matter not only foreign, but repugnant to the Theravāda Buddhism introduced in the 11th century by Anorata. It is a medley of alchemical recipes, of formulæ for the discovery of the *chintāmaṇi*, or philosopher's stone, of *yogī* precepts for the attainment of *siddhi* or magical powers, of popular medicine and wanton rules based on the *kāmasutras*, all of which ideas are of a distinctly Tāntric character, among them being embedded a vast amount of purely indigenous superstition and old time customs not to be found anywhere else. These works also are referred to as based on Arī teachings, so that the influence of these strange followers of the Buddha is making itself strongly felt even at the present day. This is borne out by the story of Ajjagoṇa, the only Arī whose name has been preserved and popularly known as the "Great Arī." He is reputed to have found the philosopher's stone and to have thereby produced a vast amount of gold which enriched the country. He has become, so to say, the patron saint of modern Burmese alchemists.

As a matter of fact, the Arī did not, as the chronicles would give us to understand, completely disappear after their persecution by Anorata in the mid-eleventh century. Of this we have a proof in the inscription of the Nandamaññā temple above mentioned. The effects of this persecution were merely of a temporary nature, since, at the beginning of the XIIth century, they flourished at Min-nan-thu, and had temples and monasteries built for them by the king and his ministers. Anorata's persecution, on the contrary, had the unexpected result of spreading the sect in remote parts of Burma, and its remnants, though not styled Arī, are still existent among a large number of Shan monks, among whom the original doctrine has been forgotten, though the

[1] The longer title is: *Ādikappakumbhā-ākyam.*

[2] Sylvain Lévi, *Le Népal*, Vol. 1, p. 117, a very short analysis of it is found in the same volume p. 272 and continued at p. 351.

[3] *Cf. Le Népal*, 1, 249; A. Barth in *B. E. F. E-O.* p. 83; F. Benoit, *L'Architecture: L'Orient Médiéval et Modern*, p. 408.

characteristic laxity of morals has persisted. Amongst the Burmese themselves at the Burmese capitals and other places of some importance, a degenerate form of Arī may be said to have lasted well into the XVIIIth century; the manuscripts of the Arī seem to have disappeared, as well as the right to the *jus primae noctis*, the animal sacrifices and the easy doctrine about the remission of sins; but the spirit of the old sect survived in the love of good cheer, copious drinking and women. The greatest part of this transformation is no doubt due to the great religious reformation of Buddhism carried out in the XVth century by king Dhammacetī, as recorded in the Kalyani inscriptions.[1]

The last mention by name of the Arī belongs to the opening years of the XIVth century, the scene now being Pinya, near Ava, where a new dynasty had just been founded after the fall of Pagan had been brought about by the hordes of Kubilai Khan. It is recorded that a number of Arī took service with prince So-yun—a statement which calls to mind the warlike bishops and monks of the Middle Ages in Europe. We know from an inscription of king Sinbyushin, dated 1557 A.D., that the severest blow dealt to these old practices was the prohibition by royal edict of all offerings of intoxicants and animal sacrifices to the Nats.[2] From this tim downwards, the name Arī[3] drops out of daily use, and an expression, equivalent to "boxing-monks" takes its place; these boxing-monks are often referred to as *Arī-gyī-do-anhway*, that is, the "Descendants of the Great Arī." They were numerous at Pinya, Ava and Sagaing and seem to have been well patronized by the sovereigns. They were so called owing to their love of sports, especially boxing, of which they gave public exhibitions. They set all monastic rules at nought, were great drinkers, and had a weakness for the other sex; they kept their hair about two inches long, wore a kind of cylindrical hat and robes of a colour not orthodox; they dabbled in alchemy and popular medicine, and were reciters, for a consideration, of mantras; they sold amulets and recipes for the attainment of magical powers; and they bred, rode and sold horses and exercised themselves in the use of arms. They were powerful at Ava in the XVth century, in the reign of king

[1] Taw Sein Ko, "*Kalyāni Inscriptions, Text and Translation*," Rangoon, 1892.

[2] A strange custom, almost amounting to human sacrifices, is recorded in the *Vohāralīnatthadīpanī Kyam*, p. 62. It is said that, when the rains were scarce—a pretty frequent occurrence in Central and Upper Burma—a post was planted in the river so that its summit was fifteen or twenty feet above the water; below was spread a net; a man had to jump from the top of the post. If he died in the meshes of the net, it was a good omen; it would rain abundantly. Things were no doubt arranged for the good omen to be as regular as possible, for the practice was abolished in the XVIth century by king Sinbyushin just mentioned. It is the same king who also put a stop, in the Shan States of Moe-meit and Hsipaw, to funeral human sacrifices where, on the death of a chief or high official, his slaves, men and women, were slaughtered and burned or buried with him (inscription on a bell at the Shwezigon pagoda, Nyaung-U, not yet published).

[3] Ari is the phonetic transcription of the name; it is written *arañ*; following the written form, E. Huber (*B. E. F. E-O*, 1909, p. 584) derives this word from *Araññaka*, basing himself on the Thai inscription of Rāma Khombeng at Sukhotay, in which the word *Araññika* occurs, and which he took to be the same as the Burmese "Ari" in its full form. But M. L. Finot (opus cit.) has shown that Araññika is a proper name, that of a "monastery in a forest." Pāli words ending in ññ(a), are never abbreviated in Burmese, but always retained in their full form. Moreover, the Ari were not ascetics living in forests, like the Buddhist and Brahman Araññakas, but lived together in large monasteries in or on the outskirts of villages. The word Ari comes from Ariya, "noble"; Pāli final *y*(a) becoming in Burmese regularly ñ which is always pronounced ī: *cf.* vinaya=Burmese vinañ, pronounced, wini.

Paṭhama-Min-gaung; the chiefs among them had free entrance to the palace at any time of the day, and there, it is said, they often drank so immoderately as to be sent back to their monasteries in palanquins. They are still mentioned in the XVIIIth century, when a thousand of them suddenly sallied from Ava and put to flight a party of Talaings, with whom the Burmese were then at war. Their decline and final disappearance—though no doubt not their influence,—is placed at the end of the XVIIIth and beginning of the XIXth centuries.

From what precedes it may be stated of the Arī: 1. That they were a Buddhist sect, belonging to the Northern School, who came to Pagan from Bengal or Northern India about the VIth century. This is confirmed not only by Tibetan sources, but by the frescoes of the Paya-thon-zu and Nandamaññā temples at Min-nan-thu near Pagan. 2. That they ministered to the superstitions of the people, and were the priests of the Nāga and Spirit-worship then prevalent in the land, and officiated at the bloody sacrifices connected with this indigenous worship. 3. That they were, about the VIIIth century, profoundly influenced by Tāntrism, (whose rapid encroachment about that time is a feature common to Hinduism and Buddhism), a system of sorcery and witchcraft which, among the Buddhists had for its aim the attainment, by spiritual means, of desired objects, whether material or otherwise, and by means of mantras, charms and alchemy sought to realize dreams of invulnerability, invisibility, etc. 4. That they were also addicted, as revealed by the frescoes, to grossly immoral practices resembling those of the "left-hand" or *vāmācāra*, owing to *Śākta* influences generally, and perhaps more particularly to intercourse with the *Vajrayānas* and *Sahajiyas* of Bengal and Nepal. 5. That they did not disappear, as has been hitherto thought, in the XIth century after Anorata's persecution, is attested by monasteries and temples, the dedication of which is recorded in inscriptions after that time. 6. That under the influence of the great restoration of Buddhism in Burma carried out by king Dhammachetī in the XVth century, and the prohibition of all sacrifices by king Sinbyushin a century later, left-hand practices and bloody hecatombs were stamped out; but the Arī, under the name of "boxing-monks," continued to exist till at least the end of the XVIIIth century. 7. That Arī immoral practices are still not uncommon among certain classes of the Shan monks. Among the Burmese this is attributed to the dispersion of part of the Arī caused by their momentary persecution in the XIth century.

CHAS. DUROISELLE.

a. PAYA-THON-ZU TEMPLE AT MIN-NAN-THU, PAGAN.

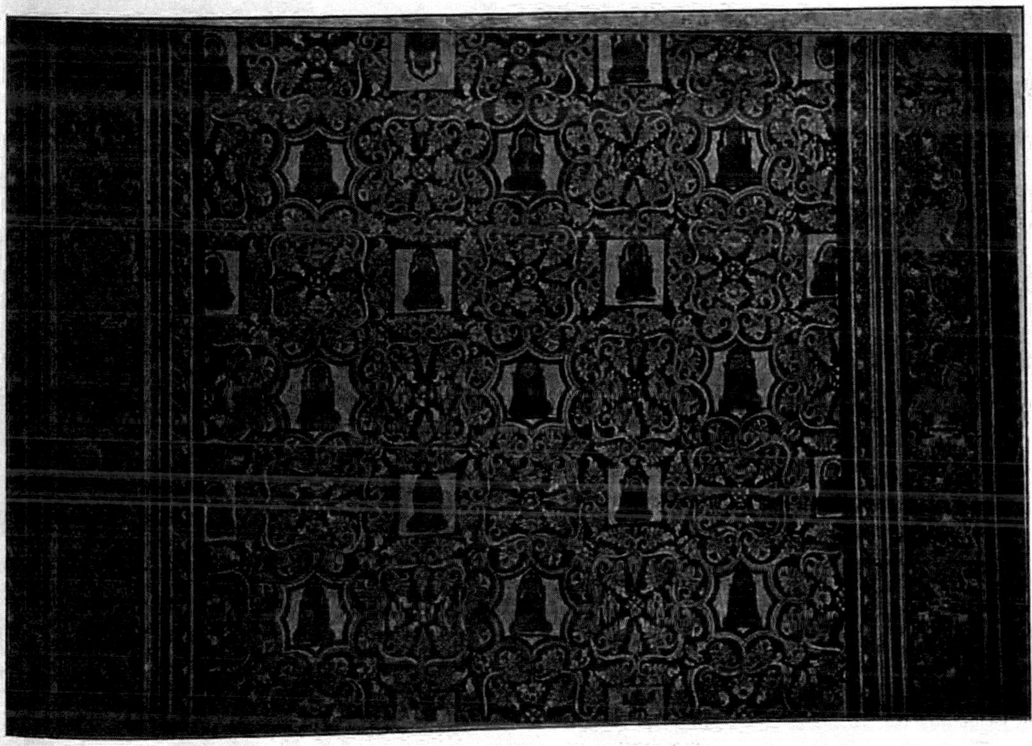

b. PAYA-THON-ZU TEMPLE: FRESCO. (2'-3" × 3'-2½").

Photo-engraved & printed at the Offices of the Survey of India, Calcutta, 1917.

a. 1′ 3″ × 1′·4½″.

b. 1′·4½″ SQUARE.

PAYA-THON-ZU TEMPLE FRESCOES.

Photo-engraved & printed at the Offices of the Survey of India, Calcutta, 1917.

a. 1'. 1" × 1'. 3½".

b. 1'. 4" × 1'. 5".

PAYA-THON-ZU TEMPLE FRESCOES.

Photo-engraved & printed at the Offices of the Survey of India, Calcutta, 1917.

PLATE LI.

a. 1'-6" × 5-[illegible]".

b. 2'-4" × 1'-4½".

PAYA-THON-ZU TEMPLE FRESCOES.

Photo-engraved & printed at the Offices of the Survey of India, Calcutta, [illegible]

a. 7½" × 1' 3¾".

b. 11" × 1' 3¾".

PAYA-THON-ZU TEMPLE FRESCOES.

a. 7" × 1'-3½".

b. 1'-11" × 8".

c. 2'-10" × 8½".

PAYA-THON-ZU TEMPLE FRESCOES.

THE SCULPTURED PILLAR ON THE INDRAKILA HILL AT BEZWADA.

BEZWADA is an important junction on the East Coast section of the Southern Mahratta Railway and is situated on the north bank of the river Kṛishṇā. A populous city and a busy centre of trade, it is fast rising into importance, so as even to eclipse Masulipatam the chief town of the Kistna district, in which it is situated. The two conical hills of Bezwada, now known as 'Telegraph Hills,' between which the river Kṛishṇā flows, lend a picturesque view to the city and have been objects of attraction from very early times. The one on the north bank of the river which abuts on to the city, has by its natural caverns, rock-cut recesses, ruins and rich treasure-trove been recognised as the more historic of the two, and carries with it the popular tradition that the Epic hero Arjuna fought on this hill with the pseudo-hunter Śiva, in order to obtain from the latter the weapon called *pāśupata astra*. The hill is, consequently, still called Indrakīla in Sanskrit and Arjunikoṇḍa in Telugu. Antiquarians are prone to identify the hill with the Pūrvaśilā mentioned by the Chinese pilgrim Hiuen Thsang in his description of the capital of the Danakaṭaka country. As a fact, however, Bezwada is many miles away from Danakaṭaka (Dharaṇikōṭa), which, ordinarily, would be the capital of the country of that name. The latter, too, is not located between two hills with the Buddhist convents, Pūrvaśilā and Avaraśilā, on them, as the pilgrim's account would require it. Though it may thus be difficult to decide upon the exact position of the Pūrvaśilā monastery, it may be pointed out that the excavations made on the southern slope of the Bezwada hill have yielded some valuable Buddhist antiquities, and that in the period mentioned by Hiuen Thsang Bezwada was believed to have been a well known capital-town of the Telugu country. The Ṭēki plates of Chōḍagaṅga, which belong to the 11th century A.D., state that Vijayavāṭa (*i.e.*, Bezwada) was the hereditary capital of great kings from the time of the Chalukyan adventurer Vijayāditya (of about the 6th century A.D.), who left Ayōdhā on a victorious campaign against the south (Dakshiṇāpatha). Bezwada thus appears to have been a city of some recognised importance from very early times, whatever its position may have been with reference to the Pūrvaśilā monastery. An old inscription of about the 9th century A.D.

discovered at Bezwada some years ago, calls the town by name Bejavāḍa. The Indrakīla pillar inscription of about this same period published below, calls it Pechchevāḍa. A still earlier record (*An. Rep. on Epigraphy* for 1917, p. 116) of the 8th century supplies the form Bījavaḍa. The form Vijayavāṭikā, which often occurs in the early and later Chalukyan copper plates as a synonym for Bezwada must have been only a Sanskritisation of the earlier form Pechchevāḍa, Bejavāḍa or Bījavaḍa.

The tradition already referred to about the north 'Telegraph Hill,' Indrakīla, is mentioned in a mutilated slab dug up in the court-yard of the Mallēśvara temple at Bezwada, which bears on it an inscription of about the 12th century A.D. It states that the name Mallēśvara of the Śiva-*liṅga* in that temple, was given to it by the *Mahābhārata* hero Arjuna, who was a famous wrestler (*malla*). Evidently, the wrestling capabilities of Arjuna therein mentioned must be understood with reference to his hand-to-hand fight with Śiva on the Indrakīla hill, when wresting the *Pāśupata* weapon from him. Still earlier epigraphical evidence confirming this same tradition is supplied by a sculptured pillar recently discovered on the top of the Indrakīla hill. It is 5 ft. 6 inches high with a moulded top and sculptured panels or inscriptions on its four faces (Pl. LIV). The ten carved panels bear bas-relief representations of the several scenes of Arjuna's penance on the Indrakīla hill, his fight with Śiva and the bestowal of the *Pāśupata* weapon. The pictures are very interesting, being contemporaneous with the inscription, which on palæographical grounds, has to be ascribed to about the 9th century A.D. The picture story, like the inscription, begins on the north face, where in the topmost section, under a floral arch, is seen the figure of Brahmā standing with four arms and four faces, of which three alone are visible. In his two upper hands he holds symbols, which are not quite clear, but must have been the lotus (?) (in the left) and the rosary (in the right). Of the two lower hands the left holds evidently the water-pot (*kamaṇḍalu*) with a rope tied to its neck, and the right is raised in the attitude of affording protection (*abhaya*). At the right bottom of the figure near the leg is the swan, the vehicle of Brahmā. In the second niche of the same face is seen Arjuna standing on one leg with his right hand raised and holding the *gāṇḍīva* bow, in the posture of one performing penance. His left hand placed on the hip appears to be mutilated. The two niches together thus illustrate the first scene of the story, *viz.*, Arjuna's going into the Indrakīla forest and performing penance, apparently under instructions from Brahmā or meditating upon him.[1] The second scene is depicted on the south face. Here, in the upper niche and also under a floral arch, stands Vishṇu of four arms with disc (?) and conch in his upper hands, his lower left holding the club and his lower right in the *abhaya-mudrā*. Near his right leg stands a boar, which evidently represents the giant Mūkāsura, who had assumed that form.

[1] The *Mahābhārata* says that Arjuna performed penance under the direction of his elder brother Yudhishṭhira who told him thus: तेन त्वं ब्रह्मणा तात संयुक्तः सुसमाहितः । देवतानां यथाकालं प्रसादं प्रतिपालय । तपसा योजयात्मानमुग्रेण भरतर्षभ । Thus it appears as if the penance was directed towards Brahmā. But the inscription published below states that it was directed first towards Mahēndra.

The only way to make an end of this terrible giant was to incite him to disturb the penance of Arjuna, and Vishṇu evidently decides to do so. Hence the representation of Vishṇu and the boar together. In the section below this is Arjuna shooting (the boar) with his left hand, being as he was, a *Savyasāchin* 'able to draw the bow with the left hand.' In the third scene on the west face of the pillar, below a plain arch, are Śiva and Pārvatī seated together on a throne with the bull Nandi below their seat. The symbols in the hands of Śiva are not clear; but the left hand of Pārvatī holds a lotus-bud, while her right is stretched apparently round the back of Śiva. The god and goddess are concerned with the penance of their devotee Arjuna, and, with the object of granting him the desired *Pāśupata* weapon, they decide to appear as a hunter and a huntress. This scene is represented in the second section of the same pillar. The pseudo-hunter, according to the story, aims at the boar (not represented in the picture), and there ensues a hand-to-hand fight for the quarry, in which Arjuna naturally suffers defeat. This is pictured in the third main section of the west face below which again, in a separate section, are depicted some figures which might be taken for the *bhūta-gaṇas* of Śiva's following. The discomfited Arjuna not knowing that his opponent, the powerful hunter, was Śiva himself, worships a Śiva-*liṅga*, the phallic form of Śiva, in the hope of acquiring more energy and skill to defeat the hunter. This is evidently the scene meant to be represented in the top section of the east face, where we find a *liṅga* on a pedestal. The flowers thrown by Arjuna on the Śiva-*liṅga*, are found no longer on the top of the *liṅga* but on the head of the hunter. Arjuna concludes that the hunter must be a crafty wizard, and tries to shoot at him as shown in the middle section of this face. Lo! His hands could not move and the arrows would not fly. At last Arjuna recognises Śiva in the person of the hunter and begs his pardon by kneeling down and praying with folded hands. Śiva and Pārvatī in their true glory appear before their pious devotee as represented in the bottom section of the east face. Śiva holds the trident in the right upper hand and in his lower the weapon *Pāśupata*, offering it to the kneeling Arjuna. The lower left hand rests freely on his waist and the corresponding upper, which must have held an axe, is not distinct on the photo.

Mr. R. D. Banerji has given a very interesting account of some Gupta sculptures of about the 5th century A.D. from Chandimau in the Patna district, which also illustrate this same story of the *Mahābhārata*.[1] Bhāravi, one of the early Sanskrit poets of India, was perhaps the first to use the theme for his exquisite poem the *Kirātārjunīya*. In much later times too, Ananta-bhaṭṭa, the author of the *Bhārata-Champū*, related the same story in a very charming and impressive style.

The object, however, with which the Bezwada pillar under reference was set up on the Indrakīla hill, was not primarily to commemorate the story of Arjuna's fight with the god Śiva. As recorded in the inscription, a certain Trikōṭi-Bōyi or Trikoṭṭi-Bōyu son of Kaliyama-Bōyi of Pechchevāḍa, et sup this

[1] *Arch. Surv. Rep.* for 1911-12, pp. 161*ff*.

pillar as a memorial of his own fame, in order to secure merit for his race. Trikōṭi-Bōyi, it is stated, was no other than the demigod (*Yaksha*) who under the direction of Indra had (in the Dvāpara-age) served as a guide to Arjuna, leading him to the inaccessible Indrakīla, whereon to worship Śiva and acquire from the latter the *Pāśupata astra.*[1] This *Yaksha* was born in the Kali-age as Trikōṭi-Bōyi at Pechchevāḍa (Bezwada), as the result of a curse (not specified). In virtue of his friendship with Arjuna in his former *Yaksha*-existence, Trikōṭi-Bōyi knew that (this) Indrakīla, on which he set up the pillar, was the very spot at which Arjuna had displayed his skill in acquiring the *Pāśupata astra* from Śiva.

This dedication by Trikōṭi-Bōyi of the pillar under reference on the top of the Indrakīla hill, must have been plainly due to the strong belief current at the time that the Indrakīla of Bezwada was the very hill on which Arjuna performed his severe penance, fought hand-to-hand with Śiva as wrestler (*malla*), and acquired the *Pāśupata* weapon. It is very singular too, that the subject matter of the inscription thus recorded in all seriousness of a lithic document in characters of about the 9th century A.D. is after all only the perpetuation of a traditional belief in the *Mahābhārata* story. Still more peculiar is the way in which the record is engraved, the lines being read from the bottom upwards. The document was written by a certain Vijayāchārya who is not known from other records.

The text and translation of the inscription are appended below. The alphabet is Telugu and the language of the inscription is Sanskrit. The palæography calls for a few remarks: (1) the secondary *ā*-sign is added to consonants by prolonging the left prong of the *talakaṭṭu* down the left side (with an occasional sweep to the right) or by carrying it straight up vertically. Both these signs are found mixed up in the letter *pā* of *śāpā* at the end of l. 8. The signs for *i* and *ī* affixed to consonants are sometimes distinguished, the latter by a loop added to the curl-end of the former; the *u*-sign is indicated by adding a tube to the bottom or by an inverted hook attached to the left side of the letter; *śrū* in l.3 is very peculiarly formed with the *ā*-sign added at the top and the *u*-sign on the side.[2] The *ē*-sign is marked both at the top (as in medieval Telugu) and at the right side. It is sometimes also added below the letter. The *ō*-sign adopted in the inscription is very much like the modern form of it; but *ē* and *ā* are separately added to express the compound sound *ō*, in *bō* (l.9), *mō* (l.11), *lō* (l.14) and *śō* (l.17). *Au* is expressed by the *ā* and *ai* signs, in *lau* (l.9). The consonants are all regularly formed as we must expect to find them in the alphabet of the 9th century A.D. The *anusvāra* is frequently used and marked by a small dot at the right top corner of the letter.

Text.[3]

North face.

1. [4]Arjjuna[ḥ*] Phalguṇa[ḥ*] Pārttha[ḥ*] Kirīṭi[5] Śvētavāha-

[1] The story, as related in the *Mahābhārata*, does not refer to any *Yaksha*.

[2] Ordinarily the tube is bent down or the hook doubled to express long u; see remarks on palæography at page 55 of *Epigraphia Indica*, Vol. X.

[3] From estampages. Read from the bottom upwards.

[4] There seems to have been a symbol for *ōṁ* and two vertical strokes, preceding the word *Arjjunaḥ*.

[5] Read *Kirīṭi*.

BEZWADA AND THE PILLAR ON THE INDRAKILA HILL.

(a) NORTH.

(b) SOUTH.

(c) WEST.

(d) EAST.

Photo-engraved & printed at the Offices of the Survey of India, Calcutta, [illegible]

2. naḥ[| *] [1]Vībhatsur=Vvijaya[ḥ] Kṛishṇaḥ Savyasāchī Dhanaṁ-
3. jayaḥ[|| *] Svasti[|| *] [Śrū]yatē khalu Dvaita-vanē Pāṇḍavā-
4. n=dṛishṭvā tat-pakshapā[tē]na vyagrō[2] Arjjuna Indrakīlaṁ gatvā
5. Vi[shṇu]-sā [hāyyatō] tapasā Mahēndram=ārādhya tad-upa-
6. [3]dē[śāt] Mahēśvaram-ārādhayataḥ [4]Pā[śu]pāt-āstr-[ā]-
7. [r*] t [th*]aṁ ch=āti-gahanam=Indrakīlaṁ [5]ayaṁ Yakshaḥ prāpa-
8. [6]yāshyati tvām=ity=ādishṭāvan[7]=iti [|| *] Sa cha Yakshaḥ [8]śāp-ā-
9. ntarāt=Kalau Pechche[vā]ḍa-[Ka]liyama-Bōyi-putraḥ[9]
10. Tri[kō]ṭi-Bōyi-nāmā dhārmmikaḥ prādu[rabhū]-
11. [d=ya*][ś=cha] Karṇna[10] iva [ba]la-parākram-ōpētō vadā-
12. nyaś=cha (|) Mātalir=iva sarvva-kāryya-kuśala[ḥ*] [svā]-
13. mi-bhaktāś=cha[11] (|) Hanūmān=iva vidi[ta]-janm-ānta-
14. [r-ā]va[tārō][12] sva-k[u]l-ōttama-charitaś=cha (|) saḥ p[ū]-

South face.

15. [13]rvvam=Arjjuna-maitryāj=ja[nm-ā]ntara-vēdī tat-Pā-
16. śupat-āstr-āvāpti-kalā-(n)nidhānam=Indrakīlē
17. [sva]-yaśō-nidhim=iva sva-kul-ābhivṛiddhayē
18. stambham=āsthāpayat | Indrakīlō giri-
19. r=yyāva(t)d=yāvach=ch=ēyam=mahā-nadī [| *] Tri-
20. [ko]ṭṭi-Bōyu-dharmmō=yaṁ [14]sthēyān=tāvad=bhavēd=i-
21. ha|| [15]Vijāyāchāryyasya likhitaṁ|| |—

Translation.

(Lines 1 to 3.) Arjuna, Phalguṇa, Pārtha, Kirīṭī, Śvētavāhana, Bībhatsu, Vijaya, Kṛishṇa, Savyasāchī, Dhanaṁjaya.[16]

(Ll. 3 to 8.) Hail! It is indeed well known that seeing the Pāṇḍavas (*in a distressed condition*), in the Dvaita-vana (forest), Arjuna with the love (*that he bore*) for them, became distracted, went to the Indrakīla (*hill*) (*and*) with the assistance rendered by Vishṇu worshipped Mahēndra by penance; (*and the latter*) directed (*him*) thus—"This *Yaksha* shall lead you to the inaccessible Indrakīla"—in order that he may worship Mahēśvara (Śiva) through his (*i.e.*, Indra's) initiation and obtain the (weapon) *Pāśupata astra*.

---

[1] Read *Bībhatsur=*.

[2] Read *vyagrō =rjjuna*.

[3] Read °*dēśān=Mahē*°.

[4] Read *Pāśupat-*.

[5] Read °*kīlam=ayaṁ*.

[6] Read °*yishyati*.

[7] Read =*ādishṭavān=*.

[8] Read *Yakshaś=śāp-ā-*.

[9] Read -*putras=Tri*°.

[10] Read *Karṇṇa*.

[11] Read -*bhaktaś=cha*.

[12] Read -*āvatāras=su-*.

[13] Read =*pūrvvam=*. Four lines of Telugu of about the same period, not deeply cut, are seen at the top of l. 15. They are much damaged and cannot be made out.

[14] Read *sthēyāsa-tāvad=*.

[15] Read *Vijay*°.

[16] These names of Arjuna are generally repeated by people in order to avoid the evil effects of thunder

(Ll. 8 to 10.) That same *Yaksha*, as the result of a curse, was born in the Kali-age as the pious son of Kaliyama-Bōyi of Pechchevāḍa (*and was*) named Trikōṭi-Bōyi.

(Ll. 10 to 18.) And he, who like Karṇa was united with strength and prowess and was charitable; like Mātali, was capable of (*doing*) every business and was loyal; like Hanūmān knew of (*his*) appearance in former existence and was the best-behaved of his race; becoming aware of (*his*) previous birth (*as Yaksha*), in virtue of his old friendship with Arjuna, planted on Indrakīla (*this*) pillar, the treasure of skill (*displayed by Arjuna*) in obtaining that *Pāśupata astra*, for the increase of his race, just as (*if it were*) a treasure of his own fame.

(Ll. 18 to 21.) As long as the mountain Indrakīla (lasts), as long as this big river (*Kṛishṇā*) (*exists*), may this pious deed of Trikoṭṭi-Bōyu remain steady on this (earth).

(L. 21.) The writing of Vijayāchārya.

H. KRISHNA SASTRI.

THE SITE OF PADMĀVATĪ.

THE city of Padmāvatī is mentioned in the *Vishṇu Purāṇa*[1] as being one of the three capitals of the Nāgas, the other two being Kāntipurī and Mathurā, but the Purāṇa gives us no information about the city beyond the bare mention of its name. A fuller allusion to it occurs in the *Mālatī-mādhava*, by the well-known Sanskrit poet Bhavabhūti, who is generally believed to have lived in the early years of the 8th century[2] A.D. The play[3] tells us that Mādhava (the hero of the play) was sent to Padmāvatī by his father from Kuṇḍinapura, a town in Vidarbha,[4] where he was a minister of the local king, to study the science of logic (*anvīkshikī vidyā*). Here he fell in love with Mālatī, daughter of Bhūrivasu, minister to the king of Padmāvatī, whose name is not mentioned. From this it appears that about Bhavabhūti's time Padmāvatī was probably the capital of a kingdom and an important seat of learning, to which students even from distant parts of the country used to resort. But the most important part of the information about Padmāvatī for which we are indebted to Bhavabhūti, is the description of the geographical surroundings of the city which he has given in the play referred to. From the minuteness and accuracy of the description Bhavabhūti appears to have been thoroughly familiar with the city and the country around it. As the references to Padmāvatī in *Mālatī-mādhava* supply the most important clue to the location of its site, they deserve to be quoted here in detail :—

मकरन्दः (माधवंप्रति) :— तदुत्तिष्ठ पारासिन्धुसंभेदमवगाह्य नगरीमेव प्रविशावः[5]।

सौदामिनी :— एषास्मि सौदामिनी भगवतः श्रीपर्वतादुत्पत्य पद्मावतीमुपागता। . . . . . भोस्तथाऽहमुत्पतिता यथा सकल एव गिरिनगरग्रामसरिदरण्यव्यतिकरश्चक्षुषा परिक्षिप्यते। साधु साधु।

---

[1] Wilson's Translation of *Vishṇu Purāṇa*, p. 479.

[2] Dr. Bhandarkar's preface to his second edition of *Mālatī-mādhava*, p. xvii.

[3] The scene of the play is laid in the city of Padmāvatī.

[4] Modern Berar.

[5] *Mālatī-mādhava*, Dr. Bhandarkar's second edition, p. 191. Wilson in his *Theatre of the Hindus, Mālatī and Mādhava*, Act. IV translates the passage thus :—

Makaranda :—Let us hence
Bathe where the Sindhu and the Pārā meet,
And then reseek the town.

पद्मावती विमलवारिविशालसिन्धुपारासरित्परिकरच्छलतो बिभर्ति ।
उत्तुङ्गसौधसुरमन्दिरगोपुराट्टसंघट्टपाटितविमुक्तमिवान्तरिक्षम् ॥

अपि च

सैषा विभाति लवणा ललितोर्मिपंक्ति-

. . . .

अयमसौ भगवत्याः सिन्धोर्दारितरसातलस्तटप्रपातः ।

. . . .

अयं च मधुमतीसिन्धुसंभेदपावनो भगवान्भवानीपतिरपौरुषेयप्रतिष्ठः सुवर्णबिन्दुरित्याख्यायते[1] ॥

From Bhavabhūti's description we gather the following information about the geographical position of Padmāvatī :—

(1) That Padmāvatī was enclosed by the two rivers Sindhu and Pārā (*Cf.* the word परिकर in the text quoted).

(2) Not only was it enclosed by the two rivers, but it stood on their confluence (*Cf.* Makaranda's words in Act IV).

(3) That there was a waterfall in the river Sindhu in the vicinity of the city. (तटप्रपात in the original text means '(water) falling from a precipice' and not 'falling of the banks' as Wilson understood it).

(4) That the confluence of the Sindhu and the Madhumatī was not far away from the city, and that on this confluence was (a *liṅga* of) Śiva, known by the name Suvarṇabindu.

(5) That the river Lavaṇā flowed close by the town.[2]

---

[1] *Mālatī-mādhava*, Dr. Bhandarkar's second edition, pp. 371ff.
For translation quoted below see Wilson's *Theatre of the Hindus, Mālatī and Mādhava*, Act. IX.

Saudāminī :—
From the tall mount Śrī Śaila, I, Saudāminī,
Have sought the royal city Padmāvatī,
. . . . .
How wide the prospect spreads-mountain and rock,
Towns, villages, and woods, and glittering streams!
There where the Pārā and the Sindhu wind,
The towers and temples, pinnacles and gates,
And spires of Padmāvatī, like a city,
Precipitated from the skies, appear,
Inverted in the pure transluscent wave.
There flows Lavaṇā's frolic stream,......
Hark! how the banks of the broad Sindhu fall,
Crashing in the undermining current.

(The last two lines of Wilson's translation do not convey the idea in the original text. The correct translation would be
'Here is the waterfall in the Sindhu, tearing the earth.)
Where meet the Sindhu and the Madhumatī
The holy fane of Swarṇabindu rises,
Lord of Bhavānī whose illustrious image
Is not of mortal fabric.

[2] Mr. K. H. Dhruva of Ahmedabad draws my attention to a verse in the *Sarasvatīkaṇṭhābharaṇa* Sanskrit treatise on poetics, of the 11th century A.D., which mentions the rivers Pārā and Sindhu, a monastery (*vihāra*), a forest of a Nāga king (*phaṇipati-vana*), a hill and a great city (as constituting a single scene). The verse probably refers to the city of Padmāvatī and its precincts. It runs thus :

पथः पाराऽपारा तटभुवि विहारः पुरवरं ततः सिन्धुः सिन्धुः फणिपतिवनं पावनमतः ।
ददर्श दृश्वो गिरिरिति गिरिरिव पुरतो विभावाः मालामिलल्लितवचनाभिर्भिजवती ॥

H. H. Wilson first identified Padmāvatī with Ujjayinī[1] (Ujjain); next he located it 'somewhere in the modern Aurangabad or Berar,'[1] as he thought it might be identical with Padmapura,[2] the home of Bhavabhūti, which is described by the poet himself as situated in Vidarbha (Berar). But there is no ground for the identification of Padmāvatī with Padmapura beyond a little similarity in name. Lastly, Wilson placed Padmāvatī at the modern Bhagalpur[3] on the Ganges.

As the *Vishṇu Purāṇa* mentions Padmāvatī, Kāntipurī and Mathurā as capitals of the Nāga kingdom, Cunningham thought that the site of Padmāvatī was to be looked for 'within some moderate distance of Mathurā'. He, therefore, rejected Wilson's identifications and himself identified Padmāvatī with the town of Narwar,[4] situated about 150 miles to the south of Mathurā. He based his conclusion on the discovery of some Nāga coins at Narwar, and on its situation in the vicinity of the four rivers mentioned among the geographical surroundings of Padmāvatī in *Mālatī-mādhava*, which he appears to have known from Wilson's translation. Cunningham's identification, however, though much nearer the truth than Wilson's, still missed the exact place: for the discovery of the Nāga coins could prove nothing more than that Narwar formed part of the Nāga territory, while he lost sight of the precise details of the geographical position of Padmāvatī, as one who approached the subject only through Wilson's translation was likely to do.[5] But though his identification of the town is not correct, he is entitled to the credit of having rightly identified the four rivers Sindhu, Pārā, Lavaṇā and Madhumatī in Bhavabhūti's description, with the modern rivers Sind, Pārbatī, Nūn and Mahuar respectively.[6] The right identification of the city was reserved for Mr. M. V. Lele, who identified it with Pawāyā[7] (Pawaia of the Gwalior Gazetteer maps), now a tiny village about 25 miles to the north-east of Narwar and some 12 miles by cart track from the Dabra Station on the Great Indian Peninsula Railway. The position of this village agrees so well with all the details given in *Mālatī-mādhava*, that there remains no doubt as to the correctness of its identification with Padmāvatī.

A reference to the map reproduced on Pl. LV will show that the village stands on the confluence of the Sind and the Pārbatī, just in the fork formed by the two rivers. About two miles to the south-west of the village is a picturesque waterfall in the Sind at the spot indicated in the map. This is undoubtedly the waterfall alluded to in *Mālatī-Mādhava*. Again, about two miles below Pawāyā, the Mahuar joins the Sind and near the confluence is a platform supporting a *liṅga*. Although the platform is much later than *Mālatī-mādhava*, it obviously marks the site of Suvarṇabindu Śiva referred to in the work. The

[1] Wilson's *Theatre of the Hindus*, Vol. II, *Mālatī and Mādhava*, p. 95, note †

[2] *Ibid.*

[3] Wilson's *Vishṇu Purāṇa*, p. 480, note.

[4] *C. S. R.*, Vol. II. pp. 307f, and *C. M. I.*, pp. 21f.

[5] Wilson's translation of the passage in question is very free as will be seen on comparison of the text and translation quoted above.

[6] *C. S. R.*, Vol. II, p. 303.

[7] *Mālatī-mādhava sāra āṇi vichāra*, a pamphlet in Marāṭhī, p. 5.

river Nūn flows at a distance of not more than four or five miles from Pawāyā. Narwar also is shown in the same map, and it will be clear that the situation of this place which is not less than twenty-five miles from the confluence of the Sind and the Pārbatī does not tally in any respect with that of Padmāvatī as described in *Mālatī-mādhava*.

Besides the literary evidence cited above there are other proofs also in support of this identification. The archæological remains at Pawāyā, to be described further on, show that it is the site of an ancient city which was in existence at least as early as the 1st or 2nd century A.D. and continued to be in a more or less prosperous condition until at least the mediæval period. From the numerous Nāga coins that are found in the early brick ruins at the place, it is clear that the ancient city was for a long time under the rule of the Nāgas. The Allahabad pillar inscription of Samudragupta indicates that the flourishing period of the Nāgas preceded that of the Guptas, as Samudragupta has included the name of Gaṇapati Nāga in the list of kings whom he violently exterminated.[1] One thus naturally expects to find among the ruins of a Nāga capital traces of Gupta or pre-Gupta art, and this expectation is not disappointed among the ruins at Pawāyā. At Narwar on the other hand there are no traces of any brick or stone monuments referable to the pre-mediæval period. Thus on the ground of monumental evidence also, Pawāyā rather than Narwar, is to be identified with Padmāvatī.

Tradition also points to the same conclusion; for the people of Pawāyā have preserved a story that their village is the city of Padmāvatī which, they believe, was the capital of a large kingdom in ancient times. The names of two kings, moreover, have survived in legend. One is Dhundapāla (Dhanyapāla ?) and the other Punnapāla (Puṇyapāla ?). The former of these, they say, was a universal ruler (*chakravartin*) of Padmāvatī. One warm day, while seated at court he perspired, and feeling offended he ordered his servants to seize and chastise the sun, the cause of the trouble. Enraged at this blasphemy of the monarch, Vajāga Devī, the guardian deity of the city, uttered a curse to the effect that *the city would be subverted*. The name of the dynasty to which this Dundapāla belonged, is not recorded in the legend. Long afterwards, the city is said to have been under the Paramāras. Punnapāla was a prominent king of this line who founded the fort[2] and the stone *ghāṭ* on the confluence of the Sind and the Pārbatī (Pl. LVII*a*). The legend may be taken for what it is worth. But this much of it may be accepted, *viz.*, that Pawāyā is the remnant of Padmāvatī, the capital of an ancient kingdom.

Still another proof in favour of this identification is the name of the village. Pawāyā is sometimes called Padam Pawāyā. Pawāyā appears to be a corrupted abbreviation of Padmāvatī. Another instance of the ending *vatī* of a place-name having changed into *vāyā* is seen in an inscription dated v.s. 1341, discovered by me at Surwāyā, a place about 40 miles to the south of Pawāyā. The

---

[1] Fleet, *Gupta Inscriptions*, p. 13.

[2] The present form of the fort is, however, attributed to the Kachhwāhas of Narwar, tributaries of the Delhi throne.

inscription gives the name of the place as Sarasvatī which has obviously been corrupted into Surwāyā. The prefix 'Padam' appears to have been added to 'Pawāyā' in memory of the original longer form of the name.[1]

The foregoing proofs taken together are manifestly sufficient to establish the identity of Pawāyā and Padmāvatī. The phrase 'the Nāgas of Narwar' coined by Cunningham to denote 'the Nāgas of Padmāvatī' is therefore a misnomer.

The archæological remains at Pawāyā, so far as I am aware, have not hitherto been described by any archæologist. The ruined site on which the village of Pawāyā stands covers an area of some two square miles, and resembles generally the site of Besnagar near Bhilsa. The extent of it is shown in dotted lines in the map on Pl. LV from which it will be seen that the ruins are not confined in the fork formed by the confluence of the Sind and Pārbatī but extend beyond the two rivers, indicating that the city proper stood in the fork while its suburbs spread beyond it. Brick walling is found under ground at several places in the area covered by the ruins and the ground all over is studded with pieces of old brick. The ruins have long served as quarries for brick wherewith to build village houses. Indeed, all the houses at Pawāyā and at the two adjoining villages Pānchorā and Chhidori on the other side of the Sind, are constructed of bricks quarried from these ruins,[2] and the Pawāyā fort, which in its present form is said to date in the Muhammadan period, is partly built of the same old material. Many a structure in the ancient ruins must thus have been destroyed during the past few centuries, though there are manifestly many more that have survived.

During the rains, when the surface earth is washed off, small copper pieces of ancient coinage are found in numbers among the ruins. In a single day's halt I was able to procure from the villagers some thirty coins which when cleaned proved to be the coins of the Nāgas, almost the same types as those figured by Cunningham on Pl. II of his *Coins of Mediæval India*. Twenty of the coins belong to Gaṇendra, six to Deva or Devendra, one to Skanda, and the rest are defaced and doubtful.

Lying scattered among the ruins, too, are various sculptures ranging in date from the 1st or 2nd century A.D. to the late Gupta period, the most interesting of which is an image of the Yaksha Māṇibhadra (Maṇibhadra). It is lying in a field, a short distance from the gate of the Fort, at the spot shown in the map, and is said to have been turned up by the plough three or four years ago. The sculpture is of white sand-stone and represents an image of Maṇibhadra in the round, standing on a pedestal (Pl. LVII *b* and *c*). Its height from neck to foot is 4′ 10″; the head however is missing and in other respects also the image is somewhat mutilated. The right hand is broken off from the elbow, a portion of the arm is also chipped. From the position of what is

[1] In the *saṅkalpa* or solemn declaration of vow which an orthodox Hindu has to make before commencing any religious ceremony, he has to specify the place where and the day on which, the ceremony is performed. In the Sanskrit formula of such a *saṅkalpa* used at Pawāyā, the place still continues to be mentioned by its ancient name traditionally handed down as '*Padmāvatī-mahā-saṅgama-kshētrē*.'

[2] An entire old brick used in a modern house at Pānchorā was found to measure 19″ × 10″ × 3″.

left, it would appear that the hand was raised up to the shoulder. The left hand is lowered and is grasping a money bag. Only a small part of it is broken. A well defined fold of flesh is portrayed around the throat and another fold below the chest, both treated in a very conventional manner. The dress consists of a waist-cloth and a scarf. The former reaches down below the knees and is tied round the waist by a plain band knotted in front. Folds of the cloth hang between the legs and are visible from both the front and the back. The scarf or upper garment has one of its ends wrapped round the left arm and the other end crosses the fore-arm and hangs behind in folds. The sacred thread (*yajñōpavīta*) passes across the belly. The ornaments comprise a rich necklace consisting of a number of jewel or pearl strings knotted and hanging down in tassels on the back, an armlet on the right arm, and a bracelet on the left wrist. There was a plain nimbus round the head, which has left its traces on both sides of the neck. The modelling of the figure is ungraceful and the execution is rough.

The front face of the pedestal is inscribed. The inscribed face measures 1′ 9″×9″. The upper edge of the pedestal is worn away and some vowel marks in the first line of the inscription have disappeared or become indistinct. The language of the inscription is Sanskrit, which however contains a few solecisms,[1] and the characters are Brāhmī of the 1st or 2nd century A.D. This age is also borne out by the style of the sculpture. The inscription contains 6 lines of writing and the text is in prose. It records the installation of the image of Māṇībhadra (Maṇidhadra),[2] on the 12th day of the 2nd fortnight of summer in the year 4, during the reign of King Śivanaṁdi, by the members of an assembly, devoted to the deity. In the latter portion, it invokes the blessing of the god on the donors of the image whose names are specified. The inscription reads :—

Text[3] (for facsimile, see Pl. LVI).

1. [Rā*] jñaḥ Svā[mi] Śiva[na]ṁdisya saṁva[tsa]rē chaturth[ē[4]] gr[ī[4]]shma-paksh[ē[4]] dvitīyē 2 d[i]vas[ē]

2. dv[ā]da[śē] 10 2 ētasya pūrvāy[ē] gaushṭhyā Māṇībhadra-bhaktā garbha-sukhitāḥ Bhagavatō

3. Māṇ[ī]bhadrasya pratimā pratishṭhāpayaṁti (1*) Gausṭhyaṁ Bhagavā āyu balaṁ vāchaṁ kaly[ā]ṇābhyu-

4. dayaṁ cha prītō diśatu [1*] [B]rāhma[ṇa]sya Gōtamasya[5] Kra[mā]rasya Brāhmaṇasya Rudradāsasya Śiva[ttra]dāyē

5. Śamabhūt[i]sya J[ī]vasya Khaṁ[jabala]sya Śiva[nē]mis[y]a Śivabha[dra]sya [Ku]makasya Dhanadē-

6. vasya dā.

King Śivanaṁdi to whose reign the inscription refers itself is unknown from any other source.

---

[1] In the transcript given below the mistakes in the original text are not corrected.

[2] Monier-William's Dictionary gives Maṇibhadra as the name of a brother of Kubera.

[3] From the original stone.

[4] The marks of these vowels have become indistinct by the wearing away of the upper edge of the stone.

[5] This word is engraved above the line.

Another interesting sculpture is a monolithic palm-capital (Pl. LVII*d*) lying in a field near a large brick-mound about a mile to the north-west of the village and a short distance from the northern bank of the Pārbatī river. The sculpture is of white sand-stone fairly well polished on the surface. The capital is shaped like a cylinder tapering towards the top, covered with three courses of palm-leaves, with a closed bud at the top and bunches of fruit in the intervals between the leaves. The top-bud and the uppermost course of leaves point upwards while the other two courses point downwards. A lion rampant is seated on a leaf in the lowermost course. The capital is in a mutilated condition, the preserved portion measuring 5′3″ in length. The pointed top of the bud, many of the leaves, the head of the lion and the base of the capital have broken off. The base is, however, sufficiently preserved to show a circular mortice which clearly indicates that the capital must have crowned a pillar. I searched for the shaft of the expected pillar in the vicinity but did not succeed in recovering it. Excavations of the surrounding ground may perhaps reveal it.

The top of the brick-mound near which the capital is lying, has been tampered with, at the point where a small pit and traces of a later platform in which lime mortar and plaster have been used, are visible. But the lower portion of the body of the mound appears to be intact. Halfway up the same mound is lying a four-sided bracket capital. One of its sides is plain and a dwarf (*kīchaka*) with hands upraised is carved on each of the three remaining sides. The necks of the dwarfs are adorned with necklaces somewhat in the Gupta style. The top of the capital is rough dressed. The sculpture appears to belong to the late Gupta period. It is possible that at this spot there once stood a stūpa or a temple with a *toraṇa* and a column connected with it.

In a field, a short distance from the mound, there are fragments of some figural and foliage sculpture referable to the Gupta age. The peasants of Pawāyā have collected some broken images, most of them in the late Gupta style, on a *kachchā* platform, towards the north of the village. These, they say, have been picked up from the neighbouring fields. Among them is the lower portion of a statue of a mother and child, seated on a *mamchaka* or chair, somewhat resembling the statues of the Seven Mothers in the Besnagar museum. Another image represents *Namdi* with a human body and a bull's head. I also saw lying under a tree a small votive statue of a seated Buddha, with the Buddhist creed in characters of the 7th or 8th century A.D. inscribed on the pedestal.

The fragmentary relics described above cover the period from the 1st or 2nd century A.D. to the 7th or 8th century A.D. The buildings that are still standing belong to a later period. Most prominent among these is the fort with a stone *ghāṭ*, built just in the fork formed by the confluence of the Sind and the Pārbatī (Pl. LVII*a*). Tradition assigns the foundation of the fort to Punnapāla, a Paramāra prince; but in its present form it is said to have been the work of the Kachhwāhas of Narwar, who were tributaries of the throne at Delhi. The fort is built mostly of brick laid in mortar, old bricks quarried from the more ancient ruins being visible here and there in the structure. It covers an area of about 40 acres. The wall is strengthened with a number of bastions all in brick. There is only one main entrance, in the north-west corner and a small postern door in the south-east corner leading to the stone *ghāṭ* behind. The *mahals* or palaces in the fort are now fallen to ruins, and the whole fort area is covered up with jungle.

There are numerous indications of Pawāyā having been in the possession of the Muhammadans in mediæval times. Remains of at least five *maqbaras* and a mosque apart from less important ruins stand within a mile's distance of the village. Most of them are of brick and lime mortar and consist of domed rooms devoid of any special architectural merit. From their style they appear to be of the early Mughal period.

Another building worthy of mention in the vicinity of Pawāyā is a temple of Śiva known as Dhūmēśvar Mahādēva, situated about two miles to the south-west of the village, near the waterfall in the Sind to which I have alluded above. It is a fairly large building of stone, brick and mortar, set on a high stone plinth and approached by flights of steps on three sides. The temple faces approximately east and comprises a *sanctum*, an *antarāla*, a *sabhāmaṇḍapa* and an entrance porch. The *maṇḍapa* is divided into a nave and two aisles and is a two storeyed building surmounted by a dome. The cell is crowned by a spire, and the porch by a roof in the Bengal style (Pl. LVIII*a*). This temple is apparently about three centuries old. It is said to have been built by Bīr Singh Deo, a Bundela Chief of Orchhā who flourished in the reign of the Emperor Jahāngīr. In the bed of the stream below and overlooking the waterfall is a solid building locally known as the *Nauchaukī* (Pl. LVIII*b*). The edifice is traditionally believed to date from the time of Prithvīrāja Chauhān of Delhi, but its construction hardly bears out this tradition ; more probably it is contemporary with the Dhūmēśvar Temple.

A small platform supporting a stone *liṅga* and very probably marking the site of Suvarṇabindu in the *Mālatī-mādhava*, has been alluded to above as lying about two miles to the east of Pawāyā on the confluence of the Sind and the Mahuar. The platform is built in stone and lime mortar with a certain proportion of older bricks. It rises in two steps and at the western end is about 5 feet in height. The top of the platform measures 17′×16′. The *liṅga* appears to be old, but the *śāluṅkā* is made up of plaster and is evidently modern. The lower portion of a statue of a mother and a child seated on a *maṁchaka* is lying at the foot of the platform. The style of the anklets and the girdle which the mother is wearing point to the late Gupta period as the date of this statue. The platform occupies precisely the position of the Suvarṇabindu Śiva described in the *Mālatī-mādhava* and, although the present platform is undoubtedly a later structure, there is every reason to believe that it marks the site of the older monument.

To summarise the foregoing remarks, the geographical position of Pawāyā agrees in all respects with that of Padmāvatī in the 8th century as described by Bhavabhūti. The brick remains and the fragments of sculptures scattered among them attest the existence here of an extensive city from at least the first or second century A.D. down to the late Gupta period. The numerous Nāga coins found in the ruins further prove that the city was long under the sway of the Nāgas. All these proofs combined, establish the identity of Pawāyā with Padmāvatī of the *Vishṇu Purāṇa* and of the *Mālatī-mādhava* of Bhavabhūti. This identification is supported by legend as well as by the present name of the place. Legend has preserved the memory of a powerful kingdom with its capital located here, and also of Paramāra and Kachhwāha rulers. The *maqbaras* and other Moslem monuments indicate that the place was occupied by the Muhammadans in the fifteenth and sixteenth centuries. The site is well worthy of trial excavations, which, if fruitful, would be likely to throw light on the obscure history of the Nāgas.

M. B. GARDE.

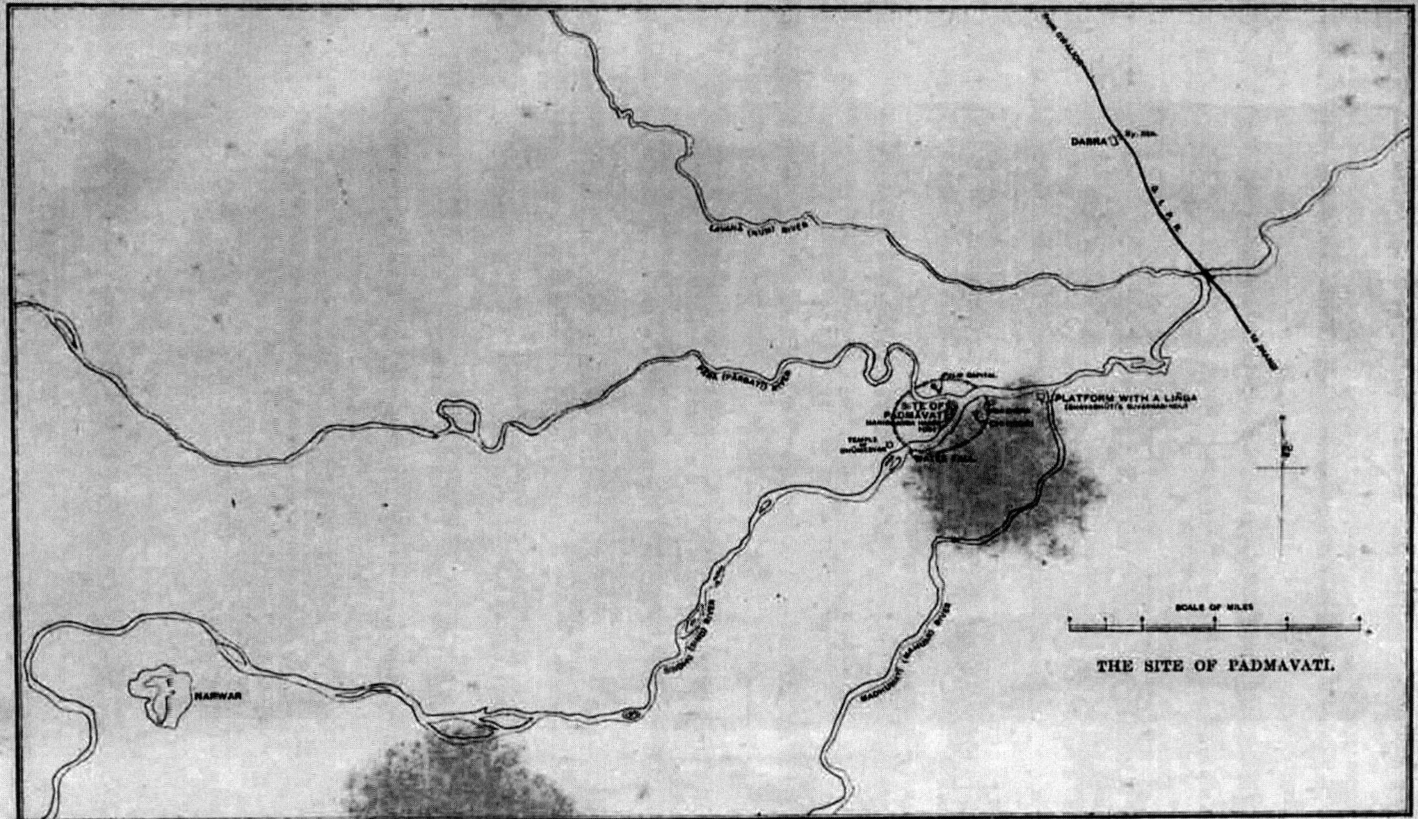

THE SITE OF PADMAVATI.

INSCRIPTION ON THE BASE OF THE MANIBHADRA IMAGE AT PAWAYA.

Photo-engraved & printed at the Offices of the Survey of India, Calcutta, 1917.

THE SITE OF PADMAVATI.

a. Panoramic view of Pawaya.

b. Manibhadra image, front view.

c. Manibhadra image, back view.

d. Palm capital.

INSCRIBED SWORDS IN THE DELHI MUSEUM OF ARCHÆOLOGY.

IN the year 1913-4 a considerable number of very interesting exhibits were acquired for the Delhi Museum of Archæology, and among them were three inscribed swords of 'Alī Mardān Khān, Shāhjahān, and Aurangzeb respectively.[1] The swords were purchased from curio dealers, who knew nothing of their history, and consequently the very little information we have about them is chiefly to be derived from their inscriptions.

1 *'Alī Mardān Khān's sword.*[2] It is a curved bladed sword, of the type usually called a scimitar. The blade, made of *faulād* (steel) with excellent *jauhars* (watering), and inlaid with gold at the back, measures 2′ 7¾″ in length and 1⅛″ in breadth. The hilt has an ivory grip with a gold plated cross-guard inlaid with enamel, and a pommel shaped like the head of a ram. The wooden scabbard is covered with red velvet and furnished with a gold mounting and two sling rings, ornamented with inlaid work like the cross-guard of the hilt.

The sword contains two inscriptions written in *nasta'līq* characters and inlaid in gold, one being on the back and the other on a face of the blade.

Inscription on the back of the blade.

این شمشیر خاص از حضور شاه عباس خلد الله ملکه و سلطانه بخانه زاد علی مردانخان سرفرازی یافت سنه . . . . .

Translation.

"This sword of honour had the honour of (bestowal) by His Majesty Shāh 'Abbās (may God perpetuate his country and his kingdom) on the slave 'Alī Mardān Khān. The year...."

As indicated by the inscription, the sword was presented by Shāh 'Abbās Ṣafwī the King of Persia (1587-1629) to 'Alī Mardān Khān. The latter was a native of Persia whose real name was 'Alī Mardān Beg. He was the son

[1] For other exhibits, see *Annual Progress Report* of the Superintendent, Muhammadan and British Monuments, Northern Circle, for the year ending 31st March 1914, pp. 21-25.

[2] See plate LIX, figure 1.

of an old, and faithful servant of Shāh 'Abbās, named Ganj 'Alī Khān, who had received the title of *Arjmand Bābā* from his patron sovereign, and had been appointed by him first Governor of Kirmān and afterwards of Qandhār, when the latter place was taken from the Emperor Jahāngīr in the year 1032 A. H.[1] (1622-3 A.D.). After the death of Ganj 'Alī Khān, 'Alī Mardān Khān was appointed Governor of Qandhār in his place in the year 1034 A.H. (1624-5 A.D.), and the titles of *Khan* and *Bābā* II were conferred upon him. But disgusted with the tyranny of Shāh Ṣafī (1629-42), the grandson and successor of Shāh 'Abbās, he surrendered Qandhār to the emperor Shāhjahān in the year 1047 A.H. (1637-8 A.D.), and took refuge in Delhi, where he was received with great honour and raised to the high rank of Amīr-ul-umarā.[2]

It appears that the sword was presented to 'Alī Mardān Khān after he was made Governor of Qandhār, as he is addressed in the inscription by the title of '*Khān*', which was conferred upon him with that appointment. It was apparently brought to India in the year 1047 A.H. (1637-8 A.D.), when he took refuge at the court of Shāhjahān. Later on it came into the possession of Sa'ādat 'Alī Khān, the Nawāb of Oudh (1798-1814), who inscribed his name on its blade in the year 1214 A.H. (1799-1800 A.D.)

Inscription on a face of the blade.

يا علی العلی

وزیرالملک نواب سعادت علیخان بہادر - ۱۲۱۴

Translation.

"O 'Alī the exalted!

Wazīru-l-Mulk Nawāb Sa'ādat 'Alī Khān Bahādur 1214 A.H. (1799-1800 A.D.)"

2. *Shāhjahān's sword.*[3] This sword has a slightly curved blade made of *sakhelā*,[4] measuring 2' 8¼" long and 1" wide and bearing a small engraving of an umbrella, the emblem of royalty, inlaid in gold.

The hilt with cross-guard and circular pommel is inscribed with the ninety-nine attributes of God, inlaid in gold. The Persian inscription, also inlaid in gold letters at the back of the blade, records that the sword belonged to the Emperor Shāhjahān. It is engraved in *nasta'līq* characters and runs as follows :—

لا اله الاالله محمد الرسول الله

هست این شمشیر خاص ثانی صاحبقران • شاه غازی بادشاه بحروبر شاه جهان

ل ۱۷. ص ۱. ن ۲۸ نصرت بخش

---

[1] *Bādshāh Nāmah* of 'Abdu-l Ḥamīd Lahori, Persian text (*Bib. Ind.*), Vol. II, pp. 26-7.

[2] *Maāthirul-umarā*, Persian text (*Bib. Ind.*) Vol. II, pp. 795-807 ; *Elliot's History of India*, Vol. VII, p. 64.

[3] See plate LIX figure 2.

[4] *Sakhelā* is an Indian term applied to a kind of steel. It is distinguished from *faulād* in its properties of being elastic and having a lustre, while the latter is brittle and contains veins or streaks running through it which are called *jauhars* (watering).

THE SITE OF PADMAVATI.

a. DHUMESVAR TEMPLE NEAR PAWAYA.

b. WATERFALL IN THE SIND RIVER AND NAUCHAUKI, PAWAYA.

INSCRIBED SWORDS IN THE DELHI MUSEUM.

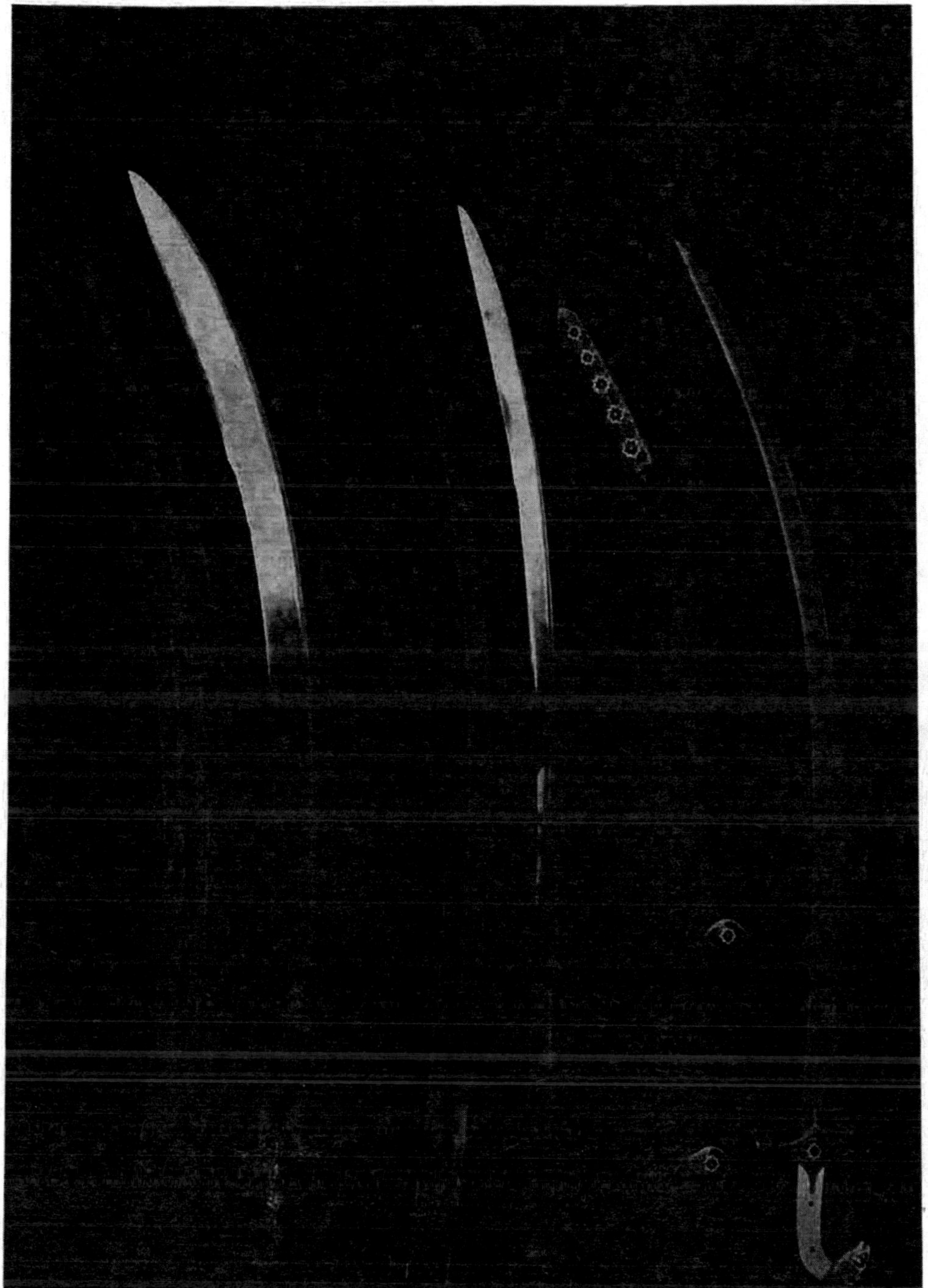

3 2 1

Photo-engraved & printed at the Offices of the Survey of India, Calcutta 1917.

Translation.

"There is no God but Allāh and Muḥhammad is His prophet. This is the chief sword of the second Ṣāhibqirān (Lord of the happy constellation) the King champion of faith, the emperor of sea and land (named) Shāhjahān........ Nuṣrat Bakhsh (the bestower of victory)."

The letters and figures written disconnectedly at the end of the inscription have some mysterious meaning not apparent; while Nuṣrat Bakhsh (the bestower of victory) appears to be the name of the sword. It is a long standing practice with Muhammadans to give names to their favourite weapons, especially their swords. *Dhulfiqār*, the name of a two-edged sword of 'Alī, the son-in-law of the Prophet, is well known throughout the Muhammadan world. Abulfazl, the prime minister and historian of the emperor Akbar, says "All weapons for the use of His Majesty have names, and a proper rank is assigned to them. Thus there are thirty swords, (*khāçah* swords) one of which is daily sent to His Majesty's sleeping apartments."[1]

3. *Aurangzeb's sword.*[2] It is a curved bladed sword, with the peculiarity that one face of its blade contains *jauhars* of *faulād* and the other the lustre of *sakhelā*. A sword of this kind is called *chap* in Indian dialect. The blade, which is inscribed with the names of God and 'Alī and bears a small engraving of an umbrella inlaid in gold, measures 2′ 10½″ in length and 1⅜″ in breadth. The punch mark on the blade near the hilt contains the following words :—

شاه عالمگیر غازی - ۱۱۱۲

Translation.

"'Ālamgīr the Emperor, champion of the faith, 1112 A.H. (1700-1 A.D.)"

The hilt with cross-guard and circular pommel, which is inlaid with gold and silver, is not the original one, which is said to have been sold to Baron Rothschild. The scabbards of Nos. 2 and 3 are modern and are not of special interest.

ZAFAR HASSAN.

---

[1] *Āin-i-Akbarī*. English translation by Blochmann, Vol. I, p. 109

[2] See plate LIX, figure 3.

SHPOLA STŪPA, KHYBER.

SOME 27 miles to the West-North-West of Peshawar and a few yards to the north of the road leading to Landikotal in the Khyber pass, is a rock which rises to about a hundred feet above the level of the surrounding fields and thus dominates the valley around. On this rock is situated a stūpa, which seen from the south-east seems to be entire, but which in reality is almost completely ruined on the remaining sides. (Pl. LX, *a* and *b*.) In this respect, as also in some others which we shall notice presently, it resembles the *stūpa* near Usman Khattar which stands out as a landmark in the Taxila valley.

The Shpola Stūpa lies near the village of Sultan Khel in the neighbourhood of Lalabeg. The name is probably old, but is not referred to either in the accounts of the Greek historians of Alexander's invasion or in the itineraries of the Chinese pilgrims Fa-Hien and Hiuen-Thsang. That the place was formerly situated in the kingdom of Gāndhāra is, however, fairly certain from the description given by these writers. It is equally clear that the stūpa was one of the most important in this kingdom, if we may judge from the profuseness of its figure decoration and its situation on the great ancient trade route. The pity is that it cannot be identified with any monument mentioned in the Buddhist records.

The only account of this monument that I know of, is contained in a paper read by William Simpson before the *Royal Institute of British Architects* in January 1880,[1] and even here we find only a passing notice of it without any measurements, drawings or photographs. In view of its size and the well preserved character of its details, the account which I am now able to publish of it will, I believe, be of considerable interest. Thanks to the courtesy and kindness of Mr. Pears, I.C.S., Political Agent, Khyber, who accompanied me on my visit to the site, I was able to inspect it in person in January last. Needless to say that but for Mr. Pears' assistance it would have been impossible for me to bring away photographs and measurements of the Stūpa, as it is situated in Independent territory.

It will be seen from the plan (Pl. LXI) that the Stūpa is raised on a rectangular plinth supported at the bottom by a massive retaining wall founded on

---

[1] *Trans. R. I. B. A.*, 1879-80, pp. 40-41.

solid rock which, at the N.-E. corner, is still standing to a height of 25 feet. This rectangular plinth is built in three slightly receding tiers and decorated with mouldings of the familiar "torus and scotia" form. The uppermost of these tiers on the east side is divided into thirteen bays flanked by pilasters with semi-Corinthian capitals about 8′ 9″ high. Three of these bays, namely one at each corner and the third in the middle, were built as niches 6′ 3″ deep. In all the bays, including the niches, traces are found of a central image of a seated or standing Buddha with two devotees or attendants on either side. Above this was the berm or circumambulatory path nearly 19 feet in width. The dome of the stūpa springs from a short cylindrical drum which is 8′ 9″ high and adorned at the base by torus and scotia mouldings surmounted by a continuous frieze of small seated Buddhas, 1′ 6″ high. These images, as well as the figures and mouldings in the bays already mentioned, bear traces of crimson and yellow paint. The top of the drum is ornamented with a modillion cornice which projects 1′ 10½″ beyond the base of the dome, while the body of the dome itself is relieved by a dentil cornice at a height of some 7 feet above the base, which results in the optical illusion that the lower part of the dome seems to curve inwards to a slight extent. The top of the dome is crowned by the remains of a modern picket hut and no traces are descernible at present of the old relic chamber. But the Khan of the neighbouring village whom I questioned on the subject, averred that, in his grand-father's time, there existed a square chamber at the top and that a few gold coins were obtained from it. All that one sees now, however, to support this statement is two trenches taken cross-wise, probably by some one in search of relics.

The dome of the stūpa is nearly 100 feet in diameter and 45 feet in height. It is probable that the stair leading to the top of the base was on the north side as mentioned by Simpson,[1] but not much is left of it at the present day. Like the Bhallar Tope, the Shpola Stūpa is built of massive limestone blocks with smaller stones intervening and with an inner core of rough rubble filling. The face seems to have been finished off with a coating of stucco which at places is more than an inch in thickness.

In its conspicuous situation, its general plan, and in the magnitude and strength of its construction, the Shpola Stūpa bears a striking resemblance to the stūpa which dominates the valley of Taxila and also dates apparently from about the same period, namely the third or fourth century A.D.[2]

Among other remains in the immediate neighbourhood of this building I noticed a few small stūpas and a monastery, all to the north. Remains of early monuments are also traceable on a hill about a hundred yards to the north-west of these.

V. NATESA AIYAR.

[1] Fergusson's statement that the steps were on the east is incorrect as there is no break in the decorations of the plinth on this side. See *History of Indian and Eastern Architecture*, Vol. I, p. 93.

[2] Since writing this article a few decorative stucco reliefs were discovered in the neighbourhood of this stūpa by a Military Works Overseer and acquired for the Peshawar Museum through the kindness of Mr. Pears.

SHPOLA STUPA, KHYBER.

a. SHPOLA STUPA FROM EAST.

b. THE SAME FROM S.E.

SHPOLA STUPA, KHYBER.

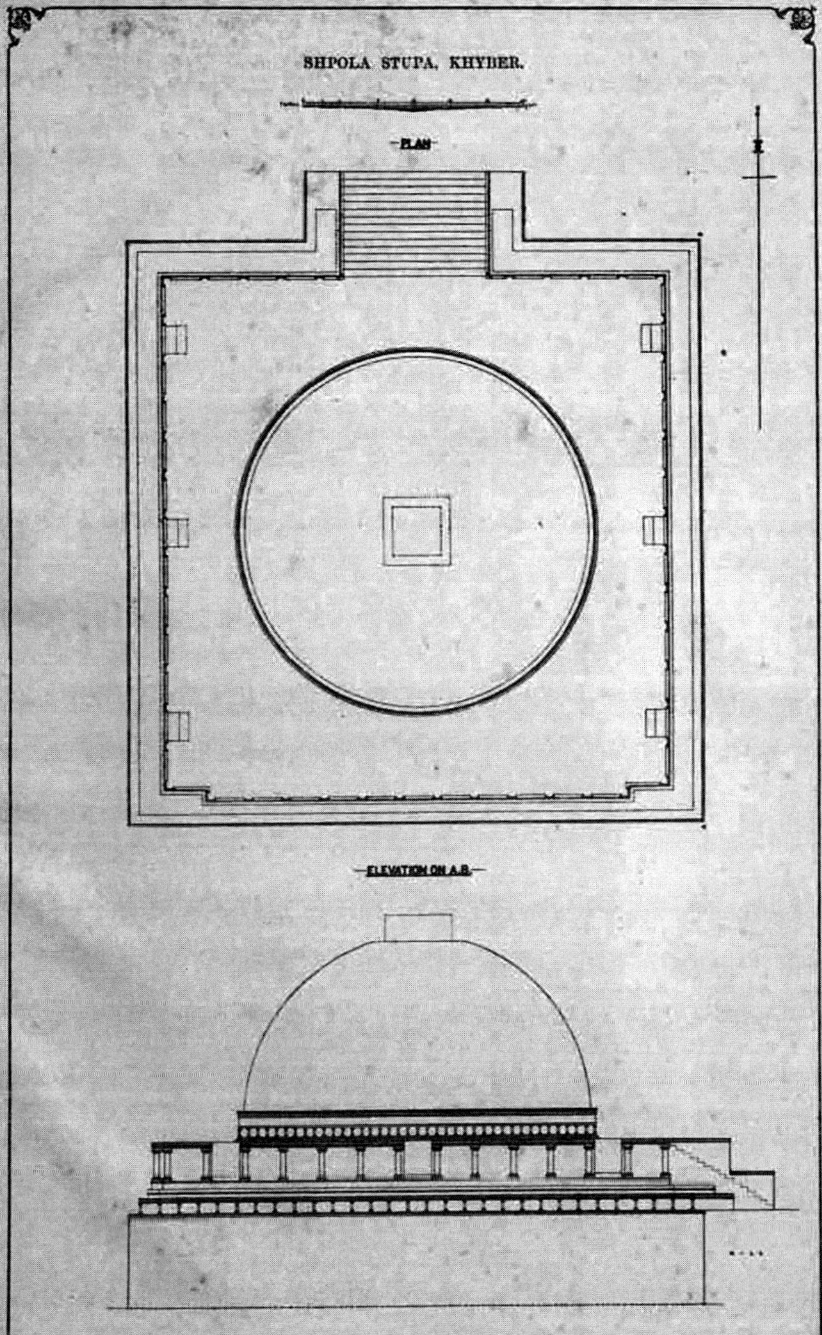